THE CHILDREN OF LA HILLE

Modern Jewish History

Henry Feingold, *Series Editor*

THE
CHILDREN
OF
LA HILLE

ELUDING NAZI CAPTURE
DURING WORLD WAR II

WALTER W. REED

Syracuse University Press

For a listing of books published and distributed by Syracuse University Press,
visit www.SyracuseUniversityPress.syr.edu.

ISBN: 978-0-8156-3422-5 (cloth)   978-0-8156-1058-8 (paperback)
978-0-8156-5338-7 (e-book)

Library of Congress Cataloging-in-Publication Data
Reed, Walter W., 1924– author.
    The children of La Hille : eluding Nazi capture during World War II /
Walter W. Reed.
        pages cm — (Modern Jewish history)
    Includes bibliographical references and index.
    ISBN 978-0-8156-3422-5 (cloth : alk. paper) — ISBN 978-0-8156-1058-8
(pbk. : alk. paper) — ISBN 978-0-8156-5338-7 (e-book)   1. Jews—France—
Montégut-Plantaurel—History—20th century.   2. Hille (Montégut-Plantaurel,
France)   3. Jewish children in the Holocaust—France—Montégut-Plantaurel—
Biography.   4. Holocaust, Jewish (1939–1945)—France—Montégut-
Plantaurel—Biography.   5. World War, 1939–1945—Jews—Rescue—France.
6. Montégut-Plantaurel (France)—Ethnic relations.   I. Title.
    DS135.F85M6547 2015
    940.53'18350830944735—dc23   2015031724

Manufactured in the United States of America

To my parents, Rika and Siegfried,
who gave me life twice—
at birth and when they sent me away.

Contents

Illustrations

Preface

This is a story of heroes of the Holocaust. The heroes are the parents of young Jewish children. The heroes are the women of a Belgian rescue committee. The heroes are young Swiss people who risked hardship in Vichy France over security at home to save refugee children's lives. They are ordinary French country folk who befriended and hid Jewish children. Above all, the heroes are the children themselves. They endured hardships and persecution and escaped across hostile and closely guarded borders. Some even chose to become Resistance fighters and Allied soldiers. And they include a humanitarian Swiss pastor who started to research and write this book until premature death intervened in 2003.

I was one of the children, but I never intended to write a book. In fact, for fifty years I had no contact with any of my wartime companions. I was able to emigrate from Vichy France to the United States in 1941, served in the US Army in France and Germany until 1946, and then put the whole history of Nazi persecution behind me. In 1943 I became a US citizen, changed my name from Werner Rindsberg to Walter Reed and never looked back.

During a return to southern France in 1997 to show my family the sites of my wartime children's refugee colony, we discovered for the first time what happened to my La Hille companions after I left them in August 1941. From several excellent memoirs published in the 1990's and through personal contact with rediscovered La Hille companions all over the world I learned the astounding details of their persecution and of their desperate attempts to escape.

When Swiss theologian and historian Dr. Theo Tschuy decided to write a carefully documented history of the Children of La Hille in early 2002, I enthusiastically offered to support and assist him, for I felt that the complete story of our colony would add meaningfully to the understanding of Nazi persecution of Jewish children.

My new friend, Theo Tschuy, decided from the beginning to focus this history on the topic of "children as victims of war" and to base his book entirely on thoroughly researched documentation. Regrettably, incurable cancer terminated Theo Tschuy's life in late 2003 before he could complete the research of our history. Gradually the obligation to carry on his intentions and his work became my mission and my objective. It is now my book as well as his. Above all it is the book of all the Children of La Hille.

Prologue

In my desperate situation I appeal in the twelfth hour for help from your organization. In mid-January I will be forced to leave the German Reich. As I do not know where this questionable fate will take me, I beg you fervently for the kindness to accept my only, lovely, and dearly loved daughter, so that I might go off on the road into the unknown with lighter heart and tranquility."

"No one can imagine the pain of becoming separated from one's loved ones for an unforeseeable time unless they are, as I am, directly affected. Please accept heartfelt and sincere thanks from a heart-broken father."[1] So wrote Leopold Tauber of Vienna, Austria to the Belgian Rescue Committee for Jewish Refugee Children (CAEJR) about his 12-year-old daughter Lilly on December 23, 1938.

And on March 8, 1939, Mrs. Ruth Strauss of Erfurt, Germany, wrote "you are the last straw to which I cling [to save my 11-year-old son]. . . . I would gladly undergo any sacrifice to know [that he is] in good hands. If you cannot help me, I don't know where to turn in my desperation."[2]

What could move devoted parents to send their young children to foreign countries and entrust them to strangers, with the strong possibility that they might never see them again? And how do children react and get along when they are separated from their family at such a tender age?

As the persecution of Jewish citizens by hate-crazed Nazis intensified in the late 1930's, frightened parents were forced to consider sending their children away in order to save their lives. After the horrifying attacks and atrocities against German and Austrian Jews during the infamous Kristallnacht ("Night of the Broken Glass") in November 1938, Leopold Tauber and Ruth Strauss were joined by thousands of Jewish families who tried to find refuge for their children in Western European countries.

About 10,000 Jewish children were admitted to England after Kristallnacht through the so-called "Kindertransports," and many hundreds more were able to escape to Holland, France, and Luxembourg. Still virtually unknown today are the efforts by the Belgian Jewish rescue committee members who procured their government's permission for the temporary stay of nearly 1,000 young refugee children from Germany and Austria.

More than one million Jewish children were brutally murdered by the Germans and their satellite helpers during the Holocaust. Thousands of others were displaced, separated from their families, and hunted by their German and cooperating oppressors in other countries until the final days of World War II.

After the German forces invaded Holland, France, Luxembourg, and Belgium on May 10, 1940, our Belgian caretakers managed to load ninety-three Jewish boys and girls from two Brussels children's refugee homes onto one of the many refugee trains headed for southern France.

Saved thus for a second time, we were fated to endure severe hardships under the French Vichy regime (in the unoccupied southern zone), and in 1942 the La Hille children were again hunted by our Nazi enemies, assisted by French police cooperators. Yet the devoted Belgian rescue women, and later newly-recruited Swiss caretakers, spared no effort to protect and sustain our group.

The Secours Suisse aux Enfants (Swiss Children's Help Society) moved our colony to the isolated Château de La Hille in early 1941, and in spite of the hardships, arrests, and persecution, all but eleven of us were able to escape to the United States and (illegally) to Switzerland and Spain, or to remain hidden in France until the liberation in 1944. Today we are collectively referred to as "the Children of La Hille."

Many never saw our parents and family members again because, though determined to save their children, they were unable to escape the Nazis' mass slaughter themselves.

The purpose of this history is to shed light on how innocent children were persecuted and brutalized by a nation gone berserk. But it is also to bring to light the incredible courage of our parents, the devotion and successes of rescuers and caretakers who were determined to counteract the oppressors' intentions, and, not least, the heroic actions of the children themselves. Because of our never-ending difficulties, we grew up fast in a turbulent world.

THE CHILDREN OF LA HILLE

◇ 1 ◇

Please Take My Children

For the Children of La Hille, the takeover of the German government by Adolf Hitler and his Nazi party (Nationalsozialistische Deutsche Arbeiterpartei, or "NSDAP") on January 30, 1933, was a non-event.

The oldest boys and girls were barely nine years old and the youngest was born three years later. We continued to go to school and were not yet aware that our parents and all other Jewish German citizens were about to be persecuted by our own government and vilified incessantly by local fellow citizens. Some of us lived in large cities like Berlin and Frankfurt; many lived in much smaller towns and villages like mine. Austria was still a free country.

Yet within a few months, laws and regulations passed by the Nazi government would deprive our parents of their livelihood and of their legal rights as citizens. The daily lives of Jewish adults and the fate of their children would change drastically.

Less than eight weeks after the Nazi takeover (on March 23, 1933), its majority in the Reichstag (the German legislature) passed the Enabling Act, which granted Adolf Hitler the legal authority for dictatorship. Three days later, Hitler met with Propaganda Minister Josef Goebbels in Berchtesgaden to outline stringent anti-Jewish measures.[1]

Throughout Germany, even in small towns and farm villages, the Sturmabteilung (or "SA"), the Nazi party's brown-shirted blue-collar foot soldiers, began boycotts against Jewish stores and businesses. Placards and graffiti on store windows warned shoppers not to buy from Jewish merchants. Shoppers who defied the warnings were harassed and threatened by the SA hoodlums.

Between spring and October 1933, the Nazi government passed laws to fire Jews from civil service positions, to restrict their practice of law, and to ban Jews from cultural, arts, and entertainment enterprises.[2]

While these actions and laws were aimed at adults, children did not escape the abuse. They were maligned and attacked by classmates in schools and on the streets and became, of course, aware of the plight of their parents. The recollections of the La Hille children paint a vivid picture:

"My father died when I was ten years old and mother and I moved in with my grandfather," recalls Ruth Herz, who was born in the village of Holzheim, Province of Hessen. "He ran a small grocery store, but after the Nuremberg laws were passed, housewives did not want him to deliver to their homes anymore. They didn't mind, however, if a small girl brought the groceries. I became the delivery girl for the Christian customers. Since I was the only Jewish child of school age, going to and from school became a problem. The other children, who had joined the Hitler Youth, harassed me constantly."[3]

In a modest neighborhood of Berlin, eight-year-old Ruth Schütz became aware of the Nazi harassment of Jews from several directions. "On the sidewalk in front of my father's store a nasty verse was written in giant letters: 'Germans, don't buy from the Jewish pigs!!'" she writes in her autobiography, *Entrapped Adolescence*.[4]

At dawn on Sundays, many men wearing brown uniforms would pass by our house. Their marching songs echoed the length of the street: "Today we own Germany, tomorrow the entire world." It was scary to see the masses marching in their brown uniforms, waving flags, and banging on drums.

At school all the girls now gathered in the courtyard before the start of classes. Every morning they raised the swastika flag on the flagpole. The headmaster of the school would shout, "Heil Hitler," and all the children would yell loudly after him, "Heil Hitler!" Only I, a child eight years old, would stand without saying a word and wait for the end of the ceremony.

When I left school, a gang of boys bothered me, hit me, and sang rhymes degrading Jews. I ran to my father's store. I hoped that one of the passersby would get involved, yell at the boys, come to my help, but nothing happened.[5]

Many of the other German-born Children of La Hille endured harassment and experienced the fears and humiliation of their families in similar fashion after 1933. Hordes of SA thugs often marched in lockstep in every community, sometimes in dramatic nighttime torch parades. The aggressive national anthem was often accompanied by a fight song that contained the words "Wenn das Judenblut vom Messer spritzt" (when the Jews' blood squirts from our knives). It sent chills down Jewish children's spines.

In Austria, the Nazi hatred of Jewish people was unleashed suddenly and cruelly on March 12, 1938, as German troops invaded their country (in the so-called "Anschluss," which means "reconnection"). It seemed as though the eager Austrian Nazis had been waiting to emulate and even exceed their German comrades in persecution of the Jews.

Helga Schwarz, then nine years old, who lived with her parents and with younger brother Harry in a three-room apartment in the center of Vienna, remembers early incidents of the period. "Near our apartment was a pleasant park and 'Maman' [Mom] took us there in the afternoons after school. One day after I had a dispute with a little girl with whom I had played in friendly fashion five minutes before, her mother sprang up, approached and insulted my mother, called her a dirty Jewess with nasty children, and spat in her face. I was frightened and overwhelmed to see Mother treated so badly. We never went back to that park," Helga writes in her biography, *Le Prix de la Vie* (The Value of My Life).[6]

Viktor Weinberg, a Viennese attorney, had been counselor to Austrian chancellor Engelbert Dollfuss who was assassinated by Nazi agents on July 25, 1934. Viktor reportedly also served Dollfuss's successor, Chancellor Kurt von Schuschnigg. Weinberg's son Robert recalls being baptized as a Catholic with his parents and his sister

Peggy at ages six and three in September 1937. "One morning in April 1938, in our Catholic school, the children were ready to say morning prayers and [make] the sign of the cross."

"Sternly the teacher said 'No, not today. Today we do it differently. Today you do as I do (she extended her arm and hand forward) and repeat 'Heil Hitler'! And we did it without realizing that our life would never be the same. I raised my arm and gave the Hitler salute only that once. When I told my parents of that incident, my father said 'we are leaving at the end of this week.'"[7]

At the border they were thoroughly searched for undeclared valuables by Nazi guards who even looked into Baby Percy's diapers.[8]

These examples of awakening to an uncertain and threatening future mirror what happened to hundreds of thousands of Jewish girls and boys in Germany and Austria between 1933 and 1938. The harassment and the loss of employment and income of their parents were accompanied by constant attacks and vilification from fellow students, and even by some teachers.

"The Germans closed the doors [to the cinemas] in our faces . . . , to the swimming pools, and to the ice skating rinks," Ruth Schütz Usrad recalls in her biography.[9] "At the entrances of the cafes they hung signs saying: "Jews and Dogs Are Not Wanted."

The Nazi persecution of the Jews had intensified with the racial laws passed in 1935 (the so-called Nuremberg Laws, which defined who is a Jew and forbade sexual relations and marriage between Jews and non-Jews). As of September 30, 1938, Jewish physicians could no longer practice medicine, and a similar prohibition on Jewish lawyers became effective on November 30.[10] Beginning on January 1, 1939, male Jews of all ages were required to add the middle name "Israel," and women and girls the name "Sara."[11]

At the suggestion of Swiss officials, the Nazis required, by decree of October 5, 1938, that the German passports of Jews be stamped with the letter "J".[12]

Yet all this was only a mild prelude to what took place throughout Germany and Austria on November 9 and 10, 1938: the orchestrated pogrom, which later became known as "Kristallnacht" (Night of the Broken Glass)—a hammer blow spreading panic among all Jewish citizens. It also triggered the emigration of thousands of very young and teenage children without their parents, and it leads us to the beginning of the story of the Children of La Hille.

Here is how Kristallnacht affected them:

"During 'Kristallnacht' the wild mob locked all the residents of the home in a school building and we all expected to be incinerated alive", recalls Inge Berlin Vogelstein, a then fifteen-year-old apprentice caretaker at the Dinslaken, Germany, Jewish orphanage. "I shall never forget the scene of all these young children, who had been raised orthodox, saying the appropriate prayers when facing death—without any adult prompting. There was no panic—they were just getting ready."[13] In addition to Inge Berlin, trainee Ruth Herz Goldschmidt and seven-year-old resident Alfred Eschwege were at the Dinslaken home that day (and all later became Children of La Hille).

Inge Berlin also describes what happened at the home of her parents in Koblenz in the Rhineland:

> When I returned to the undamaged residence of my parents, they told me that a former colleague of my father—a younger man with two children—appeared at their front door in full uniform and said: "Mr. Berlin, if anyone comes to harm you, they will first have to get past me." And this is how my parents were spared from harm.
>
> But that did not dispel their fears for my younger brother, whom they had innocently sent to school that morning. They didn't dare go into the street, but that's when a caring, dear neighbor woman volunteered to find my brother, which she accomplished resolutely. For me, it's important to underscore the courage that this must have taken.[14]

In the village of Mainstockheim, Bavaria, population 1,100, there were loud knocks on the front door of the Rindsberg house in the early hours of November 10. Brown-uniformed local SA thugs hauled my father, Siegfried, and me (I was fourteen years old) out of the house and onto a truck already packed with other local Jewish men.

Without explanation we were driven to the county jail in nearby Kitzingen where the synagogue had been set afire two blocks away.

My mother Rika and my two younger brothers were not taken and another young teenage prisoner and I were sent home three days later, without explanation. My father and many other local adult Jewish men were shipped to the Dachau concentration camp and mistreated there during the following month. (This is the author's own experience, who later changed his name to Walter Reed from Werner Rindsberg.)

The nationwide atrocities of Kristallnacht were orchestrated at the instigation of Nazi propaganda minister Josef Goebbels, who was attending a Nazi commemorative gathering in Munich and issued the order of extreme measures against the Jews. Within forty-eight hours Jewish homes and shops all over Germany and Austria were plundered, damaged, or destroyed, and the Nazi mobs damaged or burned more than 1,000 synagogues. The sacred contents, Torahs, and prayer materials lay strewn and burned in the streets. About 30,000 Jewish men were arrested and brutalized in concentration camps, mostly Dachau, Buchenwald, and Sachsenhausen.[15]

The trigger for the Kristallnacht atrocities had occurred on October 28, when the German Foreign Office gave orders to arrest and deport some 17,000 Polish-born Jews across the Polish border. Many had lived in Germany for decades. The Polish authorities refused to accept them and thousands were stranded inside the Polish border. Herschel Grynszpan, the seventeen-year-old son of one deportee, decided to revenge himself by murdering the German ambassador in Paris. Instead, he killed Ernst vom Rath, a lower-ranking embassy staff member, who died on November 9. Looking for an excuse, the Nazis blamed the murder as the cause of the widespread public reaction and revenge in order to justify the organized atrocities.

The November atrocities struck like lightning on Jewish families' futile hopes that the Nazi regime would fade away or tire of persecuting its Jewish citizens.

In fact, Hermann Göring, the Nazi chief for economic matters and head of the Luftwaffe, convened a large meeting at his Berlin headquarters on November 12. He announced that a letter written on order of the Führer requested that "the Jewish question be now, once and for all, coordinated and solved one way or another." Furthermore, the Führer had asked him the day before by phone "to take coordinated action in the matter."[16]

While Jewish families and the German public were not informed about these new orders, the Kristallnacht events set off a mad scramble to emigrate. Foreign countries were reluctant, even uninterested, to accept refugees. Some did make limited exceptions for children and younger teenagers.

It is in this atmosphere that thousands of parents reached the desperate decision to send their children away to foreign countries, to unknown camps or orphanages, and to families of strangers. Many surely feared that they might never see their beloved children again, yet instinct and escalated forebodings told them that in order to save their loved ones, they must do the unthinkable.

Each of the Children of La Hille had such courageous and selfless parents. They gave us life twice: at birth, and again in the aftermath of Kristallnacht.

◇ 2 ◇

Refuge in Belgium, 1938–1940

O ur Children Became Just Letters—The Rescue of Jewish Children from Nazi-Germany" ("Aus Kindern wurden Briefe—Die Rettung jüdischer Kinder aus Nazi-Deutschland"). That was the title and theme of a historic exhibition held in Berlin from September 29, 2004, to January 31, 2005.

"Our children are gone; all we now have is their letters." Nothing could better describe the heart-rending decisions that my family and thousands of other frightened Jewish parents faced in Germany and Austria following the terror of Kristallnacht. In desperation they searched, begged, and cajoled their local and national Jewish social service agencies, as well as those in nearby countries, to accept their children for emigration, and probably to save their lives.

Mrs. Julie Rosenthal wrote to the "Rescue Committee" in Brussels on December 3, 1938, "My husband was arrested in our apartment in Vienna on November 10 and is now in Dachau. Because my husband (who had been working in Yugoslavia) had been unable to send support for me and for our child (we are living with my in-laws) and I could not find any employment in Vienna, I had to sell our furniture in order to live on the proceeds. In order to save my poor child from the worst fate, I beg you with all my heart to accept her so that she might soon be in more favorable circumstances and in the hands of good people. You know how difficult it is for a mother to give up her beloved child, but I hope that with God's help to soon find the possibility of emigrating with my husband so that we can be reunited with her."[1]

Arnold Schelansky of Berlin-Wilmersdorf also wrote to the Belgian Committee on December 19: "This morning I was summoned

8

to the emigration office and was ordered to leave Germany with my family within four weeks. Considering this horrible situation, I beg you from all my heart to allow the immediate acceptance of our two sons in Belgium (born in 1922 and 1926). It would be a great relief to know they are safe outside Germany."[2]

Iakar Reiter of Dortmund, Germany, wrote to the committee on March 16, 1939, seeking to place his two sons, aged thirteen and eighteen. "On November 10, 1938, I was taken into protective custody [*Schutzhaft*] and kept in a concentration camp until the end of December. Now I have no more possibility of earning money and we must give up our apartment in April. It will then no longer be possible to keep our children. I therefore beg you most humbly to do all possible to bring our younger son Leo (thirteen years [old]) to Belgium."[3]

No one knows how many such letters were sent by desperate parents to foreign countries, although the partial archives of the Belgian Rescue Committee at Centre National des Hautes Études Juives (CNHEJ) alone contain many—all with similarly urgent pleas.

The cruel events of the Kristallnacht pogrom were widely reported in foreign countries and drew special attention and action in Jewish circles. In England, Jewish leaders persuaded the government to authorize the immigration of unaccompanied children, which became known as the "Kindertransports" (children transports). Some 10,000 children from Germany, Austria, and eastern European countries were brought to England in 1938 and 1939 under this special permission.

One can only guess at the fears and heartaches of the parents and relatives who were anxious to send their children to a strange land where they did not speak the language, where they were in the hands of strangers, and at an age when family care and love are most needed and valued. "Into the Arms of Strangers" is the appropriate name of a movie about these Kindertransports to England.

In Belgium, Max Gottschalk, a prominent attorney and Jewish leader, launched a special mission immediately after Kristallnacht, with far-reaching results. He had already occupied prominent positions in the Belgian government and in academia, as well as on the Geneva-based Bureau International du Travail (International Labor

Office). Beginning in 1933 he created and presided over the Comité d'Aide et d'Assistance aux Victimes de l'Antisémitisme en Allemagne (CAAVAA, or Aid and Assistance Committee for Victims of Anti-Semitism in Germany).[4]

Immediately after Kristallnacht, Gottschalk founded a new committee composed of about a dozen well-to-do and highly placed Belgian Jewish women whose aim became the rescue of Jewish children from Germany and Austria. Known as the Comité d'Assistance aux Enfants Juifs Réfugiés (CAEJR, or Jewish Refugee Children's Aid Committee), it was first chaired by Mme Renée deBecker-Remy, the daughter of Belgian financier Baron Lambert and, through her mother, a descendant of the Rothschild banking family.

Although she remained very active, Mme deBecker-Remy was soon succeeded by Mme Marguérite Goldschmidt-Brodsky, the wife of Alfred Goldschmidt, who was a prominent industrialist and the treasurer of the Belgian Red Cross. A brother-in-law, Mr. Paul Hymans, was a Belgian cabinet minister.[5]

Another prominent committee member was Mme Lilly Felddegen, Swiss-born (and non-Jewish) spouse of another Belgian Jewish business leader. Her extensive private archive of these and later events became a vital resource for this book.

The activism, high-level relationships, and incredible devotion of these prominent women became important factors in the fate of the Children of La Hille. Our story begins with the creation of the women's committee.

Very little has been known of their vital role in the Holocaust until now—rescuing and then safeguarding nearly 1,000 Jewish children from Germany and Austria. Throughout the committee's activities, Gottschalk remained a vital supporter and connector for their work, almost like a godfather (in the best sense of that term).

As soon as the committee opened its office in November 1938 on rue DuPont next to the main synagogue building of Brussels, pleas from German and Austrian parents, such as those quoted above, started to pour in. As in other countries, the political climate for accepting refugees was not favorable in Belgium because unemployment and the Nazi aggression against their Austrian and Czech neighbors preoccupied the population and the politicians.

By guaranteeing that the children would stay in Belgium only until they could be accepted in other countries and that the committee would closely supervise their care and placement, the women initially were able to obtain entry permits for 250 children up to age fourteen.[6]

Although a small paid staff worked at its rue Dupont office, the committee members were personally involved in all phases of the selection and daily care of the children.[7]

Correspondence in the committee records indicates that hundreds of German and Austrian Jewish families made direct contact with the committee, as did local Jewish welfare offices of the two countries on behalf of families of their city or area. The "grapevine" network of desperate parents who discovered the Belgian "Comité" through family friends and relatives probably played a major role in the selection of the children. This interaction emerges from letters in the committee files written by Bavarian parents known to the author.

Nearly 1,000 Jewish children were brought to Belgium or cared for by the Committee between November 1938 and May 1940 (when the Germans invaded Belgium). Exact numbers are difficult to establish but different reports and correspondence support this estimate. Correspondence between Belgian Justice Minister Joseph Pholien and Prime Minister Paul-Henri Spaak documents that Minister Pholien twice authorized quotas of 250 immigrant children, plus an unannounced additional 250.[8]

The age limit was fourteen and the committee was held responsible for the children's upkeep and suitable placement. Each refugee child was required to be registered with the local police and local authorities had to be notified when a child was moved to a different location.

The archives of the Sureté Publique (Public Security) in Brussels contain records of many of these children, with each assigned an identification number. In the final organized "transport" that arrived on June 15, 1939, the last child (David Blayman of Bonn, Germany) was issued Number 678.[9] On December 10, 1939, committee staff reported to Mme Felddegen (who by then had emigrated to New York) that 570 children were then already under the committee's care.[10]

Typically, German and Austrian families were notified to send their children to the Jewish Welfare Office at Rubensstrasse 33 in Cologne on a specified date, where the group would be assembled and sent by train to Brussels, accompanied by personnel from the Belgian Red Cross. The last such transport, on June 15, 1939, was composed of twenty-nine girls and boys. Toni Steuer from Essen, Germany, and Hans Bock from Berlin were almost three years old, while the oldest, Eleonore Fischbein, also from Berlin, was eighteen years old. Nine of this group would remain together for several years as part of the "Children of La Hille," including the author.[11]

It is not known how many times such organized groups were assembled in Cologne for the trip to Brussels. In fact, many of the children under the committee's care had crossed the Belgian border illegally, while others had come to Belgium with a single parent who could not take care of them, or they had been sent to relatives who placed them with the committee for various reasons. Because these single arrivals often were not recorded as "immigrants" by the authorities, their total number is not traceable.

From January 2 through 8, 1939, at least seventy Jewish children crossed the Belgian border illegally at Herbestal, carrying one-way train tickets to Brussels and Antwerp. All were turned back to the Aachen, Germany departure point.[12] Children who arrived illegally often were brought to the Salvation Army in Brussels and transferred to CAEJR for assignment to private homes or to one of its several children's homes. Mme deBecker-Remy negotiated with Justice Minister Pholien about "legalizing" twenty-eight of the clandestine arrivals by counting them as part of the 250 children specified in the immigration quota.[13] In return for granting the third contingent of 250 children, "Mme deBecker promised not to ask for any additional permissions during the next three months," Mr. Pholien reported to Mr. Spaak.[14]

Committee and government negotiations made the organized escapes possible, but they could not calm the trauma and anguish of the children and of their parents. The parents—who had done everything possible to send them away—were especially worried that they might never see their beloved children again. A few examples of the departure from home of some La Hille children illustrate the desperation and the trauma:

Ilse Wulff Garfunkel recalls that when she was thirteen, "We lived in Stettin and my parents accompanied me to Berlin where we said good-bye to each other before I continued by train to Cologne. At that time, my parents knew they were going to Shanghai, but they had not told me about their plans. They felt I had a better chance to grow up in 'civilized' Europe."

"Much later I realized how difficult our separation must have been for my parents, who probably wondered whether they would ever see me again. On the train a girl who sat next to me was crying bitterly and it took a great deal of willpower on my part not to do the same."[15]

Susi Davids, daughter of Paul and Irma Davids, lived in Wuppertal-Elberfeld (in Germany's Ruhr area). "After Kristallnacht my parents did not let my brother Gerd or me out of the house except to buy us new clothes with which to leave Germany," she recalls. "In December 1938 we [Susi and brother Gerd, age eleven] were put in a compartment that was completely full. I did not cry, nor did any other child. I was far too busy examining and eating my favourite chocolates. I was delighted to receive a whole box to myself, as sweets were always controlled at home by my parents. I just remember saying good-bye to my parents among a crowd of other parents." At that time, Susi was just eight years old.[16]

Else Rosenblatt, oldest of four sisters, explained the dilemma faced by her parents in an interview with German cable channel 34 at a reunion in France in 1993: "I remember that we had to go from Garzweiler to Aachen and the meeting point was Cologne. That is where I saw my parents for the last time. At that time we hoped that we would be reunited later. I was thirteen years old and my three

1. Ilse Wulff with her mother in Stettin, Germany, 1938. Reproduced with permission from the United States Holocaust Memorial Museum Photo Archive.

sisters were younger. . . . My mother did not want us to leave but my father stated that things in Germany would only get worse. 'You have to leave. You cannot stay here because it is much too dangerous. Your mother won't leave and I will stay with her, but you must go'. And that's how we arrived in Belgium."[17]

Herbert Kammer came to Belgium with his father Georg from their home in Vienna. He was seven years old. His mother was able to emigrate from Vienna to England and work as a domestic (as did some other mothers, but they could not bring their children). Eventually Herbert came under the care of the committee and was able to flee with the Children of La Hille.[18]

Friedl Steinberg of Vienna says she "did not arrive in Belgium via a Kindertransport."[19] "I walked from Aachen to Eupen [then in Belgium] on foot. We were arrested by the German border police at the 'Dreiländerblick' [Three-Countries Vista] at the Belgian border, detained and questioned and sent on our way to Belgium, the laughter of the German border police following us."

"I was in the company of a clever young boy from Berlin who had offered my mother [she was waiting at an Aachen hotel for a *'passeur'*—an illegal border guide] to take me for a walk because I had felt very ill. This 'walk' in Aachen turned into a ten-hour hike through fields and woods, with border police dogs barking like mad. My mother, who had stayed in Aachen, had no idea what happened to us until I could send her a telegram three days later. There was a quota for children coming to Belgium and I probably replaced one on the quota who did not come," said Friedl, who was fourteen years old at the time of these events.

Emil (Émile) and Joseph Dortort (fifteen and eleven years old), from Bottrop, Germany, were picked up by Belgian police after they crossed the border illegally. "They brought them to me and I did what I could for them," wrote Mme Lilly Felddegen to their cousin in Philadelphia. "The older (boy) is so serious and watches so well on the younger brother."[20]

On Christmas day 1938 Mrs. Findling of Cologne accompanied her three little boys (aged eleven, eight, and six) and her nine-year-old daughter Fanny by train to Aachen. From there she sent them alone with round-trip tickets to Brussels. The oldest son, Joseph, had tried to escape to Holland with a one-way ticket shortly before Kristallnacht, but was turned back by Dutch border officials. The children's father, born in Poland, had been deported to the German-Polish border area as part of the roundup that led to the Paris embassy murder and to Kristallnacht.

At the Belgian border, the siblings' cousin Sala met the children and turned them over to the committee in Brussels. In desperation, Mrs. Findling drugged her youngest daughter, two-year-old Regina, and smuggled her into Belgium by train with a (possibly unknown but willing) stranger. Mrs. Findling then crossed the border illegally with a paid illegal guide and lived in Antwerp for a time with daughter Fanny.

Son Joseph says he discovered his little sister at the committee office by accident. All five Findling children survived the war, the boys as part of the La Hille group.

In 1943 their mother was deported and murdered in Poland and their father became a victim of the brutal German killing squads (*Einsatzgruppen*) in Poland.[21]

Before he embarked alone on the ill-fated trip to Cuba on the SS *St. Louis* in May 1939 (the ship's odyssey across the Atlantic Ocean and back is infamous), Alfred Manasse of Frankfurt wrote to the Committee to thank it for harboring his sons Gustav and Manfred (then aged eight and four). After the aborted crossing Manasse and 213 others were admitted to Belgium and he lived in Brussels near his sons. Both Manasse parents were deported in 1942 and murdered in Poland. The Manasse boys became part of the La Hille group and survived the war.[22]

By the time brothers Julius and Kurt Steinhardt (ages eight and seven) from Aachen came under the committee's care they had already experienced the worst of family tragedies. Father Max Steinhardt had fled alone from Germany to Brussels and in August 1939 went to meet his wife and sons as they were arriving in Liège. Through a mix-up they missed each other, the father suffered a heart attack from the trauma and died without seeing his family. Sophie Steinhardt, the mother, died in Brussels of tuberculosis on February 8, 1940. Both Steinhardt boys were placed at Home Speyer by the committee and thus became part of the La Hille colony.[23]

In Vienna fourteen-year-old Edith Goldapper vacillated about leaving her doting parents. As their only child, she was especially close to them. When other young girls at the millinery shop where she was apprenticing were emigrating, she too felt the urge to escape persecution in Austria.

"Almost daily I pestered my beloved parents to take steps to get me out of the country," she writes in her diary. "Baroness Ferstel, a family friend and a relative of Belgian committee president Mme Goldschmidt, helps in the effort to get me to Belgium." When word came that she was accepted, "my dear parents supplied good advice and kept up my courage by promising to join me soon. And that consolation kept up my spirits."

"Otherwise I never would have left," she recalls. Her parents and relatives came to see Edith off at the Vienna train station on December 19, 1938, for the trip to the assembly point in Cologne. "First Mama and I embrace, then Papa, then Mama again. For the first time in my life I see Papa crying. Tears stream from his closed eyelids (he was blinded as an Austrian soldier in World War I). Mutti [Mom] also is inconsolable. So am I! I had just turned fourteen years old and now I will get to know the world; but I think that the sooner you start, the better."[24]

For Lixie Grabkowicz, also fourteen years old, the departure from Vienna to Antwerp was almost routine. "Leaving my family (mother, father, sister and grandmother) was not traumatic because I never anticipated it to become a very permanent and final separation. I had an invitation to come to my best friend's house in Antwerp and was looking forward to going there. My family took me to the train station and we said our goodbyes. I don't remember tears and wails. It was more like a trip to summer camp," she recalls.

"The hard truth and then longing to be home again came later when the stay at my friend's house became difficult."[25] Lixie was accepted at one of the Belgian committee's girls' homes.

For Werner Epstein, leaving his family in Berlin for Belgium at age sixteen also was more routine than tragic. "After Kristallnacht, I lost my job and decided, with my parents' support, to leave the country. I sold my bicycle and took the train to the Belgian border. I will never forget being on the train to leave Berlin. All of my family—father, mother, sisters, uncles and nieces—were smiling at me."

"I remember my mother tried to smile but her eyes were too wet. I was like a little kid going on vacation. I didn't know what lay ahead of me and I didn't realize that I would never see my family again. My biggest regret is that I never said good-bye."[26] Werner Epstein also was taken under the committee's wing, was deported from France in 1943, and survived Auschwitz and other atrocities.

Like many of the children rescued by the committee after Kristallnacht, thirteen-year-old Inge Joseph of Darmstadt, Germany, was able to live with a relative, Gustav Wurzweiler (her father's cousin) and his wife in a Brussels apartment.

In the book about her experiences, *Inge: A Girl's Journey through Nazi Europe*, she and her nephew, author David E. Gumpert, describe her leave-taking on January 11, 1939. "The plan was for Mutti [Mom] to travel with me on the train to Cologne. From there I was to travel with other children from Germany who were part of the Kindertransport to Brussels."

"Mutti carried on a conversation in a normal tone, as if she were merely escorting me to a relative's for a few weeks away."[27] After a few months living with the relative and then with another host family, Inge was transferred to Home Général Bernheim in Zuen, a Brussels suburb where some thirty other refugee girls were housed by the committee (at 21 chaussée de Leeuw, Saint-Pierre—later renamed chaussée de Ruisbroek). She too became one of the Children of La Hille.

While many of the children rescued by the committee came to Belgium in organized and orderly fashion, the escape and arrival of the Schütz sisters—Ruth and Betty—from Berlin was among the most daring and hazardous of those who crossed the Belgian border illegally.

After their father, Joseph, had been seized and deported in the Nazi roundup of Polish-born Jews in 1938, the family's life and livelihood had become precarious. After some relatives had succeeded in emigrating to England, thirteen-year-old Ruth beseeched her mother to let her and younger sister Betty try to emigrate to Israel or England.

Ruth began to visit several Jewish emigration offices, but was told to come back a year later because she was too young. In the courtyard of a Berlin office building she became aware of children being briefed about a children's group emigration to Belgium. "I returned to the courtyard every day until I had exact information on the date, the hour, and the train station from which this group of eighty children was supposed to leave for Belgium," she writes in her autobiography *Entrapped Adolescence.*

She laid out her plan to her mother: "Betty and I will get on the train as if on our way to England, and on the way we will join the group of children and reach Belgium with them."

"I was afraid that I would have difficulty convincing my mother to agree with my adventurous plan. But to my surprise, she too saw this as a chance for us to escape from Germany," she recalls.

The 8th of February 1939 was a cold and clear day. Wearing a heavy winter coat, a scarf, and matching wool caps, we made our way to the train station. From afar I made out a group of children who were separating from their relatives. Mother hugged us and told us the things that are said when one separates at train stations. I didn't feel any sadness at leaving her, and didn't cry. I wanted to get on the train and put an end to the nightmare of waiting.

The train passed the outskirts of Berlin and we left the compartment and passed several others. When we finally heard the happy chatter of girls, we joined them and told them that we were traveling through Brussels to England, and we would be happy to travel with them. The chaperones moved from compartment to compartment, checking the girls and affixing a tag to the collar of each girl.

We were getting closer to the border and German policemen checked the documents that I showed them and walked away. The train moved, leaving Germany and stopped on the Belgian side. This time Belgian police boarded the train. They passed from compartment to compartment and stopped near us. On our lapels was no ticket like the rest of the girls. The policemen made a sign for us to get off the train into the station. I pointed to one of the chaperones and said that he should check with her what the problem is. I grabbed Betty, who was already on one of the steps, and started to run crazily through the cars. The train continued to move, and we were in Belgium. When the train stopped again, we had arrived in Brussels.

We descended with the rest of the girls and in a large hall men and women were waiting for their children.

The hall empties and we are left to stand, squeezed against the wall in a dark corner. "What is your name? To whom are you going? You're not listed." Confusion ensues around us.

"Where did you come from? We don't have room for you. You have to go home." And I stubbornly say: "We have no home, we have no address. We have nowhere to return to." They consulted in whispers in French, and I'm trying to understand, and suddenly I hear, "Salvation Army." They want to send us to stay overnight in the Salvation Army. At this point all the dams burst. I burst out crying [and] couldn't be stopped. And Betty, in a large voice, cries after me, "No! Don't send us to the Salvation Army!"

A large woman who was already on her way out with a girl that she had just received, asked, "What's the problem?" After a discussion she turned to us and said, "Come on," and we accompanied her outside. "Is this a dream?" I asked myself. A chauffeur opened the door of a car, and I jumped into the soft, comfortable seat. We traveled for quite a distance in the night.

"Here, we have arrived," said the woman who was so kind to us, and before us was a grand villa. A young woman stood at the entrance. Around her waist was a small, white apron with a lace border, and on her head was a little white hat that gathered her hair. "Madame at your service," she said.[28]

The Schütz sisters stayed with the Padawer family for a while, then were eventually transferred to the committee's Home Général Bernheim.

Even at age seventy-eight, Henri Brunel, born in Cologne, vividly recalled the trauma. "It was wrenching for me to leave my poor parents. In spite of my young age [he was fourteen], I fully understood the frightening situation that lay ahead for them and I had the feeling that I would never see them again."[29]

At this early stage of the saga of the Children of La Hille, it is evident that fright, panic, courageous parents, and the resourcefulness of young children—and especially good luck—all became intermingled as ruthless Nazi Germans enthusiastically enacted their hatred not only of Jewish adults, but also hatred of Jewish children of all ages.

A shameful example of Nazi atrocities against children occurred at the Jewish orphanage in the town of Dinslaken, near Düsseldorf. Approximately thirty resident children were frightened and brutalized by Nazi mobs during the Kristallnacht pogrom. They were herded into the yard while SA (*Sturmabteilung*) thugs destroyed the interior of their large building.

The children were forced to join other Jewish citizens in a humiliating parade through the town. Four of the oldest boys were ordered to pull an empty hay wagon loaded with the younger children through the streets as part of a "Jewish Parade" as spiteful spectators taunted them.

Some weeks later, the acting director of the home, Yitzhak Sophoni Herz, was able to resettle the children in a vocational school in Cologne. From there he succeeded in arranging their emigration to Holland and Belgium.[30]

Among the Dinslaken orphanage children who were accepted by the Belgian committee were trainees Inge Berlin and Ruth Herz (not related to the director), Alfred and Heinz Eschwege, Klaus Sostheim and Rolf Weinmann, as well as the Steuer children. Bertrand and Hanna Elkan and Inge and Heinz Bernhard were local Dinslaken children whom the committee also rescued.

A friendly Jewish social worker arranged to include Egon Berlin of Koblenz (younger brother of Inge Berlin) in the contingent from the Dinslaken orphanage.[31] In Brussels, Mr. Dronsart, executive director of the Belgian Red Cross personally welcomed them at their hotel.[32]

Even though CAEJR members had no known prior experience with managing large numbers of children, they apparently learned quickly simply "by doing." Between November 29, 1939, and March 31, 1940, the committee raised BEF 1,206,311 (Belgian francs), then worth US$723,787, and spent BEF 942,635 (or US$565,581), leaving a balance of BEF 263,676 (US$158,206) (currency values at 1939 rate).[33] Where possible, they sought monthly support payments from the children's relatives and family friends in other countries. The children's parents were, in most cases, already in desperate financial straits and Germany would not let them send money to foreign countries.

Funds were also raised from the Belgian government and private donations. Mme Goldschmidt-Brodsky and Senator Herbert Speyer visited Belgium's Queen Elisabeth in the spring of 1939 to ask for assistance. The Queen personally donated 5,000 Belgian francs (then worth some US$3,000) to the committee, "to buy clothing and toys for the children."[34]

An organization willing to lend financial support was the Comité des Avocates (Women Lawyers Committee), whose honorary board included one-time justice minister Paul-Emile Janson, Camille Huysmans, and several university presidents.[35]

Many of the young refugees were not subsidized by relatives or friends, but host families accepted them—some with pay and many without (in early April 1940, forty-two children lived with private families without any payment, and forty others with families whom the committee paid).[36] A committee report dated December 10, 1939, shows that 330 of its children were then housed with their own parents or with relatives living in Belgium.[37]

Efforts were made to match the children with families whose values or occupations were similar to the selected child's family. Where possible, siblings were placed together. But there also were incidents where very young children had to advocate for themselves.

Helga Schwarz Assier recalls her anguish when her younger brother Harry was selected by a well-meaning couple. "No!" she cried, "you'll take both or none." As none of the families present was ready to take two children, they were placed in a group home. "And we were happy to be staying together," she recalls. Years later, with children of her own, she appreciated how distraught her parents must have been to send their children into the unknown.[38]

Committee members also attempted to place children from Orthodox Jewish families into similar environments. Insofar as possible, the committee preferred to place the children in private homes, and Mme Alfred (Louise) Wolff and other committee members toured the country to seek host families.[39] Committee members also kept a few refugee children in their own homes.[40]

2. Home Speyer building in Anderlecht, Belgium, with "A Vendre" sign, 1939. From the author's personal collection.

More than 100 children were lodged in several *foyers* (children's homes). About forty-five boys were housed at Home Herbert Speyer, a multi-story attached house in the Anderlecht suburb of Brussels. This facility belonged to, and was operated by, the long-established Foyer des Orphelins, a not-for-profit organization for orphans.[41] More than thirty girls were placed in the Home Général Bernheim in Zuen, at the northern edge of Brussels.[42]

Heide-lez-Anvers in Antwerp cared for twenty older boys and ten were placed in the care of teachers Mr. and Mme Korytowsky in

Schaerbeek. Others were housed in Wezembeek, a Brussels suburb, on the estate of the Lambert banking family.

The "Foyer des Orphelins" (orphanage)—with facilities on rue de Korenbeek, at the English Channel resort of Middlekerke, on rue du Geomètre in Brussels, and also in Louvain—played an important role as the committee's children were housed in their facilities for a time.[43] (During the German occupation of Belgium, this multi-site foyer provided refuge for a number of the committee's children who survived the war there. It employed the DeWaay couple after they returned from France in the fall of 1940.)[44]

The Salvation Army was often the first stop for children who had entered Belgium illegally (see the Schütz sisters' arrival). When the required paperwork with the Sureté Publique was completed, these children, housed temporarily at the Salvation Army, were placed with families or at the committee's children's homes.

Finding and monitoring qualified caregivers for so many children in its several facilities was another task for the leaders of the committee. At Home Général Bernheim the *directrice* (woman manager) was Elka Frank, just twenty-three years old, assisted by her twenty-five-year-old husband, Alexandre (Alex). Elka was born in Berlin; Alex in Belgium. They had met and married in Palestine, then returned to Belgium.[45] Neither had previous experience for their assignment at Home Général Bernheim.

Mrs. Flora Schlesinger, a refugee from Austria, was engaged as the cook and became a motherly friend for many of the girls. Her husband, Ernst Schlesinger, did yard and garden work and their young son Paul also lived at the home.

At Home Speyer, Gaspard DeWaay ("Oncle Gaspard") was appointed manager in January 1939. His wife, Lucienne ("Tante Lucienne"), supervised the kitchen and housekeeping. Gaspard, then twenty-eight years old (born November 15, 1910, in Verviers), had been a streetcar conductor in his hometown.[46] Lucienne was twenty-five years old (born October 24, 1913, also in Verviers), with a young daughter, when Mr. de Gronckel, general secretary of the Foyer put them in charge of Home Speyer.[47]

3. Three older girls at Home General Bernheim in Zuen, Belgium, 1939. From left: Else Rosenblatt, Lotte Nussbaum, Ruth Klonower. From the author's personal collection.

Home Speyer was named after former Belgian Senator Herbert Speyer, who had donated nearly BEF 500,000 to support Comité d'Aide et d'Assistance aux Victimes de l'Antisémitisme en Allemagne (CAAVAA, or Support and Aid Committee to Victims of Anti-Semitism in Germany).[48]

When some of the children became ill, the committee and its staff saw to it that adequate care was provided. Kurt Moser was in isolation at the Schaerbeek Hospital for three months because of an infection, as was Rolf Loewenstein at Sainte Elisabeth Hospital.[49] At least ten children were given "kinésique" (posture) physical therapy treatments for several months at the Willy B. Cox studio in Brussels, which also provided gymnastics lessons at Home Speyer, arranged and paid by the committee.[50]

For the children, now separated from their families and native homes, life in Belgium had pleasant, as well as difficult outcomes.

4. Group of boys at Home Speyer in Anderlecht, Belgium, 1939. Mme Luci-enne DeWaay is in center; Mr. Becker, counselor from Switzerland, at left, rear. From the author's personal collection.

Living with strangers or in group homes added more stress to the trauma of separation from parents and siblings, especially for the younger boys and girls. Adjusting to life where they did not under-stand the language (French or Flemish, depending on the region), having to eat foods to which they were not accustomed (endive—called chicorée—and no more home-cooked German or Austrian dishes), and going to school with children who readily tabbed them as foreigners, created emotional problems. These difficulties were offset, however, because the children (including the author) were now free of the ever-present anti-Semitic harassment in our home countries.

Correspondence was still possible with our parents who were left behind in Germany and Austria. Some of us also could visit relatives who had emigrated to Belgium. For others, living with children from different backgrounds and with "strange" habits required adjustment, but it also educated us to the idea of tolerance and respect. Most of the children came from families of modest means and many of their parents had been emigrants from Poland and other eastern countries.

5. Group of boys peeling potatoes at Home Speyer, 1939. In center with arm reaching into basket, author Walter Reed (Rindsberg). From the author's personal collection.

Luzian (Lucien) Wolfgang, who hailed from Vienna, told a German television reporter in 1993 "some of us came from well-to-do, advantaged families, but others, like me, from very poor families. My father was unemployed for many years."[51] With the number of children involved, it was inevitable that some would have behavior problems and others were placed with families who were not ideal hosts. Thus it was not unusual that the committee ladies shifted children between host families and group homes, because either the children or the hosts complained.

"In Brussels I worked as a 'mother's helper' for a Christian family," recalls Ruth Herz Goldschmidt, then seventeen years old, who had been an aide at Dinslaken. Actually I was the maid and slaved from dawn to late at night doing all the housework, yard work and supervising several school-age children."[52]

Some of the children were moved from group homes to families and back all too frequently and for various reasons. Edith Goldapper Rosenthal's diary of 1943 gives a vivid account—arriving in Brussels from Vienna in December 1938, she was personally welcomed by Mme Goldschmidt-Brodsky, and later by Mme Felddegen.

Her first placement was at the suburban Maison de Cure (previously a convalescent home) at Wezembeek-Oppem, where she met boys and girls with whom she would be associated again in the following years. Mme Goldschmidt-Brodsky personally moved her to a wealthy Russian-born host family in Antwerp. When the mother became ill and fourteen-year-old Edith was terribly homesick, she was transferred to the Home Général Bernheim in suburban Brussels.

The older children took advantage of their new environment, learning French or Flemish and also English, which was encouraged by the committee. Learning English was desirable because the main purpose of their stay in Belgium was to await permanent settlement in the United States, Canada, and other countries.

The language problem also had its lighter side. Kurt Klein, age thirteen, from Austria, always stumbled over the French word *onze* (eleven). Instead of pronouncing it "ohnz," as the French do, he pronounced the letters as they would be in German: "on-tze." Forever after his companions forgot his real first name and he became "Ontze" Klein, even when he joined the French Resistance in 1944. Fortunately, "Onze" always was full of fun and jokes, the camp clown, an attribute that would become an asset when his life was in the balance just a few years later.[53]

Committee staff reported that the children at Home Speyer and Home Général Bernheim received a "medical visit" once a month and

6. At Home General Bernheim in Zuen, Belgium, 1939. From left: Hanni Schlimmer, CAEJR Committee staff member Elias Haskelevicz, and Dela Hochberger. Reproduced with permission from the United States Holocaust Memorial Museum Photo Archive.

that "Rabbi Ansbacher provided Jewish religion lessons." In 1939 the Hanukkah holiday was celebrated with a theater visit arranged by Mme deBecker-Remy and presents were handed out to all the children, "who were in seventh heaven."[54]

The children of school age were enrolled in Belgian schools, some of the boys in a vocational school, specializing in skills like carpentry, horticulture, and locksmithing.[55] The older girls from Home Général Bernheim also attended a vocational school.

On many weekends the ladies of the committee took children of the group homes for outings to Brussels museums and to special events, often in their chauffeur-driven luxury cars. This had varying effects on the children. Some enjoyed the experience; others have complained even sixty-five years later that the women were "showing off" and made the children uncomfortable when they visited their elaborate homes—obviously not what the kindly hostesses intended. Many of the children also were taken on outings and excursions to the Belgian countryside, including some of the lovely vacation spots in the Ardennes forest. Gaspard DeWaay practiced a kind of discipline at Home Speyer that grated on the older boys who may have been spoiled at home and were advancing into their teenage years. His overly strict methods for dealing with children may have been acceptable to some at the time, but his approach was not well suited for the management and guidance of refugee children.

The recollection of the children and some of the correspondence of committee members reflect the tension that prevailed at times at Home Speyer.[56] On the other hand, Home Speyer and the other sites had counselors like Mr. Becker from Switzerland, who related well to the youngsters and operated without friction.[57] The Home Speyer boys also interacted well with "Tante Lucienne" (Mme DeWaay) who did her best to act as substitute mother for the refugee children under her care.

The last known "transport" of children from Nazi Germany arrived in Brussels on June 15, 1939. Some of its twenty-nine girls and boys were destined to stay together throughout the adventures of the next four years. All child refugee transports to Belgium were being halted and it was only with determined effort that this final small number of children could be admitted, states a letter from the committee to the Jewish congregation of Leipzig, Germany, dated June 8, 1939.[58] Inge Helft, age thirteen of Wurzen, was the only "lucky child" of the Leipzig group to be included, the letter states.

While life in Belgium was a great improvement over the children's experiences under the German-Austrian regime, new concerns would soon arise. The German invasion of Poland in September 1939 produced the "phony war" (declared, but not pursued by France and England) and was regarded with apprehension by Belgian citizens. It also became worrisome for the older refugee girls and boys who retained unpleasant and vivid memories of their lives in Germany and Austria.

Confident propaganda by Western countries, which extolled the deterrent of the French Maginot Line and the "impenetrable" Fort Eben-Emael near Liège in Belgium, bolstered Belgium's hope to defend the border against a German attack. The young Jewish refugees soon learned and joined in singing the popular refrain, "Nous allons pendre notre linge sur la Ligne Siegfried" ("we'll be hanging our laundry on the Siegfried Line"—the German counterpart of the Maginot Line).

More than 100 of the children on the committee's lists succeeded in emigrating from their temporary Belgian refuge in 1939–40, as intended by their host government and by the Belgian caretakers.[59] At least 47 went to England, 25 to the United States, 7 to Holland, 5 to Palestine, 4 to Chile and 1 to Shanghai.[60] Among those who received US visas and emigrated were Rainer Laub, Adolf Herbst, Karl-Heinz Goldschmidt, Gerhard Hirsch, two Jülich brothers (Otto and Karl), Henriette Hahn, Marianne Scheuer, Helmuth Cohn, and Hannelore Kaufmann.[61]

Fate, more than planning, sometimes played a major role in the children's lives. Susie Davids's mother, Irma, was able to leave Germany by finding a job as a domestic for a well-placed couple in the English countryside near Birmingham. Her father, Paul Davids, was living with in-laws in Belgium. In August 1939 the mother's English employer brought Mr. Davids, Susie, and her brother Gerd to England for a two-week vacation. They were preparing to board the channel ferry at Dover on September 4 to return to Belgium. When England declared war against Germany on September 3, they were "stranded" and fortunately stayed in England.[62]

◇ **3** ◇

Second Escape, May 14, 1940

On the morning of Friday, May 10, 1940, readers of the daily Brussels newspaper *Le Soir* found a routine front-page photograph of the Belgian princes Baudouin and Albert opening the Hunting, Fishing, Sports and Tourism Exposition at Brussels' Centenaire Palace Hall the day before. And they could also read that "the advance of the German forces in Norway had been slowed." But that morning those same readers also heard unaccustomed waves of airplanes overhead and then the frightening thud of bombs falling nearby. The much-feared German invasion of Belgium, Holland, Luxembourg, and France had been unleashed, and it would dramatically change the lives of the Jewish-German and Jewish-Austrian refugee children who had only recently found safety and hope in Belgium.

The sound of numerous airplanes in the Brussels sky put the whole population on edge, concerned whether the Belgian forces would be able to repel the German attack. On the radio they heard bulletins offering mostly reassuring news.

Here is how these events affected me and our other refugee children:

"A low and continuing thunder awoke me from my sleep. Suddenly I heard the noise of the windows in our room shaking, and a clear, high sound, like screams of fear. I jumped out of bed to learn what was happening and there was lightning and an explosion and then again lightning and an explosion, and then a strange silence in anticipation of new explosions. The air-raid sirens started to shriek, making a long and nerve-racking noise," recalls Ruth Schütz Usrad, who was living at Home Général Bernheim.[1]

32

Edith Goldapper Rosenthal recounts in her diary: "We hear artillery fire outside. Yes it is May 10, 1940, and the war in Belgium has begun. We are overcome by panic. With every sounding of the alarm we bound into the basement [of Home Général Bernheim]. In our free time we attempt to dig a bomb shelter and we use it."[2]

Similar emotions prevailed at the main boys' refugee home, Home Speyer in Anderlecht. We older boys knew only too well the threat that German success posed for all of us, while the younger ones may have noticed the commotion but were more concerned about the interruption of their playtime and when it would be time for their next meal.

At first, the population relied on the optimism of the prewar months. Two days after the attacks, *Le Soir* reported that blackout material was being sold and that people had not panicked. The story said that the radio was playing "Nous allons pendre notre linge . . ." (the previously-mentioned clothes-hanging song), "Madelon," and "Auprès de ma blonde . . ." (a romantic soldiers' ditty). A front-page article on May 12 concludes, "Belgium deals, intact and determined, with this new confrontation which has descended upon it."[3]

But on page 3, *Le Soir* reported that forty-one persons were killed and eighty-two wounded by the bombing raids in the Brussels area. The Defense Department claimed that fifteen Nazi planes had been downed. The adult populations of Holland, Belgium, and northern France remembered all too well the ravages caused in their regions by World War I and they fled southward, panic-stricken, in a mass exodus by train, car, bus, on bicycles, on carts, and on foot. Four million French, Belgian, and other refugees, trying to flee before the German advance, were on the roads or camped in makeshift shelters.[4]

By May 14, fear and panic had deepened for our Jewish refugee children's groups. That day Elka Frank, director of the Général Bernheim girls' home, told her protégées to pack their belongings and to wear extra layers of clothes for their flight from Brussels. Her husband, Alex, was a Belgian soldier, guarding a military airfield, so the young home director was on her own and worrying about the safety of her more than thirty girls.

The DeWaays at Home Speyer also told us to get ready and pack lightly for departure, but to carry food rations. Both groups met that afternoon at the Schaerbeek rail station in central Brussels, which was packed with anxious refugees, waiting for transportation to the south. By evening our group of ninety-three boys and girls was told to climb into two separate freight cars and the train took off into the unknown late that night, each freight car packed with refugees fleeing the city.

The children of our two refugee homes were joined by others who had been placed with families or who were siblings of a child at either home.[5] Edith ("Ditta") Weisz Kurzweil was summoned to rush from her foster home, where the host family was fleeing to the countryside, to join her brother Hansl Weisz at Home Speyer before our group left for the train station.[6] The oldest children were just seventeen and the youngest, Antoinette Steuer, would soon be four years old.

Some of the children later credited a brother of Alex Frank, who had worked for the Belgian government, as facilitating the access to the refugee freight train. Others proclaimed that the Women's Committee had abandoned the children while saving themselves. That allegation is contradicted by a recorded interview of committee member Mme Alfred Wolff in the 1950s.[7]

Mme Wolff recalls being left alone at the committee office on May 10 and directing some children who had been placed with individual families to join the two fleeing groups (see previous paragraph). She also recalls that Committee President Mme Goldschmidt-Brodsky was out of town but returned the day of the invasion. Mme Wolff also stated that Mme Goldschmidt-Brodsky "had turned over a large sum of money to the Foyer des Orphelins to assure the future of the children" (the Foyer owned and managed the Home Speyer facility). Records in its archive indicate that the funds deposited for this purpose by Mme Goldschmidt-Brodsky were, in fact, given to Gaspard DeWaay before the children departed.[8]

This is supported by a statement of Mme Lucienne DeWaay, who told Dr. Theo Tschuy in 2003 that her husband, Gaspard, met with Mme Goldschmidt-Brodsky in Cahors, France, in August 1940 when the couple moved back to Belgium. During this visit he allegedly returned to her the remaining funds not yet spent for the children whom he had led to France. The Foyer archive also contains a copy of the receipt that details the funds turned over by DeWaay to his successor, Alex Frank, and signed by Frank on September 6, 1940.

A strong contradiction to the "abandonment" accusation arises from subsequent well-documented actions of several Women's Committee members. Mmes Felddegen and de Becker had emigrated to the United States before the German invasion, as had Max Gottschalk. However, already on November 14, 1939, Marguérite Goldschmidt-Brodsky had written to Lilly Felddegen in New York, "although the current fears have calmed down, I have made an agreement with the president of the 'Foyer des Orphelins' that our children and our funds would be transferred to them if ever we became unable to take care of our little protégés. In that case our office would be dissolved immediately and all files would be transferred by my secretary, Mademoiselle Chevron, to the Foyer headquarters. Fortunately children would be in less danger than adults."[9]

It is unlikely that either Elka Frank or Gaspard DeWaay had the authority, as staff employees, to evacuate the ninety-three children under their care to an unknown destination without committee approval. Both were under thirty years old and Lucienne DeWaay was six months pregnant with their second child. In a letter to the Joint Distribution Committee in New York from Cahors, France, dated July 16, 1940, Marguérite Goldschmidt-Brodsky stated "the children escaped with the Belgian director[,] Mr. DeWaay, his wife and two female teachers," implying that she was fully involved in the escape process.[10]

Not all of the committee's young refugees were on the escape train the night of May 14. On May 10 the Belgian Justice Minister, panicked by the surprise German attack, had decreed that all German nationals over the age of eighteen were to be interned in order to protect Belgium against suspected saboteurs. These arrests included anti-Nazi German and Austrian refugees, as well as Jewish men and older teenagers who had fled from the Nazis. Thus Walter Kamlet, Heinz Storosum, Werner Epstein, and Ernst Schlesinger, husband of the girls' home's cook, Flora, and Elias Haskelevicz of the committee office staff were first interned and then evacuated to France in closed box cars.

Many of these men and teenagers ended up in French internment camps. Those named here eventually were freed and rejoined the children's colony in France. In her letter to the American Joint Distribution Committee in New York, Mme Goldschmidt-Brodsky specifically asked that "the Joint" representatives in France "help free two of our older boys from the internment camp of St. Cyprien, Kurt Moser and Berthold Elkan."[11]

As the train slowly steamed out of the Brussels station on May 14, the feeling was "go fast, go fast." Yet, to us fleeing children the train seemed to be crawling, undecided which way to turn. The Germans took over Brussels just two days later, but we were not to know this until much later. Fleeing for one's life makes even the most primitive conditions bearable. With only straw on the floor and without toilet facilities, the escape train ride was no picnic. It became all the more frightening since no one could provide answers about the route being taken or the destination. At the time, the most important thing was to get away.

Especially disturbing was the uncertainty over whether the French, British, and Belgian armies were winning or losing. Unlike today, news traveled slowly and rumors replaced information. As we read the train station signs, it became apparent that our refugee train was heading toward northwestern France, and then turned southward. Amiens, Rouen, and Alençon likely were among the way stations, but soon the train seemed to seek its way through territory unknown to any of us.

During prolonged stops at unfamiliar stations, local French people offered beverages and sandwiches to the fleeing travelers. Finding toilet facilities or open fields became urgent daylong concerns. "There were no toilets in our magnificent freight car, so this becomes one of the most urgent problems to be solved," recalls Edith Goldapper Rosenthal in her diary. "It's dicey to get out of the car because there is no known stop and start schedule. And at night I don't dare to close my eyes."[12]

On rail sidings we sometimes saw wounded French and British soldiers in halted railcars, a stark reminder that war was underway. This was intensified one night in Abbeville. "That night the train was attacked by dive bombers. We headed for Dieppe and the train sat there for a long time," Rosenthal writes.[13] Ruth Schütz Usrad also recalls that "the last car in which Belgian nuns were traveling was hit." She adds, "we traveled through France from north to south, without seeing any of its views, its scenery or its cities."[14]

By May 18 our meandering train had traversed regions of central and southern France that we, as children, had never even seen on a map. It might as well have been Spain or North Africa. Tired of the stress of fleeing and weary from the uncomfortable train ride, we were ordered from our freight cars onto the platform of a tiny station at Villefranche-de-Lauragais, some twenty-five miles south of Toulouse. For all of us it was an unknown region and landscape, but one which we were to get to know intimately in the following three years.

Dead-tired, frightened, and wondering what would come next, we soon found ourselves in a tiny and remote village called Seyre, a few kilometers over the gentle hills from the Villefranche train station.

Our home for the next eleven months turned out to be a large empty barn building at an isolated crossroad and set in the midst of a few farmhouses. The few other buildings of Seyre were the farm homes of very ordinary citizens who spoke a strange southern French dialect (*pâtois*). In 1938, the 113 inhabitants spread over the adjoining hillsides actually were the successors of a community founded 700 years before, a fact that we didn't know or contemplate at the time.[15]

The barn was just space, two stories high with some interior walls dividing it into primitive rooms. The structure contained no furniture; there were no sleeping facilities except straw on the floor, no running water or electricity, no cooking facilities, and no toilets. Most of our boys and girls, coming from two separate group homes in Belgium, did not even know each other because we had traversed France in separate, if adjacent, freight cars.

A few hundred yards from the barn sat a lovely little château built on top of a hillside, the residence of Mr. and Mrs. Gaston de Capèle

7. View of the "Barn" at Seyre, France, where the children lived from May 1940 for nearly one year. Photo taken by the author in 2000.

d'Hautpoul, who owned much of the surrounding agricultural land and the "barn." For the first night, the ninety-three children and our caretakers simply went to sleep, exhausted from our escape and from the five-day journey into the unknown.

Who selected the site and who decided that our refugee group and our caretakers were to leave the train and come to live at Seyre, of all places? We never asked and none of the children ever knew. During a visit by the author with the then ninety-year-old Mr. Gaston de Capèle d'Hautpoul at his château in 1997, he explained that in 1939 regional government authorities had researched and identified possible sites for refugees, planning for the possibility of a German invasion. His "barn" at Seyre became one of the many sites that were designated for refugees. Mr. de Capèle was away as a French army officer and his family was living in a Toulouse apartment when our refugee group arrived on May 18.[16]

The "barn," which after 1941 has served only for agricultural storage, actually had a different and more appropriate history. Known locally as *"l'arsénal"* (granary), according to Mr. René de LaPortalière, son-in-law of Mr. deCapèle, it had been intended and built as an orphanage for some 100 children by Countess Marguérite d'Hautpoul-La Terrace in the early 1900's.

It was designed with separate dormitory spaces at each end and classroom space in the center. Proceeds from the farmland were to fund the operation of the orphanage. It was, however, never occupied until we arrived on May 18. Childless, the countess had adopted her nephew Gaston de Capèle, who inherited the properties in 1937.[17]

In our isolated rural surroundings we were unaware of the enormous flood of Belgian refugees whom the German invasion had brought to the area in and around Toulouse. The available data vary. Jean Estèbe cites unofficial figures that indicate that the population of Toulouse more than doubled (from 213,000 in 1936 to 450,000–500,000 in June 1940).[18] Rodolfo Olgiati, secretary-general of the Schweizerische Arbeitsgemeinschaft für kriegsbeschädigte Kinder (Swiss Working Group for Child War Victims) reported "conservative estimates of 1.5 million Belgian refugees in southern France" in the confidential summary of his late July 1940 inspection tour of Vichy France.[19]

A police report of June 6, 1940, records the arrival of 16,549 Belgian civilians plus 26,468 Belgian soldiers in the Toulouse area by May 27.[20] Other reports describe refugees camped out in all available public spaces in Toulouse. Thus our children's colony newly arrived at Seyre was just a tiny part of the exodus from the north.

◇ 4 ◇

Life at Seyre, 1940

When we stepped outside the next morning, we found ourselves in an unfamiliar landscape. Slightly behind the huge barn we noticed a tiny country church, and a little farther along the narrow road rose a tall iron gate. Beyond it stood a gatehouse, the entryway to the Château of Seyre. Our barn stretched along the only village street, flanked by a few small farmhouses in which some of our children and our caretakers were housed. Beyond some outbuildings behind the barn we could see a valley of farmland rising to gentle flowing hills, one behind the other. It certainly looked much different from the towns we had known in Germany and Austria.

Neither the refugee children nor the local farmers had any idea that on that day, May 19, General Gamelin was replaced by General Weygand as the French military commander and that German "Blitzkrieg" (lightning war) forces had already scored crushing advances in northern France. Within two weeks, 300,000 British and French soldiers would flee to England via Dunkirk, and by June 22, four weeks after we arrived at Seyre, French leaders would sign an unconditional surrender.

During our first week at Seyre the main preoccupations of the children and our adult leaders were how to organize daily life, where and how to procure and cook food, and these were always mixed with fear about the outcome of the war. It was difficult to learn how the battle was going, with cautious and often misleading official radio announcements as the main source of information. A family fleeing with a few children to an unknown place of asylum would have faced serious difficulties, as tens of thousands did that month all over

France. But for the five or six adults in charge of nearly 100 active and anxious girls and boys aged five to seventeen, it must have been a nightmare after our group arrived at Seyre.

A closer look at the personalities of our group brings the challenges into focus. Mrs. Elka Frank, director of the Général Bernheim girls' home, was a caring and devoted young woman (twenty-four years old), but she lacked the organizational and "knowing how-to-get-things-done" skills that our new situation required. In a day when "management" usually fell into male hands, the Home Speyer director Gaspard DeWaay logically became the adult leader of our colony.

His wife Lucienne, then almost ready to give birth to their second daughter and caring for the first one, could offer little help. Mrs. Flora Schlesinger, the refugee from Austria who had been the cook at the Brussels girls' home, continued in that role. She performed miracles preparing meals without suitable equipment, under daunting food

8. The entire group at Seyre, in the fall of 1940. Camp leaders Alex and Elka Frank are at center, last row; counselor Elias Haskelevicz, first at far right, last row; and Flora Schlesinger, cook, second from left, last row. From the author's personal collection.

shortages and, a few weeks later, rationing. At the same time she worried about her husband, Ernst, who had been interned in Belgium as a "suspect alien" when the Germans invaded. For a few weeks several of the Belgian counselors, including Miss Lea and Arthur Haulot, remained with us in Seyre as useful additional adult caretakers.

In retrospect "Oncle Gaspard" DeWaay's role and invaluable service of leading the nearly 100 threatened children to safety appears most praiseworthy. He had led Home Speyer for only a little over a year and had no previous connection with the girls from Home Général Bernheim. Mr. DeWaay was not Jewish and not a highly paid employee of the Foyer des Orphelins, as he had no special training or experience for mentoring children. And he was only twenty-nine years old.[1]

One can only guess at his state of mind on May 19 as he found himself in a remote hamlet, surrounded by uncertainty and responsible for nearly 100 children without the resources and backing of the Belgian Women's Committee and the Belgian Foyer that had employed him. Young Gaspard DeWaay, though he worked hard to face up to his responsibilities, is remembered by most of the children at Seyre as a despotic and mean disciplinarian. As described by Ruth Schütz Usrad:

> His pale face gave him a weak and sickly appearance. His blonde hair was thin, and he wore glasses with thick lenses. He looked like a clerk in a government office who had to obey those above him. He would stand in front of the dining room, and make sure that all the children lined up in threes and stood in total silence. Many long minutes would pass till "Gaspard" would give the sign that we were allowed to come in and sit on the benches. He'd wait for total silence till he gave the word, "Bon appétit."
>
> For any slight transgression, we would receive harsh punishment. He would sneak up quietly and, with a shout, catch the victim who had breached his rules, for example by speaking German. We called him "the panther."[2]

His was no easy task, for within a few days the colony had to establish a way to function and to survive.

After Maréchal Pétain, the aging French World War I hero, signed the armistice with Germany on June 22 (just a month after we arrived), France was divided into the Wehrmacht-occupied northern half and the unoccupied southern zone, dubbed "Vichy France" because Pétain's regime ruled from that city.

The Pétain government was expected to comply with Nazi desires and one of the armistice regulations required that it must deliver any person the Germans requested. The Germans soon requisitioned fuel, vehicles, food products, and other vital materials so that the population in the unoccupied zone experienced shortages and misery in daily living. Mentally, too, the population paid a price. The swiftness and totality of the German victory inflicted a heavy psychological blow to the stunned French population and this feeling was not lost on the youngsters at Seyre.

Nearly thirty of the boys and girls were too young to understand or worry about what was happening to the western European countries. Getting enough to eat and having time to play, understandably, were their main concerns. However, for those over twelve or thirteen years old, what was going on around us and what lay ahead became an unending concern. And for all there was our separation from parents, siblings, and relatives, which was compounded by the remote location of our new refuge. For quite a time we all felt isolated and had no idea what was going on in France, let alone in other European countries.

These circumstances made young people grow up fast, and many of our older girls and boys rose to the occasion. Soon the colony was organized into groups with daily responsibilities for each youngster and with the sixteen-to-eighteen-year-olds taking charge. There were the "grands" and "grandes" (older boys and girls), the "moyens" and "moyennes" (the in-between age groups) and then "les petites" and "petits" (the female and male little ones).

Each of the younger groups was supervised by one or more of the "grands" and "grandes." And many of those over twelve or thirteen

9. Map of France showing north occupied by Germany and unoccupied zone (Vichy France) where Seyre and La Hille are located.
Map by Frothingham Communications.

were assigned work in the kitchen, collecting wood for cooking,
cleaning, and play supervision. The "grands/grandes" also conducted
rudimentary classes for the younger children and supervised games
and hikes.

The oldest boys readily found work with farmers of the area
because many local young Frenchmen were away—they were either
still in the army or they had been taken to Germany as prisoners of
war. The farm work created good relationships with the local population and supplied scarce vegetables and produce to our makeshift
kitchen in the barn.

Once the Vichy government was functioning, a six-franc subsidy per child (ten francs for adults) was paid to all refugees and this seems to have tided our colony over for a time.[3] And it supplemented the funds that the Belgian Foyer had entrusted to Gaspard DeWaay. Mme Goldschmidt-Brodsky, the president of the Belgian Committee, mentioned this in her July 16, 1940, letter to the Joint Distribution Committee of New York: "The director, Mr. DeWaay, still has part of a sum of money which we had collected in Belgium and that would take care of the children for another six weeks at best."[4] Fortunately the temperatures in southern France were already pleasant and heading for summer so that everyone could be comfortably outdoors. At first the lack of a heating system and running water were not as unpleasant as they would become in the fall and winter.

By far the greatest immediate difficulty was to procure sufficient food, cooking ingredients, and milk. The nearest shopping facilities were located in Villefranche, eight kilometers away, and the local population, typical of rural France, either grew its own food or shopped at the weekly open market in town. Meat was typically bought daily from a local butcher since no one had refrigeration, but there were no shops in Seyre.

In the summer of 1940, supplying a colony of 100 children with three meals a day posed constant obstacles. Preparing meals was equally challenging and Flora Schlesinger, the cook from Zuen, assisted by Elka Frank and Lucienne DeWaay, had to make do with what little was available in a cooking area without equipment and for which the only fuel was wood gathered by the older boys from the surrounding area.

Corn meal prepared in a huge vat and varied only with seasonings or added ingredients like raisins or cheese became a daily and much-maligned staple. Water was available only from an outdoor pump and from external cisterns and was a precious commodity. Washing clothes and washing one's body depended totally upon those limited water sources.

Having once more barely escaped Nazi persecution was a relief for the teenage boys and girls, but any joy would remain tinged with worry about what might lie ahead. All the children faced the increasing difficulty of communicating with their families whom they had left behind in Germany, Austria, Belgium, or England.

Ditta Weisz (Kurzweil) described the situation in a letter to her parents in New York on July 26.[5] "One has to run around to get potatoes and when one does, it's a holiday. You cannot forget that we're one hundred people, people who eat a lot. We're always outdoors and get hungry. When we're hungry we need about sixteen loaves of bread for supper. We two are lucky because we will be leaving [Ditta and younger brother Hansl had US visas], but the others don't know what they will do and no one knows. In any case, they have a life without the least hope that this life will change. This is still all right for the little ones, but it's different for the big ones."

Such concerns were well founded, for by the end of June France had capitulated and the new regime, led by Maréchal Philippe Pétain, was getting organized in Vichy.

Historians Michael R. Marrus and Robert O. Paxton describe the new rulers: "The Vichy regime launched France on what many French people believed was a permanent new tack, the program called the National Revolution: authoritarian, traditionalist, pious, and neutral in the war between Hitler and the Allies. Vichy was also publicly and conspicuously anti-Semitic."[6]

In remote Seyre it took a while before this description became meaningful. But by midsummer, even in this isolated rural corner of unoccupied France the older girls and boys and our caretakers became aware of the "new" France and what it would mean for our interrupted lives. We had vivid memories of how we became despised and persecuted young Jews when the Nazis took over our homeland. How would the German victors deal with the Jews in their newly conquered territory and who would really govern southern France? No one could tell, but we would soon find out. As everywhere, even in this little agricultural corner, there were French people who continued to despise the German conquerors, but there also were others who became willing collaborators either by conviction or to gain some little advantage in their increasingly difficult daily existence.

The first anti-Semitic measures of the new Vichy government were signed into law on October 3, 1940, defining who was a Jew. The next day, Vichy authorized its prefects (the provincial governors) to intern Jews in special camps without cause or to assign them to live under police surveillance in remote villages—"residence forcée." Historians have established that the Germans had not requested such measures.[7]

Caution dictated that the presence of some 100 Jewish refugee children at Seyre should be kept inconspicuous. For good reason, but with customary severity, our colony leader Gaspard DeWaay forbade the children to speak German. German was our native language and many were not proficient in French. Because it was summer and there were no schools nearby, the older boys and girls informally taught the new language. Fortunately, the village was so isolated, and transportation so limited, that casual discovery of the colony was unlikely.

The older boys and girls have vivid recollections of our life at Seyre. Torn from our families and completely dependent upon each other, we became a close-knit family, trying to exist and survive in truly marginal circumstances. Many forged bonds that would last a lifetime under circumstances never forgotten.

By July the daily life of the defeated French nation became routine, but with unaccustomed difficulties for the entire population. The Germans wasted no time requisitioning fuel, vehicles, industrial equipment, and foodstuffs, and shipped them to their homeland— and this was imposed in both zones of France. The remaining French cars and trucks were equipped with special burners that used charcoal for fuel instead of the unavailable gasoline. Strange grains replaced coffee beans and food would soon be rationed.

On August 7 a new phase began for our children's colony at Seyre as Alex Frank, the husband of Elka Frank, was demobilized from the Belgian Army near Toulouse and soon was able to find his wife and the colony. By midsummer, many of the Belgian and other northern non-Jewish refugees began to return to their homes. Lucienne DeWaay had given birth to their second daughter at Seyre and the DeWaays, too, wanted to return to Belgium. They departed on September 1 and visited Mr. and Mme Goldschmidt-Brodsky, who had fled to Cahors (ninety-five miles north of Seyre) on their way north.[8] Alfred Goldschmidt, treasurer and board member of the Belgian Red Cross, which had moved its operations to Cahors, chaired its extensive repatriation activities from that city in the fall of 1940.[9]

In view of some derogatory comments about Gaspard DeWaay regarding his departure and treatment of the children, written many years later by, and quoting, some of the children, it is worth noting that Mme Goldschmidt-Brodsky wrote a letter of commendation dated September 4, 1940, in which she praised his services in Belgium and in Seyre, and cited his devotion and honesty.[10]

A group of some twenty older boys and girls addressed a letter to Mme Goldschmidt-Brodsky, dated July 26, 1940, to be delivered "on the occasion of the trip by Oncle Gaspard" (who apparently was then meeting her at an unnamed location) in which he was praised for "allowing us to still be alive and free." The purpose of the letter was to urge Mme Goldschmidt-Brodsky to do all possible to help the colony to emigrate. It was signed by the author of this book (having the name "Werner Rindsberg" at the time) on behalf of the group.[11]

As of September 1, Alex Frank took over the leadership of our colony and quickly established a "can-do" spirit and a more organized camp life. Born in Belgium and just twenty-seven years old, he had studied agriculture. After his father died, he emigrated to Palestine in 1932 intending to work on the land. Instead he found himself doing stevedore and heavy construction work. In 1934 he met his future wife, Elka, there and both joined the Communist Party.[12]

Because of his agricultural experience, he quickly established friendly relationships with the farmers near Seyre, provided farm work for some of the older boys, enthusiastically led forays into the nearby woods, and made weekly food shopping trips with the older boys to the farmers' market in Villefranche. A December 18, 1940, "Happy New Year" letter to Mme Felddegen in New York, handwritten by Lotte Nussbaum and signed by fifty-five of the older children, bears the note that "seven boys are absent, working on farms" (named are Bertrand Elkan, Werner Rindsberg, Pierre Salz, Willy Grossmann, Rudi Oehlbaum, Emil

(Émile) Dortort, and Norbert Winter).[13] The letter states that "even though this marks the second year far away from our loved ones, we will try to conclude it as though we were at home."[14]

"A father figure replaced a despotic one," states Inge Berlin (Vogelstein), then seventeen years old. "With help from his wife, Elka Frank, Alex created an orderly, viable community, with each age group assigned appropriate tasks and, insofar as possible, with regard for individual needs and abilities."[15] Under Alex, the children's groups were given imaginative names, such as the "Mickeys" (a reference to Mickey Mouse) for the youngest boys, and the "moyens" (middle boys) were renamed the "Chamois" (mountain goats).[16]

Alex Frank also turned his energy and skill to liberating a number of the older boys and girls, and also some adults, who were trapped

10. "Les Petites" (the little girls) at Seyre, France, 1940. Front, from left: Edith Jankielewitz, Toni Steuer, Toni Rosenblatt, and Laura Flanter. Second row, from left: Ingeborg Rübler, Almuth Königshöfer, Rosa Blau, and Rosa Krolik. From the author's personal collection.

11. "Les Petits" (the little boys) at Seyre, France, 1940. Center, front from left: Peter Bergmann and Martin Findling. Second row, from left: Gerhard Eckmann, Guy Haas, Paul Schlesinger, and Dela Hochberger. Last row, from left: Edith Goldapper, Lotte Nussbaum, Inge Joseph, and Ruth Klonower. From the author's personal collection.

in Vichy France internment camps. Some had been seized in Belgium and transported to France when the Germans invaded, and several were arrested after the colony arrived at Seyre. That was true of Ruth Herz (Goldschmidt) and Ilse Brünell, who were taken to the Gurs internment camp soon after they had arrived in Seyre. They were freed on October 11, 1940, and returned to Seyre.[17]

Werner Epstein, then almost seventeen years old, had been arrested in Belgium on May 10, as was Ernst Schlesinger, husband of Flora, the cook at Home Général Bernheim. They and older teenagers Kurt Moser, Berthold (Bertrand) Elkan, and Walter Kamlet, plus Brussels office staff member Elias Haskelevicz had been transported from Belgium to the St. Cyprien French internment camp near Perpignan. Epstein then was transferred to the Camp de Gurs near Oloron in the foothills of the Pyrénées mountains. He and Haskelevicz contracted malaria in the camps. Epstein nearly died of the disease and credits a Spanish refugee doctor at Gurs with supplying him with otherwise unobtainable quinine to save his life.[18] Haskelevicz remained seriously ill with bouts of malaria-caused fever after he was freed and returned to the Seyre colony.[19]

Alex Frank also was able to bring Almuth Königshöfer, a seventeen-year-old non-Jewish girl, to Seyre from an internment camp near Limoges. Her parents were adherents of Nazi opponent Pastor Niemöller.[20] To liberate these individuals, Frank used connections with staff members of the Secours Suisse (Swiss Aid Society) who were assisting refugees in the camps. But he also needed to procure residence permission from the mayor of Seyre and from the Toulouse Préfecture (regional government).

In all, he liberated eight boys and girls and one adult.[21] Frank accomplished this while leading our colony at Seyre with little adult assistance. In his letters of January 30, 1941, to Mmes Felddegen and deBecker[22] he voiced regret that he was unable to liberate the older brothers of colony members Inge Bernhard and Walter Strauss from the internment camps. He explained that because they were older they were not eligible to join the colony. Alex Frank obviously was a devoted dynamo.

By early fall 1940, the stories told by these new arrivals and frequent circulating rumors had created worrisome uncertainty and fear of worse things to come among the older teenagers. Names like Gurs, Rivesaltes, and St. Cyprien reminded us of terrifying names and places—such as Dachau—that we had similarly feared before we had come to Belgium.

◇ 5 ◇

The "Secours Suisse aux Enfants" and a Tough Winter

At 9:15 a.m. on September 23, 1940, six caring individuals were seated around a table in a small office above the backyard at 71 rue du Taur in Toulouse, just down the street from the city hall and the historic Place du Capitole. The room was at the French headquarters of the "Cartel Suisse de Secours aux Enfants Victimes de la Guerre" (Swiss Aid Association for Child War Victims).[1]

By noon that fateful day the survival and protection of most of the children then lodged at Seyre, 38 kilometers down the road, had been assured, although at the time no one had any idea of this meeting's far-reaching significance. The children never knew about the meeting, then or later.

Mme Marguérite Goldschmidt-Brodsky had approached the Swiss group's director for France, Maurice Dubois, and proposed that his organization take over the colony of her former protégés now at Seyre. She had come from her temporary residence at Cahors with a former colleague from Belgium, A. Varchaver, and had summoned Alex Frank from Seyre. In addition to Maurice Dubois, the Swiss group included his wife and coworker, Eleanor Dubois, and Mme Régine Kägi, a member of the Swiss organization's board of directors from Bern.

After Mme Goldschmidt reviewed the past history of the refugee children and our current situation, Mme Kägi explained that the Swiss organization's mission was to assist Belgian and French refugee children and that a decision to include refugees from Germany and Austria had to be made in Bern. Fortuitously the approval came by

12. Mme Marguérite Goldschmidt-Brodsky, chairperson of the Belgian Rescue Committee. Photo courtesy of Pierre Goldschmidt.

mail during the meeting. Although voicing her agreement, Mme Kägi said that political and other subsequent developments could terminate the Swiss support and Mme Goldschmidt said that she was aware that unforeseen events could change the situation.

Maurice Dubois declared that the Secours Suisse was ready to assume responsibility for the maintenance and education of the children, but that Swiss managers would have to be in charge. He added that for various reasons it would be desirable to add non-Jewish French and Spanish refugee children to the colony. He also stated that the younger children might be separated and the older ones placed on a rented farm operated to sustain the colony. Mme Goldschmidt voiced her agreement. It was pointed out that Mssrs. Frank and Varchaver had already surveyed two possible properties in the Toulouse region.

Mme Goldschmidt urged the Swiss group to retain the present adult personnel and to attempt to free Mr. Ernst Schlesinger, who was still interned at St. Cyprien. The Swiss participants declared themselves ready to take over the colony on October 1 and estimated the monthly operating cost at 35,000 French francs. Mme Goldschmidt reported that Mr. Frank currently had a net amount of 53,000 French francs at hand. She added that steps were underway to solicit additional funding from the officials of the American Joint Distribution Committee (the "Joint"). Finally she thanked the Swiss delegates for their humanitarian role in relieving the misery of so many children affected by war.[2]

In July, Mme Goldschmidt-Brodsky pleaded for help from the "Joint," explaining that she had attempted to get support from the Belgian Red Cross in Toulouse, "but they will be leaving in a few weeks. I have been able to visit the children once at Seyre but cannot return for lack of gasoline. I beseech you not to abandon these children. I know them well, they are well behaved and are very willing to adapt themselves no matter what life brings. But somebody has to care enough to lend a hand."[3]

The "Joint" in fact appropriated 75,000 French francs for our Seyre colony, responding to the appeals by Mme Goldschmidt, as well as by Max Gottschalk who had recently escaped from Belgium to New York City. The approval was confirmed by Joint Vice-Chairman Joseph J. Schwartz.[4]

Apparently Gaspard DeWaay had made the first connection with the Secours Suisse. During the summer of 1940 he had visited Maurice Dubois and obtained powdered milk for the children.[5] The colony at Seyre actually was the second to be taken on in France by the Secours Suisse in 1940. Primarily concerned with furnishing food supplies to refugees and internees, the Secours Suisse management of refugee children's colonies grew as a result of the upheaval in Vichy France and other colonies were soon established or supported.

These included the colony at Le Chambon-sur-Lignon, a nursery at Pringy near Annecy, Faverges, the Home de Cruseilles, Maison Praz sur Arly, and a nursery and maternity facility at Elne. The Swiss colonies at Montluel and St. Cergues would later play a role in the escapes of a number of teenagers from La Hille. Usually the colony directors were Swiss citizens, but the shortage of Swiss staff often resulted in adult refugees serving under these directors.[6]

The importance of connecting the colony with their new Swiss guardians was recognized and praised by Mme Renée deBecker, the Belgian Committee leader who had also escaped to New York City.

On December 2, 1940, she wrote to Mme Goldschmidt-Brodsky, "it is wonderful that you were able to place the children under the care of the Secours Suisse and I hope that they will soon be able to come here where they will be safer than over there. . . ." "Anyhow you must be very satisfied with your accomplishment because it is truly a success to have reached the agreement with the Secours Suisse and, as a result, to have achieved what is possible to once again help the children in such turmoil."[7]

As a result of the meeting in Toulouse, the Secours Suisse assumed responsibility for the colony on October 1. It was understood that efforts would be undertaken to help the children emigrate to the United States, if possible. None of those involved could foresee that this intention would never be fully achieved and that the willingness of the Secours Suisse to adopt the colony would, in the end, save most of the children's lives.

M. and Mme Goldschmidt were able to leave Cahors for Basel, Switzerland, on October 2,[8] but her active involvement with the well-being and fate of the children continued from Basel until the end of the war.

Who were the personalities of the Secours Suisse and exactly what was its role in Vichy France? The first activities established by the SAK, as the Secours Suisse was then named (Schweizerische Arbeitsgemein-schaft für kriegsgeschädigte Kinder), in France after the German invasion consisted of distributing food items. Rodolfo Olgiati, its general secretary based in Bern, Switzerland, named Maurice Dubois as the director of activities in Vichy France. Dubois was just thirty-five years old. "He is the backbone of our new team," said Olgiati.[9]

Olgiati, Dubois, and other team members belonged to the "Service Civil International," whose members were pacifists devoted to help war victims. Their first activities were to assist families and children victimized by the civil war in Spain. This is where Dubois met Eleanor Imbelli, the US-born Quaker whom he married before they moved to Toulouse. The SAK was an amalgamation of seventeen Swiss organizations that had established the refugee aid operation on January 14, 1940.[10]

By coincidence, the Vichy government had ended the subsidy payments for refugees on October 1, the very date on which the Secours Suisse took on the management of the colony at Seyre. The connection with the Secours Suisse brought welcome, if limited, improvements to the children at Seyre. Blankets were provided for everyone. The itchy straw on the barn and farmhouse floors was replaced with straw mattresses. Powdered milk and Swiss cheese were donated and added to the food supply.

On October 30, 1940, Mme Irène Frank, the Viennese-born mother of Alex Frank, arrived at the colony. She had escaped from Belgium and had become reconnected with her son and his wife Elka. Tall and slim, with a sallow face framed by gray curly hair, she soon acquired the behind-her-back nickname of "Bli-Bla." A dedicated teacher, she usually carried a book in her hand and soon began to hold classes for the younger children.[11] Although some of the children made fun of her appearance and personality behind her back, Irène Frank took her work very seriously and helped to provide structure and learning to the younger children in the camp-like setting of our colony.

"To teach forty to fifty children of varying ages and different backgrounds in a language foreign to them, to hold their interest without books, dictionaries and the other usual learning materials was not easy," she wrote in her personal diary. "Many teachers accustomed to normal situations and heated classrooms couldn't imagine functioning under such circumstances," she adds.[12]

She recalls that there was no possibility of local schooling for the youngsters aged over fourteen years. They were busy every day performing chores, "as was customary in most refugee colonies." "To save lighting costs during the dark winter months, we all slept until 8:00 a.m., except for three or four older boys and girls who helped the cook, Mme Schlesinger, by chopping wood, building the fire, fetching water from the pump, slicing the loaves of bread and setting the table. At eight o'clock came the wake-up call and soon one could hear the clatter of the children's wooden shoes on the steps and shouts like 'Ruth, come to the kitchen.'"[13]

13. Mme Irène Frank, second from left, at La Hille, France, 1941, with, from left: Toni Steuer, Henri Vos, Lotte Nussbaum, and Gustav Manasse. Reproduced with permission from the United States Holocaust Memorial Museum Photo Archive.

Like Gaspard DeWaay, Alex Frank had no training in managing children. Yet his physical activism and "let's get to work" attitude soon set the tone for our colony. Most of the older boys and girls followed his example in tackling chores and actively caring for the younger children. He announced that physical punishment would no longer be tolerated, though speaking German was still forbidden.

The older boys who joined him in chopping wood for the kitchen and carrying sacks of vegetables, onions, and potatoes became known as "les crèveurs" (a French expression for "working one's tail off"). It was actually a parody of Gaspard DeWaay who sometimes shouted "je me crève pour vous!" ("I 'bust my butt' for you") when some children misbehaved.[14]

Alex Frank also held forth about communism to the older teenagers, an ideology in which he firmly believed. However, he used this more to establish a spirit of mutual support and cooperation than as a means of making converts of his charges. He would hold to that ideological commitment throughout his life and chose to live in the German Democratic Republic (East Germany) in the postwar years.

During the early months of our stay at Seyre, many of us who had relatives in the United States and in other free countries maintained the hope of gaining permission to join them soon, and it was with that expectation that the Secours Suisse had taken responsibility for our group. Although mail was slow to arrive, some of the children were able to communicate with parents and relatives in these countries.

Only four were actually able to leave Seyre. Edith "Ditta" Weisz (Kurzweil) and her younger brother Hansl Weisz, natives of Vienna, had received US immigration visas in Belgium on May 6, but were still in Brussels when the Germans launched their invasion four days later. Ditta, living in a small group home, managed to join her brother's Home Speyer group on the May 14 refugee train to France. Their father had caught a ship to America from Le Havre on May 14. Because they did have a valid visa, the two Weisz children were able to obtain exit permission from France and transit visas to Lisbon. They sailed from there on August 31 and were able to rejoin their parents in New York.[15]

Helga and Harry Schwarz were also born in Vienna and, after futile attempts to flee to France with their mother, were able to come to Belgium thanks to "une Baronne belge" (Belgian baroness)—probably Mme deBecker—as Helga Schwarz Assier writes in her private life story, "Le prix de la vie." She recalls that the "Baronne" and her maid accompanied the group to Brussels—"the famous Baronne can rightly claim to have saved us from certain death."[16]

In early May 1940, Helga (then eleven) and Harry (six years old) were living in one of the Belgian Committee's group homes in Ostende but were brought to the refugee train in Brussels and thus found themselves part of the colony at Seyre. Their father had fled earlier from Vienna to France and joined the French army supply corps, while their mother escaped to England where she worked as a maid.[17] Although Helga wrote letters to her parents from Seyre, she never received a reply and her little brother had virtually forgotten them, she recalls in her biography.

One day in the fall of 1940, while walking toward the highway outside the village, the two siblings saw a tall, emaciated-looking man coming toward them. It was their father who had searched for them and, by luck, heard about the colony through the *mairie* (city hall) of Toulouse.[18] Harry said "bonjour monsieur," but did not recognize his father, who spoke German, which Harry had already forgotten. Mr. Schwarz took his children to Lyon and they would again be separated from him as he was hunted, but eventually all three made a narrow escape to Switzerland together.[19] Constant anxiety and narrow escapes were to become the lifestyle of the entire colony, pursued by the hate-filled German conquerors and their willing Vichy collaborators.

The plans of Alex Frank and of the Secours Suisse to rent a farm where the older teenagers would live and work never came to fruition, nor did an attempt by Maurice Dubois to enlist the older boys in vocational training in Toulouse. The *préfecture* (regional government) would not give permission for the boys' relocation.[20]

As the fall months of 1940 turned into early winter, our colony had become more of a family accustomed to each other and to our surroundings. Many of the older girls took on responsibility for the daily tasks of the colony, such as cooking, washing, and mending clothes, and the boys hauled wood and food supplies, made repairs, and improved the water supply. All helped with taking care of the younger children. Many of the older boys assisted nearby farmers with the harvest.

The younger ones lived and played within their groups and were kept busy with informal classes conducted by Irène Frank and by our older campmates. Most of this age group were too young to be very concerned about the actions and intentions of far-away Germans or about the dangers looming for family members whom they had left behind.

Manfred Tidor recalls: "I was eight at the time. I was oblivious to the danger and came away from the experience without ever knowing what might have been. Other than the absence of my parents and my sister, for whom I longed and probably cried, I was unaware that there was any danger. So I came away without the lasting traumas that must have plagued my older fellows."[21]

Yet ever-present and increasing difficulties were in the offing for all of us and for our caretakers. Scarcity of food, diseases, lack of funding, the effects of the winter weather in an unheated barn without warm clothing, the continuing war plans of the Germans, and especially the declared policies of the Vichy regime's anti-Semitism made life at Seyre fragile and precarious.

The colder climate and strong winds that soon swept over the exposed hillside of the village were intensified by the lack of adequate clothing and the draftiness of the unheated farm buildings. The children learned a new French word: *Le Mistral*, a strong and very cold wind that can blow for days in the late fall and winter. Although it is normally centered in the Rhône River valley, the unusually harsh winter of 1940 caused le Mistral to spill over the Haute-Garonne region where Seyre is located. Alex Frank wrote to Mmes deBecker and Feld-degen in New York that "the cold was especially severe because it is accompanied by icy winds and it's the heaviest winter in thirty years."[22]

"The winter of 1940–1941 was especially difficult," Ruth Schütz (Usrad) recalls in *Entrapped Adolescence*, her autobiography.[23] "The temperature was freezing and found us with no warm clothes, shoes, [or] appropriate linens. Every child had a rough, wool blanket that we called a horse blanket. Toward night, we would get organized so that three children would bunch together and cover themselves with three blankets. We wore wooden shoes, and we would wrap our feet in newspaper."

"In the morning I would break the layer of ice on the water container, and I would not give in to the group of girls for whom I was responsible about washing their hands and face. In our buildings there was no source of heat and only the afternoon soup thawed our frozen hands."[24]

Because the shoes we brought from Belgium were wearing out and not suited for farm life, many of the children were furnished *sabots*, the wooden shoes usually worn by the local farmers. Without heavy woolen socks these sabots would chafe our freezing feet in the cold weather. The sabots certainly were uncomfortable to wear.

All would remember the cold for a long time. Irène Frank, the teacher, recalls that "the 40 or 50 school-age children [seven to four-teen years old] sat with bluish-red noses and hands, which they tried unsuccessfully to rub warm. Mightily they stamped their feet, but without result. I was less heroic and wrapped myself in my old coat and wool shawl."[25]

Procuring food for his colony had become a serious issue for Alex Frank and the monotony of cornmeal (known as polenta or grits in the United States) with various flavorings as the daily main dish soon became one of the children's objects of disdain. Some vowed never to touch the cornmeal-polenta again if they ever could put their current life behind them. "Morning and evening we ate a hot cereal made out of corn flour, sometimes sweet and sometimes with onion."

"During lunchtime, [we often had] a soup made out of intestines, lard, and some type of turnip that looked like potato with the name of *topinambour* [Jerusalem artichoke], whose taste and odor were nauseating. It was food not fit for human consumption."[26]

Although he did not share his worries about scarce food supplies with any of the children, Frank bared his fears in frequent letters to Mmes deBecker and Felddegen, who were in New York and worrying about "their children" at Seyre. "The children are well behaved and in good health," he wrote in a joint letter to both ladies and to Max Gottschalk on November 3, 1940.[27]

"My main goal is to see them happy and healthy. Fortunately they do not really know how dangerous their situation is. And it must be a lot worse for their parents" (who were still in Nazi-dominated countries).

Three months later he gave more graphic details in a letter to Mme Felddegen and pleaded for food shipments from America. "In response to a telegram from the [United States] of February 20, I replied on the 21st: 'Situation of 97 children uncertain. Food supplies a major problem. Help with rice, fats, sardines, molasses, cocoa, soap, shoes, trousers most needed. Financial aid desired. Early emigration mandatory.'"[28]

He also tried to reassure her, claiming the children were in good health, due especially to adequate nourishment, "plain but healthful." After describing the discomforts of the harsh winter, he reported that "the nonexistent potatoes have been replaced by cornmeal (whose sale actually is forbidden) which is very nutritious and liked by the children." He apparently had failed to ask their opinion.

Frank foresaw looming problems in the food supply. "Already shoppers in the cities are unable to find the minimum needed for remaining healthy, and in the stores I have observed homemakers who no longer are able to find food for their families. Frankly, it is only by special effort crowned by good luck that I have been able to keep our children in an advantaged situation, but I am uneasy about the future," he reports in that letter.

He also worried about the possibility that the Secours Suisse might wish or be forced to abandon the children in the future. On January 30, 1941, he asked Mme Felddegen: "Uncertain status: Having committed itself, the Secours Suisse has assured me that they will do all in their power to help the children but unforeseeable external events could suddenly prevent them from continuing their activities in France. If that should occur, they and I, too, would like to know who would guarantee the welfare of the children, whom can we contact and what should we do with the children?"[29]

For whatever reason, Frank's description of the children's health was highly inaccurate. Probably due to the inadequate diet and nutrition, many of us developed infected body sores, which lasted throughout the winter months. Because of the inadequate sanitary conditions and because we slept on straw mattresses on the floor, the hair of many children was infested with lice. This made it necessary to shave their heads, an added degradation and frustration, especially for the younger girls.

Ruth Schütz Usrad remembers:

I received pus-like sores in my mouth, and had trouble eating the little food that I received. At night I would lie awake on the straw, breathing through my mouth to alleviate the pain. I also got pus-like sores on my arms and legs. When one would close, it would leave behind a blue, ugly mark and two more would pop up. At night pieces of hay would stick into the sores, and the pain became unbearable. I looked at my arms and legs full of blue scars, and I thought in my heart, "Would this ugliness accompany me for the rest of my life?"

The sores were still oozing pus when a new affliction came upon us: Lice. Every day the older girls combed the heads of the younger girls with combs full of kerosene, and pulled out the lice. The girls' crying and pleading didn't help, and everyone's hair was cut. From now on there were no longer girls with beautiful curls or long braids. All of us had short hair.

After that forced haircut I found Betty [her younger sister] crying and sad, and her shorn head all one big sore full of pus and lice that had roads of tunnels. Betty asked to find some solace and comfort from me, but I only knew to say to her: "Had you let them cut your hair on time, you wouldn't have reached this situation." I had to show her I was tough so she wouldn't see how horrified I was about her condition.[30]

Similar experiences are recalled by Inge Berlin (Vogelstein), then seventeen years old. She describes the severe winter, primitive sanitation, and inadequate nutrition and continues: "Worry about my parents, worry about how my younger brother (Egon Berlin) would hold up (in our camp) and, finally, lice, plus a severe and painful canker sore and jaundice epidemic probably hepatitis and all that without available medical expertise. All of these afflictions made me consider seriously to return to Belgium where my parents were living, which probably would have led to deportation and death."[31]

Berlin also recalled "that cruelly cold winter when it snowed on some of our cots, when we all tried to crowd into the kitchen—the only place where we could warm our frozen hands—until Frau Schlesinger hardly could move about to do her work, so that Alex finally had to forbid us altogether to enter the kitchen. I once asked Alex during one of my Berlin visits whether it ever occurred to him that he could have lost some of the children during that epidemic. His resigned answer: 'Yes, when I had time to think about it.'"[32]

While living conditions were primitive and the nationalistic and anti-Semitic postures of the Pétain government caused ever-present anxiety, our colony managed to maintain a lively and communal existence. Through the Secours Suisse many of us were connected with *parrains* (sponsor families) in Switzerland, some of whom contributed money for our upkeep and occasionally sent packages. They and the Swiss Red Cross also forwarded letters to and from our parents and relatives who were still living in Nazi-controlled countries.

The Viennese parents of nine-year-old Herbert Kammer had been separated by Nazi persecution—his mother, Rosa Kammer, working in England, and his father, Georg Kammer, interned first at St. Cyprien and then at Camp Recebedou, not very far from Seyre. They were able to correspond and Herbert reported, in a letter dated March 2, 1941, that he had started a stamp collection and that he wished to have them return the stamps from his letters.[33]

Sadly, his interned father wrote that he felt weak and wondered whether food packages could be sent from son Herbert's camp to supplement his diet. He also would like to see Herbert before his son leaves for America but would need to sell some clothes to get money for the bus fare to Seyre.[34] Unfortunately, the encounter never took place and Georg Kammer, was deported from France on August 24, 1942, like so many other parents.

Teacher Irène Frank had vivid recollections of the younger children and their behavior. "The youngest, Antoinette, whose parents had disappeared, spoke only French and everyone treated her as the camp mascot. [Antoinette 'Tony' Steuer was four years old]. She suffered least from being separated from her family and was spoiled by everyone. Even Alex dropped his serious demeanor when she chatted away while sitting on his lap. Her special guardian was a heavyset girl named Rosemarie whom Tony called 'Maman' and who dropped everything when her protégée called her, which happened frequently."[35]

"Manfred, the second-youngest [Manfred Manasse was five years old] was a different child. Very independent and intelligent, he was not a pleasant youngster. I believe he was unhappy and his principal weapon, whenever he felt things were not going to his liking, was to

14. At Seyre, 1940. From left: Rosemarie Cosmann holding Toni Steuer, and Ruth Klonower carrying Karla Flanter. From the author's personal collection.

scream and yell so that Alex unmercifully sent him out the door with his plate," she writes in her diary. "He always looked unkempt and uncared-for. Six months later, as my student, I found him eager to learn and bright. His main problem had been to have something useful to do and to learn."[36]

Of the middle boys, Mrs. Frank recalls "the very well-behaved model student Guy [Guy Haas, eleven years old], always cramming; the red-haired, mousy-faced Max [Max Krolik, age twelve], who didn't cram but learned in a jiffy and had an astonishing talent for math. And then there was Paul Schlesinger [age eleven], the son of our cook [Flora Schlesinger], of average talent but very alert and easygoing. Paul was understandably happy to be the only child able to live with his own parents at the colony."[37]

Several of the older girls, especially Friedl Steinberg (Urman), decorated the walls of the barn at Seyre with paintings of colorful Disney

15. One of the "Disney" paintings on the wall of the "Barn" at Seyre (still in place today). From the author's personal collection.

cartoon figures and with the emblem of the Secours Suisse. These large-scale paintings were still on those walls in 2008 as a reminder of the colony, more than 65 years after we had departed from the village.

Experienced with working in camps filled with refugees from the civil war in Spain, the leaders of the Secours Suisse kept in close touch with life at Seyre from their base in Toulouse. A Christmas holiday visit by Chief Delegate Maurice Dubois in 1940 is described in a compelling portrayal of celebration at the colony in the midst of misery:[38] "Christmas Day we were invited to the Seyre colony," writes Dubois.

> Four of us went together, Miss Renée Farny, Ellen [Mrs. Dubois], A. Varchaver [our Belgian colleague] and I. Before the celebration we visited the dormitories. It troubled us to discover that the sleeping facilities, adequate for summer, were not suitable for winter conditions.

We were relieved by the thought that, without support from the Secours Suisse, many of these children would probably be suffering in internment camps. Fortunately, the cold temperature of the dormitories gave way to one much more comfortable and friendly in the dining space, decorated for the occasion.

The tables were covered with pine twigs and on the plates we found all kinds of goodies, such as tangerines, dates, cookies, flat cakes decorated with the Swiss cross, etc. There also were little presents: pocket knives for the boys, crayons, books, and calendars. It was touching for us to watch the children look for their names on the place cards at each table.

The children had practiced songs and little skits. A festive mood prevailed throughout the meal. Group leaders took care of the younger ones with love and wisdom. Mrs. Frank, the spouse of Director Alex Frank, pulled the curtain and led the children's songs, accompanied by mouth organ music. A group of young girls sang "Là haut sur la montagne" ("High on the Mountain") in triple voice. I had never heard it sung that way.

After the program the little ones went to bed, while the older boys and girls stayed, with the girls continuing to sing. While one might criticize the director regarding especially the lack of comfort for the children, one must really congratulate him for the good behavior and the positive attitude that prevail at the colony.[39]

Similar observations were made soon thereafter by Rodolfo Olgiati, secretary of the Secours Suisse based in Bern. "The children, with their five caretakers form a rarely seen community of living together, the result of having experienced the same horrible fate and their determination to create the best outcome by helping one another," he wrote in a report after visiting Secours Suisse sites in Vichy France.[40] "The godparents whom we recruited for them in Switzerland have reason to be very proud of them."[41]

The Swiss godparents remembered their Seyre children, and Alex Frank reported that "they sent Christmas packages containing chocolate and sweets which arrived on January 15 and we had another celebration."[42] He also reported that "for New Year's the children staged plays for the Seyre villagers, similar to the ones for Mr. Dubois at Christmas, and these were well received."[43]

After the war, Elka Frank recalled the hardships suffered by the children during the winter of 1940, but added: "And yet something wonderful emerged: A true community. Yes, we were all equal. None had more than the others. We all had to work hard to survive and to make life more pleasant we made music, sang and staged plays."[44]

◇ 6 ◇

The Belgian Angels' Rescue Effort
from across the Atlantic

Soon after Mme Felddegen learned of our arrival in France she began determined efforts to bring our entire colony to the United States. She was assisted by Max Gottschalk who utilized his high-level contacts with the Belgian government-in-exile, then located in London. This heretofore unknown and intrepid work resulted in nineteen of the La Hille children coming to the United States in 1941 and 1942, at a time when rescue and emigration from Vichy France became ever more difficult. However, their courageous attempt to bring all the children to the United States did not succeed. What were their plans for rescue and why did they fail?

Mme Lilly Felddegen, the former secretary and a leading member of Comité d'assistance aux Enfants Juifs Refugiés (CAEJR) had come to New York from Belgium with her husband, Albert, and teenage daughters Eve and Irène on September 4, 1939, to attend the New York World's Fair—and they stayed. She maintained close contact by correspondence with the Belgian committee staff and with her committee colleagues in Brussels until the German invasion in May 1940.[1]

After we fled to France in May 1940, she began efforts almost immediately to bring all of us to the United States. Max Gottschalk had also escaped to New York and the two combined their efforts to rescue "their children." On December 3, 1940, Max Gottschalk wrote a detailed request to Mr. Paul-Henri Spaak, then the foreign minister of the Belgian government-in-exile in London, whom he had known well when Mr. Spaak was the prewar Belgian Prime Minister

69

and held other high Belgian government positions. After describing the history and "precarious situation of the children" then at Seyre, Gottschalk explained that the US State Department would only give them permission to enter the United States if the Belgian government-in-exile would guarantee our return to Belgium after the war. (Similar US entry permissions had been granted to British children to save them from German bombardment attacks.[2])

Gottschalk added that "the Belgian government surely would not refuse this guarantee as it had already accepted these children in Belgium originally and besides, the guarantee would only be 'platonic' since many of the children could eventually probably obtain permanent residence in the United States." He concluded by asking that the guarantee be forwarded to the Belgian ambassador in Washington, with notification to Gottschalk.[3]

Spaak responded favorably and Gottschalk received the following reply from the Belgian ambassador in Washington:

> Dear Sir,
>
> Mr. Spaak has notified me that I am authorized to inform the American authorities that the Belgian government will permit the return to Belgium, after the end of the war, of the children under the care of HIAS-HICEM, 396 Fourth Avenue, New York City, and who could not obtain permission for a permanent stay in the United States. This is in reference to the group of refugee children from Germany who, as you know, had been accepted in Belgium and who are now located in France.
>
> Mr. Spaak has asked me to contact you before I forward this permission to the American authorities. Therefore I am looking forward to your response.

This letter, dated February 19, 1941, was addressed by Count van der Straten-Ponthoz, the Belgian Ambassador in Washington, to Max Gottschalk at his office, Room 204, 71 West 47th Street, New York City.[4]

On February 24, 1941, Max Gottschalk urged the Belgian ambassador to forward the Spaak guarantee to the US State Department and explained that Robert T. Pell, assistant chief of its Division of European Affairs, had requested this guarantee in early October 1940 "in order to gain permission for the children to enter the United States."[5] The desired result seemed assured when the Belgian ambassador transmitted the State Department response to Gottschalk on April 2, 1941, with the comment, "as you will see, the American government has responded favorably to our request." The unsigned copy of the letter of March 31, 1941, from the State Department to the Belgian ambassador states:

"The Secretary of State presents his compliments to His Excellency the Belgian Ambassador and has the honor to refer to the Ambassador's Letter of February 26, 1941, regarding the visa cases of a number of German refugee children now residing in Belgium."

"The assurances given by the Belgian Government for the return of these children to Belgium after the termination of their sojourn in the United States has [sic] been noted by the Department. It may be added that as the German quota is now under-issued, it will be possible for those children who are permitted to travel and who can qualify, therefore, to receive immigration visas without any protracted delay."[6] (This exchange is presented in detail as it demonstrates the skilled efforts of Gottschalk and Felddegen, and also the determined State Department and congressional efforts to thwart refugee immigration, as described further below.)

Repeatedly Mme Felddegen had expressed her determination to bring "nos pauvres enfants" (our poor children) to safety in America. "Since Mr. Gottschalk arrived in the U.S.A., I have put myself at his disposal to do all in our power to save the children of Seyre and to bring them over to the United States," she wrote to Mme Goldschmidt-Brodsky in Basel on December 5, 1940.[7] She continued, "I have already tried to interest American organizations in the fate of our poor children, but so far without success."

"Now I have attacked the matter with all my energy but limited means and can report that I have succeeded in obtaining the help and assistance of the 'United States Committee for Care of European Children' which was founded 4 months ago to save children from England

and other countries. Mme Roosevelt is the honorary chairman and Mr. Biddle (former US ambassador in Warsaw) is the director."

She explained that since the US government had now given a conditionally favorable response to the request by Mr. Gottschalk about allowing the children of Seyre to immigrate, she was working to get a resolution as quickly as possible. As she describes the situation, "One condition is to have an American organization take care of the children and I hope to resolve this with help from the above-named organization. Another was the need for a guarantee to return the children after the war. That proved to be the most difficult, but with the formation of the Belgian government-in-exile in London, we were able to solve that."[8]

Mme Felddegen expressed similar optimism and determination to M. and Mme Dubois of the Secours Suisse in Toulouse in a letter dated February 26, 1941: "I would like to say that I am working to bring over all the children of Seyre in one group and have never let on to the American authorities that one might consider separating these little unfortunate companions for immigration. And as I am holding my ground, I expect to succeed."[9] She did not yet know that she

16. Mme Lilly Felddegen, leader of the Belgian Rescue Committee, who spared no effort to rescue "her children." Photo provided by her granddaughter Susan Johnson, with permission.

would be reduced to bringing only some of the children to America, and these only in several small groups.

Why did the promising responses from the US authorities go awry and what action did Mme Felddegen take when these hoped-for solutions failed? Historian David S. Wyman provides detailed documentation of the United States' restrictive immigration policies during this period in his book, *The Abandonment of the Jews: America and the Holocaust, 1941–1945*. "In 1938, increased German persecution of the Jews led President Roosevelt to ease the extremely restrictive immigration policy of the Great Depression and open the European quotas for full use," he writes.[10]

> This step did not, however, set off mass migration to the United States, for the combined quotas of the affected countries amounted to under 40,000 per year. Furthermore, in mid-1940 the policy was reversed. Claiming the Nazis were infiltrating secret agents into the refugee stream and forcing some authentic refugees to spy for Germany, Breckinridge Long, with the cooperation of the Visa Division, suddenly tightened the requirements for entry. This step slashed admissions by half.
>
> In July 1941, refugee immigration was cut again, to about twenty-five per cent of the relevant quotas. Behind this decline was the 'relatives rule', a State Department regulation stipulating that any applicant with a parent, child, spouse, or sibling remaining in German, Italian or Russian territory had to pass an extremely strict security test to obtain a visa.[11]

At the time when Lilly Felddegen and Max Gottschalk were trying to obtain US immigration permission for our Seyre colony children, "American consulates—with the exception of a few courageous individuals—were following instructions they received from Assistant Secretary of State Breckinridge Long: 'We can delay and effectively stop for a temporary period of indefinite length the number of immigrants into the United States. We could do this by simply advising our consuls to put every obstacle in the way which would postpone and postpone and postpone the granting of visas."[12]

Historian Wyman concludes that "since neither Roosevelt nor Hull [Cordell Hull, US secretary of state] paid much attention to the European Jewish tragedy, the main responsibility for American rescue policy fell to Long and his subordinates. Instead of sensitivity to the human values involved, Long brought strongly nativist attitudes to the situation." Wyman adds that "his subordinates shared his anti-alienism. Their attitudes influenced not only visa policy but the department's entire response to the European Jewish catastrophe."[13]

In the absence of specific documents, these realities support the assumption that the Paul-Henri Spaak guarantee, though acknowledged by the State Department, may in fact have been ignored because of the visa department's opposition to immigration.

Mme Felddegen caught on quickly to the stonewalling attitude in Washington. On March 17, 1941, she explained her understanding and frustration to Mme Goldschmidt-Brodsky:[14]

> Emigration of the children: First let me remind you that the war began 18 months ago, but it's only in the past few days that the Americans decided to offer their total support. Here it's the same everywhere—it takes forever, even though, before we got to know this country where supposedly "time is money," we always thought that their speed of action surpassed ours.
>
> Especially it is very very difficult to obtain a decision because no one wants to assume responsibility and in our efforts for the children, that's exactly the situation.
>
> It's now understood that, unfortunately, they cannot come as a total group at once. In fact I am afraid that only a small number will be included in the first group, which will soon leave France under the auspices of the "United States Committee for Care of European Children" under whose protection we need to place our young travelers.
>
> This first group will consist of a total of 100 youngsters, selected from various centers of endangered children in France and composed of various religions, not just Jewish ones. The selection in Seyre will be made by a Quaker staff person stationed in France and

we'll know from their report how many of our children will have been included in this small group.

I just hope that it won't all be too late. I am tormented by the waste of time but I cannot do anything about it. I am so happy that I was able to make these efforts alongside Mr. Gottschalk, because I am mortified of these responsibilities. . . . [I]t has always been my aim to bring all of our kids over only in one group and to leave not even one behind.[15]

The effectiveness of lobbying by Mme Felddegen and Max Gottschalk is reflected in instructions sent by John F. Rich, associate secretary of the American Friends Service Committee's (AFSC) from its Philadelphia headquarters, to Howard E. Kershner at the AFSC Marseille office requesting that his staff include "selections from OSE, the Jewish Children's Committee of Brussels (which, we understand, is now under the care of the Secour[s] Suisse of Toulouse). . . ."[16]

Luckily for the Children of La Hille, Mme Felddegen was as persistent and skilled as if we were her own children. She worked closely with two members of the Belgian rescue committee who had also been able to flee to the United States, Mme Renée deBecker-Remy, and Mme Louise Wolff, as well as with Max Gottschalk.

Mme Felddegen exchanged letters frequently with Mme deBecker between 1940 and 1945, always concerning news and developments about the possible rescue and status of "les gosses" (the kids) and "nos pauvres enfants" (our poor youngsters). Mme deBecker was especially involved in contacts with the Quakers.[17]

When the attempt to bring the entire group of children from Seyre to the United States was thwarted by the US State Department in early 1941, Mme Felddegen left no stone unturned to get as many as possible "of our children" added to the group of 100 for whom the United States Committee for Care of European Children had received a special immigration exception.[18] "In the meantime, the American Friends (Quaker) representative in France has visited Seyre to draft the list of children to be submitted to Washington, using the information which I had previously furnished with all the needed information and birth dates," she reported in a letter to Mme Goldschmidt-Brodsky in Basel.[19]

The efforts by Mme Felddegen and Max Gottschalk brought seventeen of the Seyre-La Hille children to the United States in 1941, although the children were unaware who achieved their rescue. Ten were included in the first group of 100 youngsters, rescued by the US committee, which sailed from Lisbon on the SS *Mouzinho* on June 10. They were Rosalie Blau, 9, from Cologne; Bernhard Eisler, 12, from Cologne; Alfred Eschwege, 9, from Rockhausen; Lore Flanter, 6, from Lichtenau; her sister Karla Flanter, 11, from Erfurt; Herbert Kammer, 9, from Vienna; Gerd Arno Obersitzker, 15, from Berlin; Klaus Sostheim, 15, from Mannheim; Kurt Steinhardt, 9, and Jules Steinhardt, 10, both from Aachen.

On September 9, 1941, seven more of the colony's children were included in the refugee group traveling on the SS *Serpa Pinto*, which also sailed from Lisbon. They were the three Findling brothers, Joseph, 12, Siegfried, 10, and Martin, 8, all from Cologne; Max Krolik, 12, from Leipzig, his sister Rosa Krolik, 10, born in Berlin; Manfred Tidor, 9, from Frankfurt, and Rolf Weinmann, 10, from Bielefeld.[20]

Mme Felddegen was also involved in the separate immigration of Hanni Schlimmer, 15, and me (then Werner Rindsberg, now Walter Reed), 17. Schlimmer was able to join her parents in Spain in 1941 for the crossing to the United States, and I came alone in August 1941 through the efforts of American relatives who gained assistance from Mme Felddegen in booking my ship's passage.[21]

Four other La Hille children made it safely to the United States in 1942, several with considerable help from Mme Felddegen. Willy Wolpert, 11, born in Frankfurt, and Arthur and Eva Kantor, age 15 and 13, from Vienna, arrived on the SS *Nyassa* on July 30, 1942, and little Toni Steuer from Essen had come as part of a group of fifty children on the SS *Serpa Pinto* on June 25. She was almost six years old. Both ships left from Marseille and continued after a stop in Casablanca.

17. Toni Steuer (center front) at Seyre, 1941, with younger boys, nearly all of whom came to the United States that year through the efforts of Mme Lilly Felddegen. From left: Manfred Tidor, Alfred Eschwege, Fred Manasse, Gustav Manasse, Siegfried Findling, William Wolpert, Martin Findling, and Joseph Findling. From the author's personal collection.

Instead of the nearly 100 Seyre children coming as a group, Mme Felddegen had to be satisfied to see twenty-three of us come safely to America from Vichy France in several groups. The disappointment served to intensify her efforts to bring other individual La Hille children to the United States. Her private archive contains hundreds of letters to and from the children's relatives and acquaintances in the United States in which she goaded and guided them to provide affidavits and the funds needed to buy passage from Europe. None of these produced permission to immigrate and several for whom she campaigned vigorously were later deported and murdered in Poland.

Her efforts for these other children failed because US authorities further curtailed the issuance of visas and, later, Vichy France periodically refused exit permits to those who did obtain US immigration visas. Were it not for the discovery of her extensive private archive a few years ago, the impassioned efforts she and her colleagues devoted to the rescue and safety of "her children" would never have come to light.

◇ 7 ◇

Life at the Château de La Hille,
1941–1942

On February 20, 1941, Max Schächtele addressed a regular Secours Suisse staff meeting in Toulouse, and the impact of his appeal was recorded in the minutes: "it is now Max's turn. This big talker gave us such an upbeat description of his activities that he literally had us feeling that we are part of the birth of the colony."[1]

Max Schächtele reported that "eight days ago we left Seyre, where the children were housed so miserably that Eleanor and Maurice [Dubois] had long ago concluded that they should be moved. One day, Eleanor and Anita [probably Anita Willems, Secours Suisse staff member], touring on bicycles, had discovered the 'Château de La Hille.' The building is 250 years old, renovated in 1830 and uninhabited for the past 25 years." (The château actually dates from the sixteenth century; originally it was the residence of the Rochechouart-Faudoas family. The surrounding walls were built in the nineteenth century.)[2]

The group meeting in Toulouse that day certainly was not aware that they were hearing about the beginning of a series of dramatic and perilous events lasting until the end of the war. These events would mark our colony forever as "The Children of La Hille," and La Hille as a site where collaboration, trauma, drama, and wartime heroism would weave a memorable fabric of World War II history and turmoil for innocent refugee children.

Eleanor Dubois had indeed discovered an ancient fort-like manor house in a remote corner of the Ariège Department (Ariège Province).

The Château de La Hille, surrounded by undulating hillsides along the tiny Lèze River, is located just outside the village of Montégut-Plantaurel, population then about 300, about thirty-seven miles southwest of Seyre and twelve miles northwest of Foix, the historic capital of the Ariège province. The Spanish border, which snakes along the top of the Pyrénées mountains, is about fifty miles farther south.

"We are underway," Schächtele continued. "The truck, heavily loaded with 6 tons of stuff and 20 youngsters, is ponderously climbing the winding roads which remind one of our own [Swiss] mountain highways. The château is located in a large park, surrounded by magnificent stands of trees. The view is appealing." (The author also remembers this ride and the letdown upon first seeing the rundown "château," which that day did not look like an improvement over the primitive barn at Seyre.)

"There is a heavy medieval-looking wall and an entryway like in an old fort." Schächtele then described the building's rooms and facilities

18. View of the Château de La Hille at Montégut-Plantaurel in 1941, when the refugee children arrived. From the author's personal collection.

in great detail and with obvious enthusiasm. He detailed how the children would be housed in dormitories and individual rooms and mentions the ample closet space. "There is central heating, installed 25 years ago, and with a little repair it will be functional and economical as it operates with steam. In calculating the arrangements we come up with 60 sleeping spaces but the ceilings are tall enough to accommodate double-decker bunks so that we can house everyone. The separate storehouse building can accommodate the staff and maybe even a visitor's bedroom."

"Maurice [Dubois] was fortunate to discover that the Prefect [departmental government chief] in Foix is a very accommodating man. Besides 100 beds (real iron beds with springs) he provided us with 500 kg of horsehair for the mattresses, 100 straw mattress covers and 100 pillows. It's all ready for use."[3] In light of later developments, the cooperation of the Prefect is significant and surprising. Maurice Dubois needed his authorization to relocate our colony from Seyre to the Ariège Department. "When I visited the prefect of the Ariège to obtain his permission to move our colony of Jewish children to his province, I promised to accept a ratio of one-third French children with them. But because we could not find a large enough dwelling, I was unable to keep that promise, as our château will barely hold the 100 children and the staff personnel of the Seyre colony," Dubois wrote to his Swiss superior, Rodolfo Olgiati.[4]

At the Toulouse staff meeting, Schächtele also described the young work crew: it was composed of fifteen boys, aged twelve to eighteen (including author Walter Reed), plus three girls, "all of them hard-working, but obviously inexperienced for the work and unfortunately also not very strong."

"A Spanish immigrant carpenter, Mr. Salvide, is assisted by 2 boys in making new benches and repairing three found at the château. The two strongest boys are working with the excavation (they have already shoveled between 6.5 and 7.5 cubic yards of dirt). They're all very dedicated and the blisters don't seem to bother them."

Among the boys' work crew were Egon Berlin, Charles Blumenfeld, Edgar Chaim, Joseph Dortort, Hans Garfunkel, Manfred Kamlet,

19. Swiss staff member Max Schächtele, who assisted in the preparations of the move to La Hille, 1941. From the author's personal collection.

Kurt "Onze" Klein, Kurt Moser, Rudi Oehlbaum, Werner Rindsberg, Peter Salz, Walter Strauss, and Norbert Winter. Elias Haskelevicz, of the Brussels office staff, was also among them.[5]

Schächtele reported that Ernst Schlesinger, husband of the cook, helped with supervision. He said the terrain surrounding the château offers play space, shady spots in the summer, and room for a 30 x 7 meter vegetable garden, plus space for a football field. Because the little Lèze River at the edge of the terrain flows year-around, it could be used for bathing and doing laundry, he said.

> And guess how much annual rent we are paying for this gem? Just 1,800 French francs for the château, plus 200 francs for the added terrain! The local farmers are all very friendly toward us. After I had explained what we're doing here and how limited our resources are, they were truly moved and admire Switzerland for being able to offer such generosity.

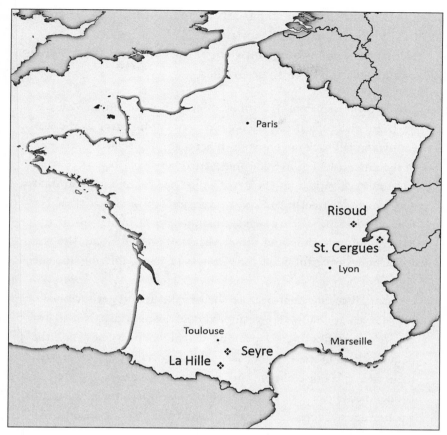

20. Map of sites in France. By Bruce Baumberger, with permission.

I have even been able to obtain potatoes, which they usually save for seeding instead of eating them. And they are furnishing us with milk, which will increase after the calves are weaned. The farmers in this region are especially glad that so many young people will be coming soon because they need help with the harvest.[6]

The majority of the children remained at Seyre, with Alex Frank in charge. He had hoped to move the colony to La Hille by April but the work at the château would not be finished that early. By that time the parents and siblings of many of the La Hille children were separated, incarcerated in camps, in hiding in France or Belgium, or left behind in Germany and Austria.

Irène Frank writes poignantly about the children's trauma of separation and isolation from their families:

> Lex [her son Alex Frank] distributed the mail at lunchtime. One day we heard the 15-year-old Ilse [Wulff] cry out in terror as she was eating and fall back unconscious in her seat. Elka [Frank] and some of the girls rushed to her side and carried her to her bed.
>
> Lex then picked up the letter which had fallen to the ground and which apparently had caused the accident and read that her father had died. [Ilse's parents emigrated to Shanghai in 1939].[7] She was an only child and the mother now was all alone. Ilse was a charming, cheerful child and this was her first suffering and she could not bear it.
>
> I recall the incident because she was the first to get such news. Others were to follow and we got to know the reactions. Not all lost consciousness like Ilse. Depending on the child's personality, the pain emerged in loud crying, silent tears or leaving the room hastily in silence. Poor children, orphaned at a young age. What crime condemned them to be chased from the warmth of the nest at such a young age to experience the harshness of a nasty pitiless world, like blossoms blown away and isolated never to ripen?[8]

As early as December 1940 Maurice Dubois had noted the scarcity of adult caretakers at Seyre. In a letter of December 27 to Rodolfo Olgiati in Bern he recounts that work and supervision were carried out by only Alex, Elka Frank, and the cook, Mme Schlesinger, as assisted by the "grandes filles et garçons" (older girls and boys). "We are aware that this staffing is inadequate," he wrote. "I know that in addition Mme Frank, the mother of Mr. Frank, as well as a Polish man [probably Elias Haskelevicz, born in Bolgrad, Bessarabia] are giving lessons."[9]

In early 1941 the Secours Suisse recruited Rösli Näf, a nurse who had served two two-year stints with Dr. Albert Schweitzer in Lambarene, Africa. Born in Glarus, Switzerland on May 9, 1911, she loved to travel and had already met Eleanor Dubois in Switzerland during a vacation from Africa. After reporting to Toulouse, she arrived at Seyre on May 6, 1941. Her two-year leadership of the colony would be difficult and controversial, yet overall, nothing short of heroic.

She recalled her arrival and impressions in a compilation of former staff members' recollections published in June 1990 under the title, "Le Secours Suisse aux Enfants dans le Sud de la France, 1939 à 1947" ("The Swiss Children's Aid Society in the South of France, 1939 to 1947"):[10]

I was received politely but with a certain hesitancy. I was instantly struck by the surprising discipline of such a large group of young children in spite of the extremely miserable living conditions, especially in the winter. Many of the children had body sores, especially on the legs. The result of the cold or insufficient nutrition? At that time their menu consisted almost exclusively of cornmeal cooked with water. The diet lacked fats and albumins. I immediately thought of adding nettles, prepared like spinach, to the diet to offset the lack of vitamins, an idea that at first scared the children more than it enthralled them.

Every drop of water had to be drawn form a faraway pump. There was neither soap nor any other cleaning material. To prevent or cure lice infestation all the boys and girls wore short hair. Before I went to sleep (the first night) I reflected on all that I had seen and experienced. I was overcome with fear and doubt, asking myself whether I would be up to the challenges before me. I realized that Mr. Frank might be uncomfortable turning the direction of the colony over into such relatively inexperienced hands.[11]

I was reassured by the thought that Mr. Frank, as a refugee who also had his wife and mother at the colony, would want to stay and then another reassurance arrived like an unexpected present: An old resident of the village was anxious to inform me that I will be dealing with very good and well-behaved children. He had been watching them closely since they arrived in May 1940 and hoped that we would experience a better future.[12]

Maurice Dubois intended for Rösli Näf to be in charge and especially to represent the colony in dealing with the local and préfecture
French authorities, while Alex Frank, the experienced agriculturist,
would work with the older teenagers internally and on manual labor
and maintenance tasks. As a Swiss citizen, Mlle Näf could more effectively protect us and represent our interests than Frank, who was Jewish, a Belgian refugee, and openly a Communist. Not long after her
start as "directrice," there would be clashes between Rösli Näf and the
Frank family, as well as with the older teenagers.

On June 1 the entire colony was moved from Seyre to the Château de La Hille. "They said good-bye to the villagers of Seyre to be
reunited with their companions as well as brothers and sisters who
had preceded them to the Château de La Hille at Montégut," Rösli
Näf reported to her superiors. "It is with sadness that the residents
watched them leave. Many of the Seyre residents, including some of
the men, had tears in their eyes."[13]

Irène Frank reflected on the hard times at Seyre, wondering what
might lie ahead: "It was a difficult life here in Seyre, a constant battle
against hunger, cold, vermin and uncertainty—but it was worth it as
we managed to achieve whatever was possible, we created a community, a unity amid diversity, a sense of communal life which helped us
to overcome much adversity. At La Hille living conditions promised to
be more favorable but would we be confronted there with challenges
of a different kind?"[14]

"The landscape was incomparably more scenic than at Seyre, the
view of the foothills of the Pyrénées a calm, peaceful countryside
which fills the lungs with pure and clear air. The château made a
welcome impression compared to the dilapidated convent [the barn
at Seyre]. All the rooms were well-lit and spacious with large windows and the dining hall was so elegant, with wood-paneled walls,
that some of the children were shy about entering," Mme Frank
remembered.[15]

"Including the staff personnel, the colony consisted of about 100
persons and it took several weeks of long workdays to convert the
château from its previous state to a suitable children's home. Every

day without rain was utilized to sow and plant the vegetable garden. Vegetables, mixed with flowers, were planted both inside and outside the castle walls," Mlle Näf reported.[16]

"Without sufficient facilities indoors, one could see the children line up each day at the river with their toilet articles to wash, the boys near the bridge (which led from the main road to the château) to the spot for the girls 100 meters downstream."

With the pleasant summer weather, Rösli Näf decided that all meals should be served outdoors in the enclosed château yard. The children were seated on benches and at tables built by some older boys under the supervision of Mr. Salvide, the Spanish refugee carpenter. It would take more work to render the château's interior more comfortable and attractive, but those tasks were delayed until the colder months when all activities would have to take place indoors.[17]

Mlle Näf states that when Max Schächtele left in mid-June, Alex Frank took on the supervision of the heavy construction and maintenance activities. There were problems with some of the water and sewage construction and it took a while before the préfecture authorized the procurement of the needed cement.

In the fall another problem caused great concern. The mayor of Montégut-Plantaurel refused to let the younger La Hille children attend the local school because an additional teacher would be needed to accommodate them. This was resolved when the school received a new teacher assigned by the regional school director. Nineteen of the La Hille children aged under fourteen years walked each day from the château to the village school, starting on October 15.[18]

Once the children were settled at La Hille, the principal task was to organize life around daily needs and to provide educational opportunities on site, since the attempt to send a number of the older boys to a vocational school in Toulouse had failed to win the approval of that city's authorities.

Mme Irène Frank continued teaching the thirteen- and fourteen-year-olds on a daily schedule similar to that of the school at nearby Montégut. By October a new teacher and mentor had arrived from Switzerland. Eugen Lyrer taught French and English to the older boys and girls, as well as shorthand and typing. Moreover, he motivated many to get interested in literature, as did Mme Frank for the younger students.

For the older teenagers Mr. Lyrer often became the instigator of lively evening discussions and educational input. Later he would become an invaluable ally to the older boys and girls when they felt compelled to flee or hide.

In December some ten of the older boys joined a weekly course in agriculture at the nearby village of Pailhès, which was organized by the education director of the Foix Préfecture.[19] Although criticized for her narrow-minded and arrogant manner in dealing with the teenagers, Rösli Näf obviously worked diligently and with foresight to maintain favorable relationships with local and departmental government officials. Sending boys to the government-sponsored course in Pailhès was part of that endeavor.

At the farm building across from the Château entrance, three heatable rooms were set up for a girls' sewing shop, a larger one for carpentry and a third as quarters for Mr. and Mrs. Nadal, Spanish refugees who arrived in the fall. Mr. Nadal would teach woodworking to some of the boys.[20] By fall of 1941 a laundry room and showers had been installed in the château, while the toilets remained outdoors.

Fresh milk was obtained from local farmers until early winter, but as supplies dwindled it was supplemented with powdered milk supplied from the Swiss headquarters in Toulouse. Monthly special food allocation coupons for children's camps from the area government were helpful but were not enough without additional supplies from the Secours Suisse office in Toulouse.[21]

In the fall the children undertook several daylong excursions into nearby woods where they gathered 300 kilos of edible sweet chestnuts as a diet addition.[22] They also plucked large quantities of blackberries and elderberries from the countryside that were used to make jam and stored for later consumption.[23]

The spirit of cooperation, taking care of each other and willingly doing the chores to maintain and improve the primitive living conditions, was obvious to visitors at La Hille and also expressed by the adult caretakers. "The children are in excellent health and well behaved," stated Alex Frank, "and some of them conduct themselves truly in outstanding fashion."[24] "We must say that the spirit of the colony is excellent and all these children are truly very well behaved. I am sending you some photos," wrote Maurice Dubois.[25]

But the poor living conditions, increasing external threats for Jewish children in Vichy France and all over Europe, plus personality clashes between the caretakers and with some of the older children also had an effect on the daily life at La Hille. Although Alex Frank had made laudatory comments about Rösli Näf on June 22—"she is very nice and very able"[26]—on January 28, 1942, he followed with a derogatory letter obviously written in frustration and illustrating the staff conflict: "Mlle Näf, with whom I have collaborated, unfortunately is an excessively opinionated person, dishonest, unfair and narrow-minded, and working for the first time with children. She has no idea about leading young people, tends to humiliate them in a moral sense and often sets a very sad example."[27] He adds that this underlies his decision to give up his responsibilities at La Hille, caused also by Maurice Dubois's obvious preference for Swiss personnel.[28]

Alex Frank's negative feelings about Rösli Näf were expressed by his mother in even angrier fashion in her diary. That Rösli Näf was headstrong and not universally liked by some older teenagers at that time also is documented in the recollection of Ruth Schütz (Usrad). She describes Rösli Näf as "quite a tall woman, about 30, and single, with light blonde hair, very carefully combed back, and dressed according to her position, without any extra color or decoration." She recalls her as "a hard-working woman, to the point, and tough enough that she wasn't taken aback by the difficult living conditions and an endless work day."[29] But she also recalls the negatives: "Sensitivity and tenderness were foreign to her, and she didn't display an ability to listen to the pains of the young ones. Every morning she checked the angle that the sheets on our beds were folded. On the door she hung a paper on which she wrote the personal achievements of each of us in folding our blankets and so on." "I was sixteen years old. The world around us was going up in flames. I was worried about the safety of my parents. The future was threatening and cloudy and our headmistress was treating us like children. In my anger one day I pulled the list off the door. The confrontation between Ms. Näf and me continued for several weeks," she recalls.[30]

Between our arrival in Belgium and the summer of 1941 at La Hille, more than two years had passed and the older boys and girls had become teenagers with their own feelings and opinions, as well as fears about the future. Many had matured quickly under these circumstances and were aware of potential dangers. We were no longer children. Most, if not all, worked hard at the tasks required to keep the colony running and to take care of the needs of the younger children. But they also were confronted with the turmoil of the times. Sixteen-year-old Lixie Grabkowicz (Kowler) expressed her frustration in a letter to her parents, who were still in Vienna: "Inside I have become a totally different person. I am no longer this former "Lieserl" [nickname for Lixie]. Life here is, and is becoming slowly but surely, unbearable. Not in a material sense because we are more or less used to deprivations and we almost no longer miss extraneous things, but in a spiritual sense it is no longer tenable. I don't know what will happen but if it doesn't end soon and some time it must end, because nothing endures forever!!"[31]

On the one hand the children's caretakers believed that the children, for the most part, were not aware of pending dangers, yet they also cite anguish over the fate of their family members left behind. "I assume that the children hardly are conscious of what is going on," Maurice Dubois wrote to Mme Goldschmidt-Brodsky in Basel on September 10, 1941. "Living isolated in their colony without any contact with the outside world, they are certainly not aware of the day's problems." Yet in a December 15 report regarding the colony he states "a number of the children are anguished by the knowledge that their parents have already been deported to Poland or are about to be."[32] That awareness is underscored by another statement in the same report: "The most important happening, without question, was the visit of four of the children at the Camp de Gurs [notorious internment camp near Pau in Vichy France] where they were able to hug their parents, for the first time in nearly two years!"[33]

The awareness and danger of being incarcerated at Gurs was also brought home to our children by the liberation from Gurs of seventeen-year-old Werner Epstein by Alex Frank, who wrote to Mme Goldschmidt-Brodsky on June 22, 1941, that he had been able to obtain a furlough for Werner, "which the Secours Suisse had been able to renew month-by-month."[34]

In March of 1941 Fritz Wertheimer, a protégé of Swiss nurse Elsbeth Kasser (at Gurs), also was liberated from Gurs and brought to La Hille.[35] Edith Goldapper (Rosenthal) notes his arrival: "My God, what tales he has told us. Gurs must be a horrible place. Those poor people, compared to them we have a wonderful life," she writes in her diary.[36] Wertheimer apparently had been brought to Gurs with his parents Julius and Klara Wertheimer in October 1940 and both died there before the end of the year.[37]

21. Fritz Wertheimer (at left) and Kurt Moser at La Hille, 1942. Both were arrested in 1943 and deported to Poland and murdered. Reproduced with permission from the United States Holocaust Memorial Museum Photo Archive.

When there was communication from left-behind parents and family members, it often contained code language, because the writers knew that all letters were being read by Nazi censors. In fact, the letters received by the children often bore the censor's mark. "The death or disappearance of one or both parents were written as 'Papa has gone to the countryside' or 'both parents suddenly had to make an emergency trip' and 'a sister suddenly became very ill,'" notes Irène Frank in her diary.[38] "Such news became more frequent and the youngsters to whom it was addressed quickly learned how to recognize the code words and the situation which was described by the ominous words."[39]

No code language was needed when Edith Goldapper (Rosenthal) learned about her parents' deportation to Poland:

Today is July 14 [1942]. Tomorrow is Papa's birthday. Just now the young Mrs. Frank [Elka] asked me to come to her room and shows me a letter she received from Mrs. Goldschmidt. She writes that my golden, one-of-a-kind, dear parents were deported to Poland. Well, I feel awful, things are blacking out in front of my eyes. It had to happen to them! That's the reward that Papa fought for Austria and lost his eyesight—that's the generous thank-you of the damned Germans.

If I had a German next to me now, I would exterminate him on the spot. I am totally devastated. They had already been threatened once before but due to good protection they succeeded to remain in Vienna. But this time it's for real, and only God knows whether I shall ever be able to see my beloved parents again. It's a heavy blow in my life.[40]

Although the deprivations, personality clashes, and ever-present fear of persecution had become detrimental aspects of daily life, camaraderie, learning new pursuits, and the attractive features of living in the French countryside provided at least some balance as the entire colony became adjusted to its new surroundings.

A number of the older boys and girls became connected with local farmers, forging bonds that, in several cases, lasted beyond the war

22. Edith Goldapper seated at Château de La Hille, 1942. Her diary contains extensive and valuable details about the Children of La Hille history. From Edith Goldapper collection, with permission from Joachim Rosenthal.

years. Inge Berlin (Vogelstein) worked at a farm near the château, Rudi Oehlbaum (Oliver) was a regular at a farm called Borde Blanque, up the hill from La Hille, and also at other farms, as did Georges Herz, Norbert Winter, and Gerald Kwasczkowski, to name a few. Ruth Schütz (Usrad), Edgar Chaim, and several others went to work and live at Le Tambouret, a farm owned by the Schmutz family, which had originally come from Switzerland. This property is located several hours' walk over the hilly countryside from La Hille (and was still in the family's possession sixty-five years later).

Although the plan for sending boys to a vocational school failed, Walter Kamlet (aged nineteen), a skilled pianist, and Heinz (Chaim) Storosum (aged eighteen), a dedicated violinist, were enrolled at a conservatory in Toulouse by Maurice Dubois. Before they left, and after their return, they performed regularly for the colony, and sometimes also for neighbors, accompanied by Edith Goldapper (Rosenthal), barely seventeen, who also played the piano.

23. Georges Herz at farm near La Hille, 1942. A number of other La Hille teenagers also worked at nearby farms. From the author's personal collection.

Literature and a small library became part of the daily cultural diet, nurtured by the two teachers, Eugen Lyrer and Irène Frank. Mme Goldschmidt-Brodsky had sent a sizeable check to Maurice Dubois from her new home in Basel, Switzerland, for the purchase of books. He suggested that they be purchased as a gift for the Jewish New Year in September, which apparently happened.[41] "At the Rosh-ha-shanah celebration we were very pleasantly surprised by your generous present. The books have brought us so much joy, especially since our library had been very limited," wrote Elka Frank on September 23, 1941.[42]

Outdoor games, excursions into the countryside, and especially swimming in a natural pond up the hillside during the good weather season made the colony into something like a summer camp, in spite of the ever-present negative factors. Irène Frank describes it:[43]

A few kilometers from La Hille flowed a little stream into a quarry, a natural invitation to go swimming. On hot days we led the children there. The Spanish sewing teacher had made some bathing attire, not bikinis for beach beauties, but respectable to comply with "higher authority."

Mr. Lyrer plunged into the water with enthusiasm, Elka [Frank] and I abstained, even though the cooling water tempted us. It became apparent that most of the children could not swim, which did not diminish their enjoyment. The older ones and those who knew how to swim took them under their wing and there was much splashing, shouting and yelling as is customary in such settings.[44]

In the fall of 1941 the children rehearsed and performed two plays in French by Molière—"Le Malade Imaginaire" (The Imaginary Invalid) and "Les Fourberies de Scapin" (Scapin's Deceits). Farmers from the surrounding area were invited to the performances and voiced their pleasure and appreciation.[45]

The Christmas holidays (already the second time since the children's escape to France) were celebrated with the arrival of Santa Claus on December 6 (the customary date for European children) and presents were prepared and exchanged.

It is worth noting that the observance of Jewish religious customs, while not forbidden, received diminished emphasis as survival in the countryside and separation from Jewish communities changed the children's priorities.

By the end of 1941, before the United States were drawn into the war, nineteen of the La Hille children had succeeded in leaving for America, seventeen of them through the efforts of Mme Felddegen and the US committee. Hanni Schlimmer and Werner Rindsberg left separately after obtaining individual visas. The vacancies created by these departures were filled by the Secours Suisse with French and Spanish refugee children.

Maurice Dubois and Rösli Näf wanted to diversify the colony in order to better protect their Jewish children and also to gain favor

24. Older boys at La Hille with Elias Haskelevicz (far right) in summer of 1941. From left: author Walter Reed (Rindsberg) shortly before his emigration to New York; Peter Landesmann (who later joined the Resistance); Werner Epstein, who survived deportation to Auschwitz; and center, with back view, author's best friend Walter Strauss, who was deported to Majdanek and murdered in 1943. From the author's personal collection.

with the local French authorities. On November 17 Flora Schlesinger wrote to Rolf Weinmann (who had arrived in the United States with the Quaker-selected group in September) that five French and two Spanish children had joined the colony.[46] Rösli Näf, as described in the September 14, 1941, minutes of a staff meeting, "was enthused about the idea of soon receiving French children for the eighteen teenagers who were to have attended the vocational school in Toulouse."[47] "This would appreciably improve relations with the authorities. The story in the 'Dépêche' newspaper in Foix that we would welcome French children assigned by the Préfecture was followed immediately by an increase in the ration of meat and of potatoes," Mlle Näf reported.[48]

Because they were living in an isolated countryside, the children of La Hille were less likely to be bothered by the authorities or by denunciation from collaborators and Nazi sympathizers who existed side-by-side with those French people who disliked the Nazis (and to whom they referred as "Boche" and "Sale Boche" [filthy German]). But many of the children had only vague notions of measures and intentions of the Pétain regime that would soon directly affect and threaten them.

Already eighty-four years old when France was overrun by the Germans, Marshal Phillipe Pétain owed his notoriety to his role in the defense of Verdun in World War I. When the French government collapsed after fleeing to Bordeaux in 1940, Pierre Laval and others persuaded Pétain to become chief of state of the unoccupied zone of France, with headquarters in Vichy. Pétain soon established an autocratic government in the unoccupied zone based on a new constitution that gave him sole power without a parliament. He surrounded himself with Ministers who believed in what he called the "National Revolution,"[49] and the regime soon launched a propaganda campaign against groups and individuals whom they blamed for the French defeat. Their targets were Freemasons, Jews, Communists, and Gaullists (supporters of Col. Charles de Gaulle, a former Pétain military subordinate who had set up a French exile government in London).[50]

There is disagreement over whether Pétain was an anti-Semite but he certainly gave free rein to his associates who were and he participated actively in the discussions of anti-Jewish decrees and signed all of them. During a Cabinet discussion of the "Statut des Juifs" ("Law against the Jews") on October 1, 1940, "it was the Marshal who was the most severe. He insisted particularly that the Justice and Education [Ministries] should contain no Jews," wrote Foreign Minister Paul Baudouin in his journal.[51]

There is much evidence that the Vichy regime persecuted Jews without prodding from the Germans. On September 3 and 27, 1940, decrees signed by Pétain empowered the prefects (regional government-appointed officials) to intern foreigners without special authorization, and on October 3 Pétain signed the "Statut des Juifs," which defined for France who is a Jew (which was different from the German definition). He followed this the next day by signing a law authorizing the prefects "to intern, assign to supervised residence, or enroll in forced labor any foreign Jews in their department [region], as they saw fit."[52] Whether they knew it or not, these decrees would soon change the lives of the Children of La Hille.

On March 29, 1941, a new Vichy law created the Commissariat Général aux Questions Juifs (CGQJ—a government bureau of Jewish affairs). The Germans had requested such an agency for the occupied zone, but Vichy officials extended it to both zones.[53] Xavier Vallat, an ardent anti-Semite, was named commissioner. Pétain now had a full-time Jew-hater in place. His second "Statut des Juifs" of June 2, 1941, included a requirement that all Jews must register with their préfecture, "a grave step which profoundly shocked Jewish opinion and was to have fatal consequences later when Jews were being rounded up and deported."[54]

The Vichy French public paid scant attention to the racial laws of 1941. "Most had other problems," writes Susan Zuccotti. "They worried about the one and a half million French prisoners of war in Nazi Germany. They worried about scarce food, clothing and fuel supplies, inadequate transportation and communications . . . and the increasingly hostile behavior of the German occupier."[55]

The older teenagers of La Hille and our caretakers learned of major events by radio and from some newspapers. Between the summer of 1940 and spring of 1941 news about the air warfare over England (the Battle of Britain) caused concern that the Germans would soon invade England. Soon after the main colony's arrival at La Hille, on June 22, 1941, the Germans launched their long-planned invasion of Russia. Their initial successes further reduced any hope that German domination of Europe would be reversed and this feeling soon penetrated to the remote area where we were living.

Ruth Schütz (Usrad) describes it well:

> We were lonely and isolated in a remote area of the country, and we knew very little about what was happening in the world. Our only source of information was a one-page newspaper the size of a school notebook that came out of the Vichy government, which served

the Germans. All the countries of Europe had been conquered by Hitler's armies. Only England had not given in and was absorbing horrible bombings on its populated cities. I knew that Germany had started a massive invasion of the USSR, and was progressing very quickly. The look of things during that year was very dark and pessimistic and left little hope for a better future. I worried about my mother who was in London, being bombed.[56]

At the end of 1941 a significant action took place in Switzerland, an action which would profoundly affect the Children of La Hille, other refugee colonies in Vichy France, and their Swiss caretakers, although the children were unaware of it. The Swiss Aid Association for Child War Victims (SAK), an association of seventeen different organizations related to helping children, was created on January 14, 1940, and Rodolfo Olgiati had been named its *Zentral-Sekretär* (general manager).[57] When Germany invaded Western Europe a few months later, the personnel who conducted the relatively benign activities of SAK encountered a rude awakening. "The directors of the SAK appeared to be totally overwhelmed by these events," writes Ms. Schmidlin.[58] She adds, "with these events in Western Europe the war scene came much closer to Switzerland."

Throughout the war the Swiss government had to face the possibility of a German invasion and therefore pursued a deliberate policy of neutrality, often bending over backward so as not to annoy the Germans. A related factor was the Swiss economic situation. The country needed coal and other commodities from Germany and in turn had to rely on selling machinery and other Swiss goods to both sides in the conflict without becoming liable to retribution. These realities indirectly led to concerns in the highest ranks of the government about the operations and actions of Swiss organizations like SAK (later Secours Suisse) in Vichy France. Further, the leaders, like Olgiati and Dubois, as members of the Service Civil and known as pacifists, were regarded with suspicion by the higher authorities in the Swiss government.[59]

These concerns led to the proposal that the Swiss Red Cross should gain supervision over SAK and especially over the Swiss services to children in Vichy France. An agreement to that effect was signed on December 17, 1941, and became effective on January 1, 1942.[60] The former SAK was now renamed "Secours Suisse aux Enfants, Croix Rouge Suisse," (Swiss Children's Aid, Swiss Red Cross). Because the Swiss Red Cross (which was founded in the 19th century as a medical resource for soldiers in battle) was part of the Swiss Army Medical Corps, its chief was *Oberst* (colonel) Hugo Remund.

With the amalgamation of the SAK, Remund became its leading official—and, not much later, the central figure in controversy and confrontations related to the Children of La Hille. Rodolfo Olgiati was named secretary of the Secours Suisse, with headquarters in Bern. Although he was admitted to meetings of the board of directors, he did not have a vote and was originally not even expected to attend board meetings.[61]

Remund lost no time in notifying a German Red Cross official in Berlin that the merger had occurred[62] and required Olgiati to resign as secretary of the Service Civil. Remund explained that because the Service Civil was regarded as a political organization in certain European circles, Olgiati's Service Civil position would be in conflict with his new connection to the Swiss Red Cross.[63] We cite these developments in detail because the prejudices and defensive attitudes of Remund and his superiors would soon become serious threats to the safety and fate of the Children of La Hille and to others under the care of the Secours Suisse in Vichy France.

By January 1942, personality conflicts and perhaps other matters increased the tension between Rösli Näf and Alex Frank. Mlle Näf's strict and somewhat impersonal method of dealing with the children contrasted with the work-related camaraderie that Frank had created, especially with the older boys. His spouse, Mrs. Elka Frank, had responsibility for the younger children ever since the arrival at Seyre.

There also was the logical desire of Dubois and the Secours Suisse to have a *Swiss* person in charge when it came to external relationships,[64] not to mention their possible concerns over Alex Frank's political attachment to communism. Frank's political orientation could well have run counter the very conservative views of the Swiss Red Cross leadership after it merged with the SAK and assumed control over the newly named Secours Suisse.

Whatever the reasons, Frank wrote to Mme Goldschmidt-Brodsky on January 28, 1942, that he was leaving the colony in order to not further disturb the prevailing harmony of the La Hille community. He indicated that his wife and mother would continue to function at La Hille and that he would always be available to assist if circumstances required his help. His intention was to do maintenance work at an unnamed château fifteen kilometers away and to return to assist local farmers in April.[65] At the same time, Frank informed Mme Goldschmidt-Brodsky that his wife Elka had undergone serious surgery and was recuperating.[66] Physical ailments would plague her for the rest of her life, aggravated by the hardships of the time and her later escape on foot over the Pyrénées.

From the Hebrew Immigrant Aid Society (HIAS) office in New York, Mme Felddegen worked tirelessly from 1941 to 1943 to bring more of the children to the United States. In her HIAS office Mme Felddegen kept, and regularly updated, a complete card file on every La Hille child, with names of relatives' addresses and parents' whereabouts, if known. An "exposé" (i.e., a summary description) regarding the colony—probably used for approaching US government and private agencies—contains a list, dated January 23, 1941, of thirty-nine La Hille children "who have US affidavits" (i.e., care-giving guarantees from relatives or friends, which were required for US visa applications). On this list are the names of eight teenage boys and girls who later were deported and murdered, as well as many who eventually fled illegally to Switzerland and Spain. Affidavits from relatives, in fact, were no guarantee that the US State Department would issue a visa to Jewish refugee children.

A separate list compiled by Mme Felddegen[67] identifies thirty-one La Hille boys and girls "who will be 16 years old by July 1941 and for whom the Committee will not care" (i.e., who were ineligible to come to the United States under the special children's quota used by the US rescue committee). Coincidentally, these older teenagers would soon be "eligible" for merciless arrests by Vichy-controlled police forces.

"As I consider the possibility of bringing our children over here as a group improbable at this time, and since we also need to find a solution for those aged 16–18, I am now collecting individual papers for each, with the assistance of their relatives and friends. We will transmit these to Washington in order to gain favorable consideration for the application for each child which you will make to the American consulate [in Marseille]," she wrote to Maurice Dubois on May 22, 1941.[68]

"It is of the utmost importance that these papers be submitted through us [the HIAS office] to remind the US government that the child is part of the group for whom the State Department earlier had given a favorable response," she added. "Whether we can indeed obtain the authorization for individual children remains to be seen." Her doubts would later be proven to be correct. "In any event, I am doing everything possible to help get the children out of France," she tells Dubois.

◇ 8 ◇

Internment and Liberation

At the beginning of 1942, the Nazi persecutors made decisions that would soon spell doom for the Jewish populations of Europe. These decisions directly affected the Children of La Hille, although they and their caretakers would not know it until mid-summer.

On January 20 Reinhard Heydrich, deputy of SS Chief Heinrich Himmler, assembled fifteen ranking Nazi government officials at a lakefront villa on Lake Wannsee outside Berlin to coordinate the next steps toward the "Final Solution" of their Jewish "problem," as the German criminals code-worded the mass murder of all European Jews.

The eminent Holocaust historian Raul Hilberg has categorized the Nazi extermination of the Jews into four phases: definition (who is a Jew?), expropriation (depriving Jews of rights and property), concentration (moving them into ghettos and deportation centers), and annihilation (mass murder).[1] Emigration, voluntary or forced, was the consequence of the first steps and that was how the Children of La Hille first fled Germany to Belgium in 1938–39, and then to France in 1940.

Zealous French and German officials were hard at work in early 1942 to carry out the diabolical German obsession for annihilating all the Jews. In unoccupied France, Vichy Interior Minister Pierre Pucheu issued an order to all regional prefects on January 2, 1942, to conduct a compulsory registration (census) of all foreign Jews and of those who had become citizens of France after January 1, 1936, "following up on an order by the Vice President of the Conseil [Admiral Darlan], according to which these (described) Jews were to be put in Foreign Workers groups or in Special Centers."[2] Penalties were to be imposed on those who failed to register. Those targeted had to decide whether it was better to stay off the list and risk punishment or to report and be easily traced and caught.

On February 25, 1942, each of the Children of La Hille filled in and signed the required registration. Rösli Näf signed for the youngest who were unable to sign their names themselves, namely Antoinette Steuer and Manfred Manasse. These forms are stored, intact, at the departmental archives in Foix to this very day. Now Vichy even knew where to find five-year-old Antoinette![3]

In May, Xavier Vallat was replaced as commissioner-general for Jewish affairs by Darquier de Pellepoix, a power-hungry and conniving anti-Semite who was fond of debauchery and psychologically flawed. The new head of the French national police network was thirty-three-year-old René Bousquet, who would soon play a pivotal role in the fate of the Children of La Hille. On the German side high-level SS and Police General Carl Albrecht Oberg, based in Paris, reported directly to Heinrich Himmler, the main Nazi leader in charge of mass-murdering the Jews of Europe. Also heavily involved in the planning was Theodor Danneker, chief of the "Judenamt" (Jewish office) for France and the notorious Adolf Eichmann, Danneker's chief.[4] As part of the preparation process, Eichmann, head of the "Judenamt" (Jewish office) of the central German security office (RSHA) arrived in Paris on June 30, 1942, bearing a brutal directive from Himmler: all the Jews of France were to be deported, apparently without distinction or regard for French citizenship. The Final Solution had begun.[5]

On August 25, 1942, Mariem Kokotek delivered her twelve-year-old twin daughters, Guita and Irene (born in Chemnitz, Germany), to the La Hille colony. They had escaped the first roundup of Jews in Paris on May 13 and managed to cross the guarded border into Vichy France. Their father, Aron Kokotek, had been interned at the Beaune-la-Rolande Camp and (as they found out later) had by then already been deported and murdered in Auschwitz. "You will be safer here," Mariem assured them, as she viewed the pleasant hills that surround the isolated château. Only a few hours after she left, unfolding events would prove that she was greatly mistaken.[6]

Word of the arrests of Jews in Paris and of a deportation from Camp Gurs had already reached the colony at La Hille. Hans Garfunkel, then eighteen years old, remembers hearing about these early deportations from BBC Radio and apprehension spread quickly among the older boys and girls. By August 24, he and Charles Blumenfeld, also eighteen, and another teenager had planned to leave La Hille and hide in nearby woods. For some reason they postponed their departure. Before sunrise on August 26 Hans rose to go to the outdoor toilet and became frightened at the sight of a gendarme in the semi-darkness. Upset and worried, he woke Rösli Näf.[7]

On Wednesday, August 26, the French police throughout Vichy France carried out a long-planned *rafle* (roundup) and brought many thousands of Jews—men, women, and children—to various internment camps in the unoccupied zone. Rösli Näf, awakened by Hans Garfunkel and by Elka Frank, made her way to the main door with a flashlight. She described what happened next in a report to the Bern headquarters of the Secours Suisse dated September 15, 1942:[8]

It is 5:10 a.m. With shaking hands I pull back the heavy iron door bolt and now I saw two gendarmes standing in front of me and I almost dropped the flashlight in fright. They asked why I seemed so frightened and I answered that it's more appropriate that I ask THEM what they are doing here. They lied and said they were on patrol and had entered to get out of the wind. I invited them inside but they declined politely. When I came back inside, Mme Frank told me that there were two other gendarmes at the back door.

Now we had no doubt what was going on. As I went upstairs to quickly put on some clothes, the stairs were already blocked by other gendarmes. They ascended the stairs like a huge multi-tentacled monster, about twenty of them. The chief of police from Pamiers [a nearby provincial city] ordered that I follow him. He said he needed to talk to me. He would not even allow me to put some clothes on. On the main floor he showed me a list of more than forty names of the teenagers over sixteen years old, plus the Jewish staff members—the two Mrs. Frank, Irène and Elka, and Mr. and Mrs.

Schlesinger. He said he had orders to arrest them all and they could bring up to thirty kg of belongings.

I shouted in his face that this was outrageous and I would never have expected that anyone would violate a facility of the Swiss Red Cross. He shrugged his shoulder and mumbled something about orders and duty. They refused when I asked that I be allowed to awaken the children so as not to scare them. Instead they allowed me only to accompany them from room to room in order to announce the brutal order.

One gendarme stayed to guard each room, all corridors and stairs were blocked and the whole château was surrounded. The adversities that the older ones had already experienced in their lives had taught them that staying calm in such circumstances will assure a better outcome. Even the girls, who usually would scream when they saw a mouse, did not panic. Calm and with teeth clenched everybody gathered their minimal belongings.

It was impossible to avoid waking the younger children, as each of their rooms was occupied by one of the older girls as caretakers and these were being arrested. They were puzzled about what was happening and cried over the commotion that was mirrored in the faces of the older ones. The police allowed us to serve a quick breakfast and then lined them all up with their belongings for roll call in the yard. They had already fetched several youngsters who were staying overnight at nearby farmhouses and made notes about three others who were working at more distant farms and whom they would find and arrest there.

They got them all. We had made their task easy (by dutifully registering everyone). Three teenagers who were over sixteen, but not on the list, were left alone. They then searched all the belongings for knives and scissors and recommended that they leave all jewelry, if any, with me. Then the sad procession went, two abreast, out of the gate and down the access road.

Our neighbors, the farmers, stood in front of their building, some of the women crying. They had always considered our children as nice and well-behaved and were fond of several who had helped them with their farm work. At the main road there was another roll call and they mounted the waiting bus.

To my question "where are you taking them?" they gave only a vague "to central Ariège, direction Pamiers" in reply. By 10 a.m. the bus started, with the little ones whose siblings were being taken away crying louder. We as well could no longer control our emotions. As he left, the police commander, partly to excuse himself, pleaded "higher orders" and expressed thanks for the cooperative attitude of the teenagers whom they were arresting. In my exasperation I answered that I was truly sorry that I had not helped the boys and girls to escape when the rumors first surfaced but I just could not believe that France would sink so low.

I cannot remember ever having been as saddened as I was returning to the half-empty château. What to do? I still had sixty children left and all my staff had been arrested, except for a Swiss teacher who had returned from a vacation in Switzerland the night before. All the dormitory bedrooms looked like a storm had raged through them. In a mirror I saw my face. I looked like a half-crazed woman, unkempt and devastated. We divided the housework among some of the boys aged twelve to fifteen and I took on the cooking chores.[9]

By coincidence, Mme Parera, the wife of a Secours Suisse staff member from Toulouse was visiting La Hille. She ran to the village of Pailhès, two kilometers down the road, to telegraph the devastating news to Toulouse, Bern, and Vichy, Mlle Näf writes in her report (La Hille did not have a telephone). The next day employees at the préfecture office in Foix confirmed that her children had been taken to the Le Vernet internment camp near the town of Pamiers, about twenty-five kilometers from La Hille. She requested that a visitor pass for her be sent to Le Vernet and returned to La Hille.

Several La Hille teenagers who were working on farms away from La Hille also were hunted down by the French gendarmes. On August 26 Ruth Schütz (Usrad) was working and living at the remote farm of the Schmutz family near Escosse (between La Hille and Pamiers):

In the early afternoon, I returned with a basket full of fresh vegetables from the garden.[10] From afar I could make out a black car in front of the home and two large men in black uniforms of the French militia next to it. They turned to me and said, "Is your name Ruth Schütz?" "Yes, that's my name." "We have an order to arrest you, and you have five minutes to collect your belongings."

To my question, "What did I do and where are you taking me?" they answered, "To a work camp. It's time you little Jews should work a little." I wanted to add, "But I AM working!" but their manner was so threatening that I kept quiet.

With the kick of a boot I was thrown into the car. The car stopped in front of the police building in the town of Pamiers. Without another word I was put into a detention cell and a heavy door was closed behind me.

I was alone in the small room, whose barred window faced the street. From my window I saw women and men wearing urban clothes, probably clerks hurrying to their house for lunch. Children moved around on bicycles, young men and women in groups went by laughing aloud. Does this all still exist in the world, and why don't I have a part in it? What type of curse has descended on me? Why are these girls walking around outside, and I am locked up behind bars?

With evening I was put into a car, in which sat a family, parents and two young children on their laps. We drove a short way and before us opened the gate to the Le Vernet concentration camp.[11]

"I'll never forget the goodbyes, it's too horrible to think about," confided Edith Goldapper (Rosenthal) in her diary.[12] "Mlle Näf is devastated. Only on the bus we learn that they are taking us to the Le Vernet Camp. After we arrived, each of us was taken to the headquarters where we had to complete 1,000 forms and were searched for false papers."

"After all that we were taken to our barrack. There were double-decker bunks. Inge and I were in the upper ones, Frieda and Ilse below. Meanwhile new transports keep arriving. It is a horrible scene.

The lights are kept on all night. Early the next morning there is another roll call."

She recalls the first full day in the camp. "All the prisoners of our section [*îlot*] go for a walk (800 of us). We join in and have good conversations and think often about La Hille. We sing a lot, which cheers up the others too.[13] Now it's day 2. We are extremely happy, overjoyed, because Mlle Näf had arrived. We cling to her and everybody else also surrounds her constantly. We really feel more protected now."[14]

Rösli Näf found out quickly that her teenagers had been taken to Le Vernet and decided to join them. She was allowed entry into the camp because of her Swiss Red Cross pin and at the camp headquarters she was greeted in Swiss dialect by one of the administrators. She was housed in a barracks of the French Red Cross and an hour later was led to the barracks of the La Hille contingent.

> My joy at finding them healthy and unmolested in simple but clean barracks was indescribable. For them my arrival brought hope that perhaps something could be done to save them. My Red Cross guide was full of praise for their excellent behavior and how they had taken charge of everything that needed to be done in daily chores.
>
> Suddenly their reports of goings-on at the camp were interrupted by the command *Fixe!!* [attention!!]. As almost 100 voices went silent, the director of the camp, an older gentleman, entered and introduced himself. In very friendly fashion he asked what I was doing there and, without hesitation, gave me permission to circulate freely in the camp provided that I would stay as long as the children remained there. That was better than what I had expected.[15]
>
> Surrounded by barbed wire, the compound of 9 buildings was patrolled by silent guards but the inmates were allowed to circulate. The boys prepared soup twice a day and each day there was a bread ration for each inmate and much fruit (it was summer time). By Saturday, August 29, I learned from Maurice Dubois by telephone that his efforts in Vichy had been successful. Once again I was all torn up inside, this time from sheer joy. I could hardly contain myself. However, the colonel (camp director) decided that the children should

not be returned to La Hille until after the departure of the other inmates. I would have preferred to spare us the sad experience of watching the others being taken away but it seemed unavoidable.

I could of course not say with certainty that our children would be liberated. I could still only offer that hope, and after the phone call, in good conscience. Later Maurice Dubois came himself for a short visit to tell the children that their stay at Le Vernet would soon be over.[16]

What led to the decision to spare the boys and girls of La Hille and did the mass arrests of August 26 really come without notice? The story behind the scene is fascinating and now well documented. At a meeting with Eichmann in Berlin on June 11, Danneker and his Nazi counterparts from Belgium and Holland were given a quota for the deportation of Jews in their territory. For France, including the unoccupied zone, it was 100,000. Upon his return to Paris, Danneker put the target for Vichy France at 50,000 and Rudolph Rahn, a senior German embassy official, set up a June 27 date with Premier Laval to make the demand official.[17]

Laval discussed the topic at a Vichy cabinet meeting on July 3 but did not mention a plan for mass deportations.[18] But the following day he set the course. On July 4, Police Chief Bousquet declared (according to Danneker) that Marshal Pétain, together with Laval, had agreed to the deportation of all stateless Jews from both zones, as a first step.[19] In early August, Danneker insisted on an additional shipment of 11,000 Jews from Vichy France in a few weeks. In order to meet the Germans' demands, now put at 32,000 Jews to be deported by the end of the summer, the Ministry of the Interior sent secret instructions to all regional prefects on August 5. In a follow-up on August 22 Bousquet ordered these prefects to take personal charge of the operation and to "crush all resistance you encounter," to deal firmly with "indiscretions" or passivity, in order "to free your area totally of foreign Jews as provided in my circular of August 5."[20]

In other words, the Children of La Hille and Rösli Näf had no idea that their fate had been decided many weeks before Hans Garfunkel heard the foreboding BBC Radio broadcasts. Others, however, were well aware and took action. On August 10 Donald A. Lowrie, the American YMCA representative in France, sent a detailed insider report to Mr. Tracy Strong, general secretary of the YMCA World's Committee. He reported knowing "about a Laval conversation with the German commissar for Jewish affairs a month earlier. When Danneker asked Laval, 'When are you going to apply to your Jews in the non-occupied zone the measures we are using in the occupied zone?' Laval answered, 'the only Jews we have are your Jews. We will send them back to you any time you say.'"

Lowrie continues: "On July 30th, through the indiscretion of Fourcade, Acting Chief of Police, we got information that 10,000 foreign Jews were to be deported. The first 3,500 were to be taken from internment camps and to be evacuated on August sixth, eighth, tenth and twelfth. The Executive Committee of our Coordinating Committee decided that we must appeal to Marshal Pétain. I left for Vichy on August third."

Lowrie describes how several visits by advocates with Laval and Pétain during the following days were fruitless.[21] Lowrie concludes his report with an observation about the reaction of French people: "The few French people who know of this situation are profoundly shocked and many have said they were ashamed of being French when crimes like these could be committed in the name of their country."[22]

In a follow-up report on August 22 sent from Geneva, Lowrie summarizes his frustration: "Representatives of our various organizations went to local capitals and to Vichy, while I appealed to Marshal Pétain in a special audience; representatives of the Quakers saw Laval. The result was nil. The old Marshal could do nothing. Laval would not. After consulting together, Cardinal Gerlier (of Lyon) and Marc Boegner, President of the Protestant Federation of France, addressed letters to the Chief of State. There has been no reply."[23] In mid-August, letters that criticized the planned roundups and deportations were issued by Cardinal Gerlier, Archbishop Soliège of Toulouse, and Bishop Marie of Montauban, among others. They ordered that these be read in their parishes.

With all of these caretakers of refugees aware of the Vichy government's plans, it comes as no surprise that Maurice Dubois also had advance information, though he apparently chose not to share it with the management at La Hille. In a memorandum written for Secours Suisse chief Colonel Remund, which records an oral report from Mrs. Dubois, the Bern staff states that Maurice Dubois had accidentally learned of the planned arrests from the prefect of the Pyrénées Orientales Department at Perpignan.

The memorandum indicates that he had phoned Bern on Monday, August 24, reporting the imminent roundups and that he was leaving for Vichy. He requested that a rendezvous with the Swiss ambassador to Vichy be arranged for him.[24] After Dubois's warning phone call to Olgiati in Bern on August 24, there was active consultation between high-placed Swiss officials about whether any action should be taken and how to protect the Swiss neutrality policy.

Urgent back-and-forth deliberations involved Edouard de Haller, the government's watchdog over, and adviser to, the Red Cross and Secours Suisse, Colonel Remund, Heinrich Rothmund, the chief of the Swiss Federal Police and border guards and Ambassador Stucki. Rothmund and Stucki agreed that "it would be both ill-timed and dangerous for the Secours Suisse and Swiss Red Cross to take the initiative in retrieving these children. As this deals with an action of the French government taken under conditions known to everyone, such an initiative will be interpreted as an act of hostile criticism with all the consequences implied in such a position. Surely the CARTEL [Secours Suisse] has other options. As for R. de Haller, he immediately recommended to Colonel Remund that he do all possible to assure that the Secours Suisse staff in France refrain from protesting."[25]

In Basel, Mme Goldschmidt-Brodsky also had learned the news quickly. On August 27 she telegraphed Max Gottschalk in New York: "Am very upset, call your attention to danger awaiting children Montégut. Must do the impossible for all. Greetings, Marguérite Goldschmidt."[26] This time, unfortunately, matters were already out of their hands.

While it is interesting to explore the maneuvering behind the scene many decades later, the incarcerated children of La Hille knew only worry and anguish, as their worst fears had suddenly become reality. The resolve and courage of Maurice Dubois stand out even more in light of the developments behind the scene.

Irène Frank, then fifty-five years old, had also been arrested at La Hille. She corroborates Edith Goldapper's recollection of the camp. "Mlle Näf's appearance created attention in the whole camp," she writes in her diary.[27] "Her tall figure, determined voice and her [Swiss Red Cross] insignia drew the attention of many inmates."

"There were a dozen very young children in the camp and some of the mothers begged her to take their innocent children. 'You have a large colony and 6 or 8 more children won't make any difference,' they pleaded. 'Please save our children. We'll try to get over it and God will reward you,' they declared. It was a terrible spectacle. No Shakespeare tragedy performed by the greatest artists could compare with this chorus of mothers ready to sacrifice everything in their helplessness in a world without humanity."[28]

Maurice Dubois's courageous intercession, probably assisted by Swiss Embassy official Decroux (see below), resulted in Vichy Police leader René Bousquet issuing the unusual order to free the prisoners from La Hille. The only written evidence of the actions taken by Maurice Dubois appears in a memorandum to Colonel Remund from the Secours Suisse staff recounting an oral report by Mme Dubois of August 30, 1942.[29]

Mme Dubois came to Switzerland on August 28 with the aim of doing all possible to reverse the measures taken against some of the residents of our colonies (in France). On that evening she received a telephone call from Mr. Dubois who had stayed in Vichy longer than intended and therefore could not join her in Switzerland. He stated that he had obtained assurances from the General Secretary of the Interior Ministry [this was Bousquet's official title], which was the only office which had issued the orders in this case, that all of the persons arrested in the Swiss colonies would be released.

Further details about this issue, as well as assurances or conditions regarding the future fate of the Jewish persons under our care are not known at this time.[30]

Mr. Dubois added that after much difficulty, and with the assistance of the Swiss chargé d'affaires (as Swiss Ambassador Walter Stucki was then in Switzerland, it appears to have been Mr. Decroux), he had succeeded in gaining access to the Vichy official.[31]

Although the imprisonment of the teenagers lasted just a week, it seemed much longer at the time. Even after the news of impending liberation by phone to Mlle Näf from Dubois on August 29, the mood was depressed, she reports in her memorandum of September 15, 1942: "There were the many other prisoners whom no one was able to help. Dear, respectable persons who had tried honestly, during their short time in France, to support themselves by farm work. Others had lived in restricted forced refugee areas, usually in small resorts. Many had attempted to flee into the mountains where they were hunted and caught by the police."[32]

Because she was housed in the same building as the guards, Rösli Näf learned on the evening of August 31 that the deportation was scheduled for the next day. By 7:00 a.m. she accompanied the French Red Cross nurse to the internment area. Soon some forty state police spread over the area and the order to pack was given. "Two of our older boys approached me pale and perturbed and their fear-filled eyes, more than their words, asked, 'are we now going too?' I shall always be thankful that I was able to answer 'no' to them. They could now help the others, the mothers with little children and those who were paralyzed with fear."[33]

Edith Goldapper (Rosenthal) describes the events:

It's September 1. The camp commander enters our barrack. His voice thunders: "You have half an hour to get ready for your departure. Pack your luggage." We all feel sickened, the pain strikes our heads, necks, stomachs and legs. We feel faint. Now that which we silently expected, deportation to the East, is becoming reality. It's just too dreadful! At that moment Mlle Näf arrives and says, "stop the packing and help the others. You will not be deported." Of course we didn't believe her and think that it's just wishful thinking on her part. But since she insists, we do believe it and we help the others.

A half hour later the commander returns and now it sounds like a death sentence as he calls out the names Kohn, Katzenstein, etc. By noon the entire *îlot* [camp section] is cleared, except for us and a few special cases. In my 17-year-long life I have never seen such a scene. These poor unfortunate beings are glad that we are being freed even while they are being herded into the unknown. My God, that's too severe! I think that there is no longer any human justice.[34]

The Näf report describes in saddening detail the loading of the train and how the La Hille children helped those who had to leave. "What a sad and sorrowful task! And then the immense disappointment that the youngest children also had to get on the train. How gladly we would have relieved the anxious parents of this great worry."[35]

Whether intentionally or by accident, Rösli Näf's report did not mention the one boy whose mother's pleadings did save his life. In early 1942 Isi Bravermann (Veleris), age nine, had been directed to move with his mother, Irene, from the tiny village of Beaucholet to the forced residence village of Aulus-les-Bains near the Pyrénées. During the August arrests, all the Jews concentrated in Aulus-les-Bains, including the Bravermanns, were brought to Le Vernet (fifty-seven persons, according to a hand-written tabulation in the Ariège departmental archives). Somehow Mrs. Bravermann succeeded in having her son Isi accompany the children who were returning to La Hille on September 2. His mother was sent north on the September 1 train from Le Vernet and deported from Drancy to Auschwitz on Convoy No. 33 on September 16, 1942. Isi survived the war at La Hille because his mother made the heart-wrenching decision to turn her nine-year-old son over to complete strangers.[36]

Rösli Näf reports that her hope of leaving on the same day as those being deported was not realized though they were assured that they could leave the next day, on September 2. Their spirits were lifted when the beloved La Hille teacher Eugen Lyrer (who had rushed back from a vacation in Switzerland) arrived that afternoon. "From many gestures and remarks one could tell how repugnant their deportation assignment was to some of the camp employees, as well as the joy in the entire camp about our liberation. We left at the same hour as the deportation train the day before but ours was headed in the opposite direction" on the main line from Toulouse to Foix.[37]

At St. Jean de Verges, fifteen kilometers from La Hille, two horse-drawn farm vehicles were waiting to load the baggage and a truck to carry most of the freed La Hille prisoners (it was Mr. Boulihar, the vegetable man, writes Edith Goldapper). "All along the road the farmers rejoiced with us. How beautiful the world seemed without barbed wire. Everything was decked out with flowers for our return."[38]

"As we neared the castle of La Hille, the younger children greeted us by singing, and with a tremendous burst of happiness. Betty [Ruth's younger sister] was so happy she jumped on me and hugged me. This happiness was strange to me. I couldn't forget the heartbreaking pictures that I had witnessed only yesterday," writes Ruth Schütz (Usrad).[39]

Irène Frank recalls the return to La Hille in glowing words:

"Bien venus chez nous" ["welcome home"] read the sign in large colorful letters on the door of the château. While I was contemplating how to notify my mother, she actually was standing by the dining hall window and rushed toward me like a young girl and we fell into each other's arms crying. Never had we greeted each other with such emotion. [Mrs. Frank's aged mother was living in a hotel in nearby Pailhès.] My mother had suffered more than I and reports were that for 8 days she hardly ate any food.

They had invited Mama for the homecoming meal that had been prepared by a couple of 14-year-olds, with guidance from Mlle Näf. Mme Schlesinger [who like Irène Frank was arrested and had returned from the Le Vernet Camp that day] was not allowed to even enter the kitchen or do any work that evening. We had a truly sumptuous "peace meal." Mr. Lyrer contributed wine, and fruit juice for the younger ones, from his own pocket. It became a happy harmonious meal (saddened only by the thought about those who, crowded into tight train cars, were then traveling toward a horrible fate).[40]

Edith Goldapper (Rosenthal) recalls similar emotions: "We owe our liberation to the Red Cross [she probably meant 'Secours Suisse,' as she did not know then of the reservations that the Swiss Red Cross had about offending the French and Germans by liberating her and her companions] and I doubt that we will ever be able to repay what has been done and is being done for us. Such wonderful human beings are hard to find today."[41]

Although the actual document ordering the liberation of the La Hille children and adults from Le Vernet has not been found, the departmental archives at Foix contain a document dated September 9, 1942, in which the mayor of Montégut-Plantaurel (where the Château de La Hille is located) certifies that "GOLDAPPER Edith has voluntarily left the Camp of Le Vernet with all the members and children of the colony of the Swiss Red Cross of the Château de La Hille on September 2, 1942, carrying out a written order of the Regional Prefect."[42] The regional prefect was located in Toulouse and Le Vernet came under his authority.

The famous French Holocaust historian and advocate Serge Klarsfeld writes in *French Children of the Holocaust* that 11,402 children under eighteen years old were deported to the murder camps from France and that only 300 survived.[43] Maurice Dubois's courage and negotiating skill had saved some forty additional teenagers and several adults whom the Nazis and Vichy collaborators had fully intended to add to the list of their innocent victims from France.

◇ 9 ◇

Hazardous Journeys across
Well-Guarded Borders

Although the rescue of the La Hille teenagers from near-deportation was like a miracle, it turned out to be only the beginning of more threats and equally narrow escapes.

On September 10, 1942, Maurice Dubois wrote to Mme Goldschmidt-Brodsky in Basel that "truly these past few weeks have been very upsetting for everyone and we are very happy that we finally could save our children. For now I think I can tell you that we have been assured that they will not be endangered in the near future. It is of course very difficult to predict what may happen in the future; everything keeps changing so quickly."[1] His prediction could not have been more accurate.

Following the arrests and liberation of the La Hille teenagers, Eleanor Dubois and Rösli Näf separately went to Bern to urge the admission of the children into Switzerland in order to safeguard them from other roundups that were sure to follow. Rösli Näf recalled:

> Even though the daily routine was resumed, my sense of safety had been shattered. I went to the Bern headquarters of the Swiss Red Cross with the urgent request to bring all the children of the colony to Switzerland. Even though they were familiar with the events at La Hille and Le Vernet, there was no interest in my proposal. Instead I was reproached for a lack of faith following the successful liberation from Le Vernet.
>
> I realized that, in spite of their knowledge of what had happened, there was no awareness of how perilous the situation had

118

become and that they neither could nor wanted to confront the reality. Although I had told no one at La Hille the purpose of my trip, the more astute of the teenagers noticed that I was not returning with good news.[2]

Eleanor Dubois, already in Switzerland, made a separate effort to gain asylum for the children of La Hille. "Like numerous other persons who spoke out about these questions in recent days, Mme Dubois had the definite impression that the anti-Semitic actions in France would continue and be extended to younger children. Mme Dubois asked that the possibility of quickly granting asylum in Switzerland to the Jewish children and teenagers in our colonies be researched."

"An exploration with representatives of rescue organizations to assess this emigration issue took place in Geneva, chaired by Mr. Lowrie of the American Unitarian Service Committee."[3]

Antonia Schmidlin[4] describes Eleanor Dubois's attendance at the August 29, 1942, meeting of the Geneva Committee, "whose objective was the emigration of all endangered young Jewish people from France. She had traveled to Bern the day before at the request of her husband Maurice Dubois."

"Ellen [Eleanor] Dubois gave a down-to-earth report about the events at La Hille. It was concluded that the Swiss Red Cross provided the only possibility of saving the threatened children in France. Therefore it was proposed to ask the Red Cross Children's Aid Society [Secours Suisse] to move the children in the Secours Suisse colonies in France to Switzerland until the end of the war or until emigration overseas becomes possible. Ellen Dubois took on the responsibility for making the contact with the Red Cross."[5]

Unfortunately for the children at risk in France, higher authorities in Switzerland had already begun to divert any rescue efforts into other channels. A September 4 meeting of the Secours Suisse in Bern was preceded a few hours earlier by a discussion between insiders Edouard de Haller (representing the top level of the Swiss government), Col. Hugo Remund (chief of the Secours Suisse), Secours Suisse secretary Olgiati and federal Justice and Police Department Chief Heinrich Rothmund.

Mr. de Haller wanted to prevent any protest against Vichy actions, limit the Secours Suisse to caring for the children and prevent their immigration and, above all, was very concerned about offending the Nazi regime. His views were presented by Col. Remund at the meeting of the Secours Suisse that followed:[6] "Messrs. Zuercher[7] and Olgiati are instructed to get in touch with the French Red Cross of the unoccupied zone, in coordination with the Swiss embassy in Vichy. This pleases E. de Haller because the approach is discrete and poses little danger for Bern. The committee's decisions follow entirely the party line: No official pronouncement, no comment to the press and a waiting posture toward the French Red Cross."[8]

The climate at La Hille was quite different from the attitudes in Bern. "At La Hille, life supposedly returned to normal, but in actuality everything was different. Anxiety spread among us, and the castle turned into a trap where we could be arrested at any moment," recalls Ruth Schütz Usrad.[9]

"A miracle happens only once. We invented many plans to escape. I returned for a short time to the Schmutz family's farm, whose peace was a total contrast to my state of mind. After a few days I received an order from the police that I must return to La Hille without delay. We now existed under the framework of forced living, and it was prohibited to leave the place."[10]

Already on September 13, French police arrested Heinz (Chaim) Storosum (almost nineteen years old) and interned him at Camp Noé near Toulouse.[11] Storosum, a dedicated violinist, and Walter Kamlet, a devoted piano player, had been ignored during the August 26 mass arrests at La Hille because they were registered in Toulouse instead of La Hille, where both had been placed by Maurice Dubois for study at the music conservatory. "Once again Maurice Dubois and his wife came to my rescue, just in the nick of time. I was already on the way to the freight car when they suddenly rushed to my side and brought me back to La Hille in their car."[12]

All the older La Hille teenagers had good reason to fear what might come next. In April at least eleven had been required to register with the préfecture office in Foix for Group 721 of the Groupement de Travailleurs Étrangers ("GTE," sometimes abbreviated "TE," or the Foreign Workers Battalion).

On January 2, 1942, the Vichy Interior Ministry had issued a ten-page order to the regional prefects signed by P. Pucheu that spelled out the requirement of assigning Jewish immigrants to the "TE" battalions. Those registered who were in occupations "useful to the national economy" could keep their present employment but would be assigned to the "TE" ranks under the "pour ordre" (on call?) designation.[13]

An examination of the Ariège archives shows that Mme "Audie" (Olga) Authié, Cabinet secretary of the Ariège Department Préfecture, had established and initialed the documents, with the handwritten remark "pour ordre" on all La Hille records except that of Émile Dortort. Among the La Hille teenager registrations on file are those of Karl Heinz Blumenfeld, Edgar Chaim, Émile Dortort, Berthold Elkan, Werner Epstein, Hans Garfunkel, Kurt Moser, Ernest Schlesinger, Inge Schragenheim, Manfred Vos, and Fritz Wertheimer. There may have been others.[14]

The "pour ordre" designation means that she signed in behalf of her superior. It is likely that there was collaboration between Rösli Näf and Maurice Dubois with Mme Authié. Both Swiss staff officials had apparently seen to it that the older boys of the La Hille colony were assigned to work for French farmers in the area under the "Mission de Restauration Paysanne" (Agricultural Rehabilitation) program established by pre-Vichy French law on April 27, 1940.

The director of this program in the Ariège Department notified his prefect on March 29, 1943, about the placement of Jews in agricultural work and lists "the following young Jews" (*all from the La Hille colony*): "Charles Blumenfeld at Mr. Étienne Savignol, farmer at Lézat sur Lèze; Edgar Chaim with farmer M. Soula at St. Ybard; Werner Epstein at M. Schmitz [probably Schmutz] at the Tourloure farm in Escosse; Adolf Nussbaum with M. Dupuy at Rimont; and Fritz Wertheimer and Kurt Moser with Mr. Milleret at the Couteret farm in Cerisols" [actually Cérizols].[15] It is a stretch to consider this farm work as "essential" enough to entitle the La Hille teenagers to this special treatment. It probably protected them from deportation, at least for a while.

Émile Dortort, for unknown reasons, apparently did not obtain this status, was drafted into the TE forces, and moved to the Sept-fonds camp north of Toulouse.[16] In Vichy Premier Pierre Laval's deal making with the Germans, foreign Jewish refugees were always available to be surrendered for deportation. "During the summer and fall of 1942 the GTE (Travailleurs Étrangers) helped fill the deportation trains to Auschwitz," state authors Marrus and Paxton.[17] Unfortunately, Émile Dortort became one of those GTE camp victims. He was sent to Drancy and from there he was deported to the Majdanek murder camp on Transport No. 51 on March 6, 1943, one day before his nineteenth birthday. His friends Bertrand Elkan (arrested at La Hille) and Norbert Winter (age nineteen) were on the same transport.[18]

The Nazi murder of Berlin-born Norbert Winter was another well-intentioned rescue effort gone wrong. Sometime in the winter of 1941, Maurice and Eleanor Dubois had come to La Hille and tried to interest the older boys in moving to the new "ferme-école" (agricultural school) La Roche, organized by the Society for Trades and Agricultural Labour (ORT), a Jewish organization started in Russia in the late 1800s. It was located at Penne-d'Agenais, about ninety miles northwest of Toulouse. Only Norbert Winter and the brothers Leo and Willy Grossmann volunteered. Although the three boys were not enthused about the primitive camp-like conditions, the Dubois couple persuaded them to stay because they would be safer in the remote country setting of La Roche.

As the Vichy police roundups intensified in mid-1942, La Roche was also targeted and the older boys hid in the nearby woods. Leo Grossmann suffered lung damage but was nursed back to health by the wife of the camp leader. Leo, the older Grossmann brother, contacted the farmer "at Lantanet" near Seyre for whom he had worked in 1940–41. Jean and Amélie Rouger agreed readily to accept him. Their nearby relatives François and Marie Ambry also agreed to hide younger brother Willy Grossmann on their farm property.

Because it was dangerous to approach the authorities for a travel permit, Leo obtained a local doctor's fake prescription for eyeglasses in Toulouse and made his way to Seyre from Toulouse without any problems. Willy followed his brother in similar fashion a week later. They were able to stay safely at Seyre under the protection of their farmer friends until the end of the war, grateful that none of the village residents gave away their secret.[19]

Norbert Winter was not so fortunate. Caught in one of the round-ups at La Roche, he was deported with several of his La Hille friends from Drancy to Majdanek on Transport No. 51 on March 6, 1943.[20]

In November, only ten weeks after the boys and girls liberated from Le Vernet had returned to La Hille, the German army moved south and occupied all of France. After the Anglo-American forces landed in North Africa on November 8, Pierre Laval had tried to persuade the Germans that he could effectively maintain neutrality in Vichy France. Hitler's military forces ignored his promise and swept south to the Mediterranean coast on November 11. For the third time in their brief lives, the children of La Hille were again under direct threat of their German persecutors.

"Suddenly we heard, via radio from Toulouse, that the Germans had marched into southern France," wrote Edith Goldapper (Rosenthal). "Without exception we knew what this would mean and are consequently afraid. I don't know how it happened, but suddenly panic prevails and we all want to flee."[21] Ruth Schütz Usrad also described the surrounding events: "The Gestapo spread out in every city and district, and started rounding up young French youth to send them into Germany for forced work. The noose around the necks of the Jews grew tighter and tighter. It was clear that in this situation no intervention by the Red Cross would be strong enough to save us."[22]

In Bern, the governing committee of the Secours Suisse also was alarmed. "It considers it its duty to once more request the Bundesrat [Swiss governing body] to review again the question of admitting the Jewish children who are in the care of our colonies in France. The situation which has developed since November 11, 1942—even though we have not received any upsetting reports so far—leads one to fear renewed actions against these children."[23]

Although the Château de La Hille is located some ten miles out in the countryside, German troops were now permanently installed in

Foix, Pamiers and other main towns of the Ariège department, within easy reach of the La Hille colony.[24]

"From now on whenever we listened to the foreign radio, we first posted lookouts at all corners of the château," recalled Rösli Näf in an August 1989 report.[25] "Especially for Jews and for political refugees the German occupation came as a heavy blow. They could literally feel the net tightening around them. Especially our older teenagers felt this fear as they had aged fast during these past two years."

With the growing anxiety at La Hille, lookouts were posted and a camouflaged hideout called the *Zwiebelkeller* (onion cellar) was created. It actually was located in an attic space near the château tower. From teacher Eugen Lyrer's bedroom a small opening hidden behind a moveable clothes closet led to a cramped space invisible from outside the building. Here a number of persons could hide during inspections and searches, which were not long in coming.

All over Europe the deportations were now in full operation. Although details were not known, the fact that children, the elderly, and persons in poor health were included in the arrests signaled even at La Hille that the destinations of the trains likely were not labor camps, as the Nazis were pretending in order to disguise their plans of mass murder.

In the remote countryside of the Ariège department, where La Hille is located, there were only three options for escaping the new arrests: hiding with area farmers, crossing the rugged Pyrénées into Spain over out-of-the-way mountain paths, or traversing some 450 miles by train and on foot, with frequent identity checks, from La Hille to the Swiss border, which was closely guarded on both sides.

> Thousands of Jews attempted to flee France, and many of the rest tried to go into hiding. It has been estimated that some 22,000 refugees of all backgrounds, many of them Jews, illegally crossed the Spanish frontier immediately after "Attila" [the codeword for the German occupation of Vichy France]. By the end of 1942 the figure had swollen to 30,000. Both Spain and Switzerland discouraged refugees and often turned people back.

In October 1942, the Swiss tightened their controls, refusing entry to anyone not provided with a normal visa issued by the Swiss consulate. Along both frontiers began a desperate traffic. Local guides took these people across, and to the hazards of police and border guards were added the hazards of fraud and robbery by some unscrupulous opportunists.[26]

The older of the La Hille children and some of their Jewish care-takers were soon fated to experience all of these difficulties singly and in small groups. This is the story of their daunting and incredible attempts to escape in order to avoid capture and certain death. Their courage and heroism, the selfless devotion of those who assisted them, as well as the tragedy of those who failed and were murdered, are the main reason this book had to be written. Between September 1942 and the end of 1944, twenty-three made successful escapes to Switzerland, eight succeeded in crossing the Pyrénées to Spain, but eleven of the La Hille boys and girls were caught, arrested, and murdered in Poland, in addition to the adult Ernest Schlesinger. Below are the details of these attempts to escape or to hide in Vichy France.

During the night of September 12, 1942, Almuth Königshöfer was the first of the La Hille teenagers to succeed on the hazard-ous mountain journey from France into Switzerland, illegally. She had left La Hille three days earlier and traveled by bus and train via Grenoble and Annecy toward what is now the Morzine ski area, east of Geneva. She hiked across the border at night from Morzine over the Col de Chésery (a mountain pass) at 6,500 feet. After making her way down the mountain on the Swiss side, Almuth continued via cable car and then by train to Lausanne where her parents Friederich and Ella Königshöfer were living after they had fled from Germany in March 1939.

Almuth and her parents were Protestant, with some Jewish ances-tors, and they were known to be anti-Nazi. This is why Almuth went to France alone at age fifteen. After the war began, she was interned three different times (because she was German), the last time at Gurs in September 1940. This is where the Secours Suisse freed her in

November 1940 and brought her to the colony at Seyre. She was then seventeen years old. When her parents' application to have her join them in Switzerland was denied by Swiss authorities, she had already decided to escape across the border on her own.[27]

Lotte Nussbaum was, like Almuth, one of the most responsible older girls of the colony. In 1942 the Secours Suisse had transferred her from La Hille to its children's home at Saint-Cergues-les-Voirons near the Swiss border east of Geneva. Nineteen years old, she became a caretaker for young children. On August 26, 1942, she was arrested there, interned at Venissieux near Lyon, and freed on August 30. Lotte and two companions pretended to go on a walk near the Swiss border at Monniaz/La Renfile and succeeded in crossing the border on October 4, 1942. She thus became the second of the La Hille group to enter Switzerland illegally. Like all others who successfully crossed the border she was questioned by border guards and then interned for some time.[28]

In mid-December, Viennese-born Lucien Wolfgang and Norbert Stückler (both seventeen) were the first La Hille teenagers to hike across the Pyrénées into Spain. Little is known about their route or the difficulties that they encountered, yet the journey on foot in winter conditions off the main mountain roads is extremely treacherous. In a biography statement written in the 1990s, Wolfgang reported, "we made the escape mostly without a guide. After 3 days we were arrested in the village of Litlett outside Berga near Manresa and brought to a jail in Barcelona. On January 3, 1943, we were released, based on a New Year's amnesty by the Franco government."[29] Both survived the war. Wolfgang served in the Free French Army and Stückler later emigrated to the United States and served in the US armed forces.

By now the question at La Hille was no longer whether it was high time to leave, but only with whom, where to, and when. "Because the USA was no longer an option, they all wanted to try to reach neutral Switzerland," wrote Irène Frank in her diary.[30] "So it happened repeatedly that at the breakfast table 2 to 3 youths would be missing, without a word to any of us, except maybe to Miss Näf."

That was the case on December 22 when Regina Rosenblatt (fifteen), Margot Kern (sixteen), Peter Salz (sixteen) and Jacques Roth (seventeen) left together on foot and by bus to Foix and from there by train via Toulouse to Lyon and Annemasse.

Rösli Näf had given them money for the trip, false identity cards with assumed names and directions to the Secours Suisse children's home at Saint-Cergues-les Voirons, close to the Swiss border southeast of Geneva.

At that colony they were assisted by Miss Renée Farny, who had worked at various Secours Suisse facilities in Vichy France before she came to Saint-Cergues. The four young people from La Hille were the first of twelve whom she helped to cross the border illegally.

"The next day she connected us with a 17-year-old French scout who led us to the border and gave us directions," recalled Peter Salz in a biography written in 1985. After some false turns and other adventures we reached the barbed wire and climbed over it. We were in Switzerland."[31] Fortunately, the Saint-Cergues colony was located only about one kilometer from the border with a wooded area called Grands-Bois separating it from the barbed wire area of the border. As would happen to all their La Hille friends who successfully made it across the border into Switzerland, the four were arrested, interviewed, and interned by the Swiss border authorities. "As we agreed to do beforehand, we lied about our age and therefore were not sent back [those over 16 might be sent back] and we had already destroyed our ID papers," Peter Salz wrote in his biography.

Copies of the border police interviews for virtually all the escapees from La Hille are preserved in Swiss archives (Schweizerisches Bundesarchiv and others). When asked about acquaintances in Switzerland, most named their Swiss *parrains de guerre* (Swiss family godparents who had been recruited by the Secours Suisse for most of the La Hille children) and Rodolfo Olgiati, secretary of the Secours Suisse in Bern ("suggested by Rösli Näf," they said). Some also gave the name Mme Marguérite Goldschmidt-Brodsky, their Belgian protector, who had fled to Basel with her husband and whose Swiss address they knew. Many contacted her soon after they arrived in the Swiss internment camps.[32]

One day later Hans Garfunkel (eighteen) left la Hille alone and arrived in the same border area. He crossed the Swiss border at about 10:00 p.m. on December 24 near the village of Monniaz.[33] Very bright and also very worried, Garfunkel had sounded the alarm the morning of the August arrests at La Hille. He too contacted his Swiss godparents immediately after he reached Switzerland and reported to Mme Goldschmidt-Brodsky by letter on January 28, 1943, about his ordeal and the fate of those he left behind.

"I came to Switzerland on Christmas eve. I traveled from La Hille to the border as a 14-1/2-year-old French boy in short pants and Boy Scout shirt! That's how I got to the border without difficulty but could of course bring nothing with me. Since then I have been able to obtain the necessities from my [Swiss] godparents and acquaintances," he wrote. "Miss Näf had done all that was possible to protect us at La Hille but the situation had become so desperate that we slept mostly at nearby farmers' and in other hideouts."[34]

Rösli Näf recalled her version of these traumatic days in an extensive report written in August 1989:

> With Jean [Hans Garfunkel] as the first one, who one night before Christmas, undoubtedly after many and serious reflections, took the rescue into his own hands, a new and very difficult period began for all of us. [She failed to recall that the others named above had left before Garfunkel.]
>
> I was aware that if I did not report his escape immediately to the police, I would place myself on a slippery slope—also with the Secours Suisse—especially since I, instead of preventing any further escapes, which would have been impossible with the older teenagers, actually assisted them, even with money when they needed it.
>
> Although Lucien and Norbert had succeeded to reach Spain, most of the others preferred to try to flee to Switzerland. Because of their relationships with their Swiss godparent families they already had a connection there. This was augmented by the offer

from Renée Farny who had already assisted others in getting across the border.

From now on we lived in constant fear. What if one of the groups were caught? I discovered what dangers are connected to illegal actions and I cursed my inexperience. In any event it was I who needed to assume the responsibility and the blame. Toulouse must be kept in the dark. But what if the police found out anyhow? How could we be sure that our (La Hille) children attending the public school wouldn't tattle?

How could I maybe quarantine the château while the fleeing teenagers were en route? Strange as it may sound, until then we had never needed medical help. Without any definite idea of how I could explain this, I found myself in the office of a nearby doctor—and I got lucky again!

The doctor grasped immediately, after I told him who I am, what I needed from him. He told me to relax and promised to announce a scarlet fever quarantine for La Hille to the local school and to the police. This even kept away visitors from the Toulouse office who had already been invited to come for the Christmas celebration.[35]

Edith Goldapper (Rosenthal) recalls the chaotic situation among the older girls and boys: "So we've reached December 21, 1942. We are aware that the deportation of Jews is imminent and that is why some have decided to get out yet tonight. Inge [Schragenheim] and Leo [Lewin] will leave tonight. They are heading for Switzerland. The leave-taking is awful. To imagine that 2 young people are venturing off into the unknown like that is upsetting," she writes in her diary.[36]

In fact several other groups quietly fled from La Hille on New Year's Eve. Seventeen-year-old Leo Lewin and Inge Schragenheim, barely eighteen, had already left together on December 20 and headed for Lyon where they made contact with the Jewish community. There they were given false identification cards and sent to Abbé (Abbot) Marie-Amédé Folliet in Annecy, closer to the Swiss border. They were hidden there for a few days by a family that asked neither who they

25. Secours Suisse staff visiting at La Hille in 1942, hosted by Colony Director Rösli Näf (at far right). To her left is Rodolfo Olgiati, general secretary of the Secours Suisse, from Bern. From the author's personal collection.

were nor where they were going. And they received new false identity cards, supposedly issued by the prefect of the Haute-Savoie Department. Leo Lewin now became Léon Dubois.

During the night of December 31 a guide led them to the border at Moillesulaz, east of Geneva. About 3:30 a.m. they were arrested and interrogated by Swiss police. Leo (Lewin) "Dubois" could stay as a refugee because he was under eighteen. He told the interrogators that he knew Mme Renée Didisheim of La Chaux-de-Fonds (his volunteer godmother), Pastor Mueller of Habkern, near Interlaken, and Mme Goldschmidt-Brodsky of Basel.

Inge Schragenheim was not so lucky. Already over eighteen years old, she was pushed back over the border to France and "with more good luck than smarts I found my way back to Annecy and then returned to La Hille," she wrote in a 1990s autobiography.[37] Lewin states that Inge was lucky to be returned to French authorities and not to the Germans. In 1943 Inge would try again and succeed in fleeing to Switzerland where she was reunited with her mother.[38]

Also on December 31 another trio, Ilse Wulff (who had turned seventeen that week), Ruth Klonover (eighteen), and Else Rosenblatt (seventeen) left together via Pamiers, Toulouse, and Lyon. Ruth joined the two others when Lixie Grabkowicz was unable to go. She recalls[39] that Rösli Näf supplied money for travel and the address at Saint-Cergues. "We masqueraded as young French students with our schoolbags but suddenly German soldiers came into our compartment on the train. We pretended to know a few German words and learned more, trading them French ones. Our schoolgirl trick also worked at the Annemasse train station."[40] Their crossing from the Saint-Cergues colony succeeded (they crossed at La Renfile)[41] and in their interviews with the Swiss border interrogators they were able to get away with their falsified ages of fifteen and fourteen. In fact the transmittal letter with their files to the federal police in Bern on February 3 states, "in light of their young age these girls should be placed appropriately by Mlle Hohermuth."[42]

Few of the escapes from La Hille went smoothly and all were undertaken with great stress, fear of arrest, and failure. This was the case with Ruth Schütz (Usrad) and Lixie Grabkowicz (Kowler), age eighteen, who also left the colony on New Year's Eve 1942. Ruth, then seventeen years old, describes the dangerous odyssey in detail in her autobiography, *Entrapped Adolescence*. With Rösli Näf absent that day, teacher Eugen Lyrer gave them money that had been sent by Ruth's mother from England, as well as bread and cheese. He directed them to an address in Lyon where they would get help for crossing the Swiss border. They left La Hille secretly and walked toward Pamiers to catch the train to Toulouse. They soon found out that even the side roads were patrolled by the gendarmes and they dove into ditches twice when motorcycles approached.

In Toulouse the day's last train to Lyon had already left and they now were faced with finding shelter before the 10:00 p.m. curfew. After a fruitless search for lodging they ended up spending the night of New Year's Eve huddled in an apartment building doorway. They were able to recover a bit in the morning, when a caring resident of the building took the two shivering Jewish girls to a church where they could at least get warm.

New Year's Day afternoon they wangled their way onto the crowded train to Lyon and successfully managed to avoid the German guards' identity checks; they carried no identification papers and had they been stopped, they would certainly have been apprehended. They carefully remembered the Lyon address that Eugen Lyrer had given them: 22 rue de Lanterne. Lixie recalled[43] that this was the address for the renowned Abbé Glassberg, a Catholic priest who helped many Jewish refugees. Because the abbé was away, his housekeeper gave them ration coupons and directions to a Christian support place. "We were without identity cards, ration cards and without money in a strange city," recalls Ruth Schütz (Usrad).[44]

> We used the morning hours to survey the churches in the city. Which one should we choose to sleep in at night?
>
> When we arrived at the home of the Christian Friends, we found people sitting at rough wooden tables, bent over their plates. Two boys near the window looked familiar. They saw us and greeted us with great excitement because they were Bertrand [Elkan] and Charles [Blumenfeld], two older boys from La Hille who had arrived several days before.
>
> They told us that there was no point in trying to get across the border into Switzerland because the Swiss government had ordered that asylum be given only to pregnant women and children. All other Jewish refugees were turned back to France, and many of them had fallen into the hands of the German henchmen who were patrolling the borders.[45]

From a French Jewish welfare organization the boys had received a little money and rented a room in Lyon. They invited the two girls to sleep in this room.

> They asked us to come just before the curfew hour and we tried to sneak into their room without being seen. It only had space for one double bed, and on it lay down 5 souls: the 4 of us, and also Friedl

[Steinberg Urman from La Hille], who had come one day earlier. We were very careful not to make any noise or be excited.

The next morning we went to the Jewish welfare organization hoping to receive a little money and some advice. When Lixie and I started to climb up to the first floor, we heard screams and curses in German. We quickly ducked under the stairwell and witnessed a nightmarish scene. The Jewish workers of that office were coming down, their hands on their heads and German soldiers pushing them with the butts of their rifles. We heard screams outside and the noise of cars leaving, and then all was quiet. Quite a while passed before we mustered the courage to leave our hiding place. We had been silent witnesses to the end of the activities of this Jewish organization in Lyon.[46]

Every day we searched through the local newspaper ads seeking farm workers, and returned to the Christian alms house to eat the daily soup. It was a watery liquid made from cabbage, squash, or turnips. It was the only food that touched our lips. Bertrand and Charles couldn't stand the hunger anymore and decided to return to La Hille. I begged them, "Please don't return to the castle. Spring is coming, and they will need helping hands in the fields. Somehow we will be able to survive."

But they were determined to return. They were stopped by the French police, interned in a camp, and sent to the East where they perished. This is how we lost Bertrand with the shy smile, and the small, bright eyes. Because he was short, we had nicknamed him "Bébé" (Baby). He was very mature in his behavior, had a sharp mind, and was loved by all. The tall and handsome Charles was always carefully dressed and combed, gracious, and with perfect manners.

Ruth and Lixie did find a temporary hideout in a convent in Lyon and later sought refuge in various places throughout the region east of Lyon. After a stay in a convent near Grenoble—Lixie says it was Notre Dame de Sion—she found a connection to the French Fortrat family and stayed with them as a domestic for eighteen months under a fake name. Ruth began a series of short-lived and precarious stays with primitive farm families and then joined the French resistance as a messenger. Neither ever made it to Switzerland.[47]

Two other groups got underway separately on December 31 in what proved to be perilous and ultimately disastrous attempts to find a route across the Swiss border.

Irène Frank in her personal diary described the human and emotional feelings that accompanied the leave-taking from close friends:[48]

> Sometimes 2 or 3 children would be missing at the breakfast table without informing anyone except perhaps Miss Näf. One day Inge Helft and Dela [Hochberger] came to see me and confided in me because we were fond of each other. Walter and Manfred [the Kamlet brothers] looked ashen and upset. I understood what the impending leave-taking meant for these infatuated young people, especially Walter.
>
> More than any, these young people who know that they must continue to fight and struggle, but from then on alone, without their beloved one to help, torn away unmercifully, a light extinguished which in such a glow and purity would never return, a wound which would never quite heal.

The day before, Kurt Moser, twenty years old, noticed that sixteen of his companions had already left the château. "I felt a vast void," he writes in his diary.[49] The next night at 2:00 a.m. he left La Hille accompanied by Kurt "Onze" Klein, who had just turned seventeen. Each carried 2,000 French francs, bread, cheese, and chocolate. The two went by bus and train to Toulouse, bought train tickets and spent the day in the station's waiting room. The train left for Lyon at 7:25 p.m. "Seated in a compartment with two French policemen and a German soldier, 'Onze' wished them 'Happy New Year' on the way between Narbonne and Beziers," Moser writes.[50] Little did they know that their own New Year would start off with very bad luck.

Moser notes that they were not "bothered" in Lyon because it was New Year's Day. It was already dark when they arrived at Saint-Cergues and they headed immediately toward the Swiss border. At first they missed the barbed wire that was strung along the border. But then, "we're in Switzerland!" A border guard spotted the pair and brought them to a small town's police station. Because they were older than sixteen, without relatives in Switzerland and without identification papers, they would be returned to France. "I tried to escape but they caught me. They drove us back on a truck and we went through the barbed wire. We're back in France. 'Onze' did not want to try it again, so we separated."

"I climbed over a high barbed-wire fence but tore my hand. There were snow flurries and I didn't know where to turn." Through the night Moser lay in the snow. "Then I ran. The hills receded and I stayed on small paths. After about 10 kilometers, a small village! I see grey-green-clad patrols. They were German border police, who took me into their office. I was back in France! They took down my false identification: Karl-Heinz Flanter, born on December 28, 1926, in Hannover. I had worked on a farm in Saverdun. They fed me and treated my hand. In the evening they took me by sled to the police at Douvaine (another nearby town). I was searched and they took my money, watch, knife and briefcase."[51]

The next morning the police took Moser to Thonon-les-Bains. He spent the night in "the dark cellar" behind bars. On January 5 he was transferred by train to nearby Annecy. At the jail gate another policeman had Walter Strauss in tow. Moser learned that Walter too was caught by French border guards. They are incarcerated together with other prisoners. The guards are nasty. He learns what happened to the other La Hille group of five and the story is not cheerful.

After interrogation by a local judge, Moser eventually was released and received the papers authorizing his travel back to La Hille, where he arrived on January 16, more than two weeks after he and "Onze" had fled. "'Flanter' once again became 'Moser,'" he writes. "Many of the older boys and girls had gone. Irène Frank had been asked to leave for violating the rules.[52]

And what happened to "Onze" Klein? He had enough of border crossings. "Onze" ran back to Saint-Cergues and from there to Annemasse. At night two German soldiers caught him on the street but his fake story during the interrogation about having to meet an uncle set him free and he caught the train to Lyon. There he was caught again and was able to go free with the same fake cover story. The German guards spoke French poorly and failed to detect his Viennese accent when he spoke French. Thus he, too, made it back to La Hille, but not without dangerous adventures, interrogations, and failing to escape to safety in Switzerland.[53]

The attempted escape of five teenagers led by Walter Strauss turned into one of the two most tragic accidents of the La Hille history (the other occurred later on the way to Spain). Like Kurt Moser and "Onze," Dela Hochberger from Berlin, Inge Helft from Wurzen, both aged sixteen, Manfred Vos from Cologne, aged eighteen, and Inge Joseph, aged seventeen from Darmstadt, left La Hille on New Year's Eve 1942. Ruth Schütz (Usrad) was to have been one of the group members but stayed behind because she felt ill and did not want to hinder the escape's success.[54] Walter, seventeen years old, from Duisburg, was one of the leaders of the La Hille colony, admired and respected by his peers (and was this author's closest friend). He also was Inge Joseph's boyfriend.

The five left the village near La Hille in the middle of the night and hiked the fifteen kilometers to the train station at St. Jean-de-Verges on the mainline to Toulouse. Arriving in Toulouse about 10:00 a.m., they separated, trying to evade the snooping German and French control personnel until the connecting train to Lyon was ready to leave in the late afternoon.[55] It is not known whether Kurt Moser and Kurt "Onze" Klein rode the same train, though the documents about their flight point in that direction. Similarly, Ruth Schütz and Lixie Grabkowicz would have been in Toulouse and on their way to Lyon that day or the next day or two.

The danger and the fears that confronted the fleeing teenagers are described graphically in the cited book by David Gumpert, nephew of Inge Joseph. Their train was filled with German soldiers and French strangers, any one of whom could have been a dedicated Nazi collaborator. Most of the La Hille teenagers did not speak perfect French and many had German accents. So silence was the order of the day and the ride to Annemasse, the target town near the Swiss border, lasted seventeen hours.

Somewhere along the way one of the Germans entered the group's compartment, looking for a chess player. Walter Strauss volunteered, moved into the player's compartment, and allowed the soldier to win some games, thus diverting attention from his uneasy group.[56] After they arrived in Annemasse, the walk to the Swiss Red Cross children's home at Saint-Cergues eight kilometers to the northeast went smoothly.

But soon a frightening and disastrous series of events would lead to tragedy for the group and to far-reaching upheavals for the entire La Hille community. The available sources provide varying descriptions of the details and of the timing, yet even a general summary is graphic enough.

After a brief stay at the Swiss children's home of Saint-Cergues, the group of five headed toward the nearby border area, which was covered with snow. A number of the La Hille refugees were guided to the border by Renée Farny, the aide at the Saint-Cergues colony. Mlle Farny apparently was not present and the five refugees had to find their own way.[57] It was pitch dark and snowing heavily when they arrived at the barbed wire. They crawled under it one after the other and continued through bushes and fields, looking for the road to Geneva. Instead they reached another barbed wire. Confused and already lost, they decided to cross that wire as well. Moving forward and hoping the road to Geneva was near, they instead encountered a third barbed wire fence. They realized that they were lost and after much discussion, continued along the fence toward some trees. Soon they saw a light at a house some distance away. It was decided that Walter would go ahead alone and explore. The others would wait for his return. If, for some reason, he did not come back, they would go in a different direction.[58]

Walter did not return as promised, and after much discussion his four companions took the fatal step of following him toward the house with the light. As they approached the building a German border guard arrested them. When they were marched to a larger building ten minutes away, conversation among the German-speaking guards indicated that Walter apparently had been caught by French soldiers who were alternating with the German border patrol. When they arrived at the Hotellerie Savoyarde, site of the German border police, they were subjected to lengthy interrogations.[59]

Two of the girls and Manfred Vos admitted their real identities and that they had come from the Château de La Hille, while Inge Joseph steadfastly stuck to her fake name and cover story, in spite of typical interrogation trickery. The German commandant, interviewing Inge for the third time that evening, pounded his desk and threatened that she would face a firing squad at 7:00 a.m.

During the night she asked a guard for permission to use the bathroom. There she found a window, pried it open and jumped to the snow-covered ground. Though a hunt was quickly organized, the panicked Inge burrowed into the snow and managed to escape.[60] The next morning, a Sunday, Inge had made her way to the Swiss Pouponnière (nursery) at Annemasse, where she encountered Mme Germaine Hommel, the director at Saint-Cergues, who was visiting there and unaware of the fleeing group. She brought Inge back to Saint-Cergues and hid her there.[61]

Word of the tragic turn of events had spread quickly. Rösli Näf had arrived at Saint-Cergues from La Hille on Saturday, concerned about the several groups of her teenagers who had planned to cross illegally into Switzerland with her support. Upset by the misfortune, Mme Hommel was anxious to meet with Mlle Näf and accidentally found her at the Annemasse train station, already on her way back to La Hille. By a strange coincidence they also spotted Walter Strauss who was being escorted, in handcuffs, by French police. The policemen allowed him to speak with Rösli Näf to whom he reported his version of what happened to his group before he was caught by a French border guard.[62] The gendarmes then led him off to a French jail where he would meet Kurt Moser, who had been apprehended after the Swiss guards pushed him back over the French border.

On Monday at noon, Maurice Dubois, chief of the Secours Swiss operations in France, telephoned Mme Hommel for details after Rösli

Näf had alerted him to the problems. He urged Mme Hommel to get the inside story from the local authorities and she connected with the German border guards at the Hotellerie who informed her about the interrogations. They referred her to the main office at Annemasse where she learned that Manfred Vos, Inge Helft, and Dela Hochberger had already been sent to Lyon, where they were delivered to the German authorities.[63] From Lyon they were brought to the deportation transit camp of Drancy near Paris, deported, and murdered in Auschwitz.

On February 18, Kurt Moser (by then back at La Hille) records in his diary that the three had written to their friends at La Hille from Drancy. "On the 9th they were deported to an unknown destination."[64] All three were indeed sent to Auschwitz from Drancy on Transport No. 46 on February 9, 1943.[65]

Encouraged by the Swiss personnel at Saint-Cergues, Inge Joseph made two more attempts to get across the Swiss border at night in the following days. She made it the second time, found the road to Geneva and came close to Lake Geneva. A Swiss guard stopped her; she was brought to a police station for interrogation, and again pushed back across the French border. The young La Hille refugees could not know that the Swiss authorities had decided on December 29 to return illegal immigrants to France if they were found within twelve kilometers of the border. Before that date they were allowed to stay if they had managed to cross the border.[66]

From a small French police station Inge was taken with twenty other "violators" to a prison in Annecy, a French city near the border area. After three days, awaiting appearance before a judge, she could not believe her eyes when she spotted her friend Walter Strauss waiting in the same courtroom. Mme Hommel of the Saint-Cergues colony, who knew the judge, facilitated their release and they traveled together on the train back to La Hille.[67]

Although he was caught, Walter Strauss was lucky to be arrested by a French border policeman instead of by the Germans. During the usual interrogation he protected his Swiss caretakers and lied that he had stolen the food and the money that they had found on him. As with all the other fleeing La Hille teenagers, it was Rösli Näf who had provisioned him with money and food. Before he encountered Inge, Walter had been taken before a magistrate at the border town of St. Julien. There Mme Hommel had vouched for him and testified about his leadership role at La Hille.[68]

What caused this tragic mishap when others of the La Hille colony were able to cross successfully in the same area? The January 8, 1943, report by Mme Hommel states that the Strauss group was caught at Machilly, a small border village near Saint-Cergues. In that area Switzerland pokes into France like a thumb. If one crossed the barbed wire from near Saint-Cergues into Switzerland, one would reach the other side of this thumb just a short distance away and be back in France. On her third crossing, Inge Joseph discovered that mistake and avoided it. Attempting this crossing in unfamiliar territory at night and in deep snow, as the group did, they had fallen victim to this peculiar border configuration.

Besides the deportation and deaths in the failed attempt, dire and reprehensible repercussions were quick to follow in other directions and up the ladder to the governing officials in Switzerland. A disgruntled staff member at the Swiss Red Cross office in Annemasse, a Mr. Kuesner, was present and overheard part of Mme Hommel's report about the arrests to her superior, Mme Marthe Terrier. Without knowing the full story, and intent to denounce Rösli Näf and Mme Hommel, he traveled to Geneva on January 5 and gave a distorted verbal report to local Swiss Red Cross authorities, including Max Zürcher. Based on what he heard, Zürcher immediately notified Col. Hugo Remund, the chief of the Secours Suisse, in Bern. Upset and angry, Remund ordered the dismissal of Rösli Näf and Mme Hommel without awaiting information from Maurice Dubois who had already been briefed by Mlle Näf on January 3 in Toulouse where she had stopped on her way back from Annemasse. Dubois in turn visited La Hille on January 5 and, with Mlle Näf, checked on the reaction of the Ariège Préfecture officials who declined to act—"toute l'affaire serait étouffée" (what happened would be swept under the rug).[69]

On January 9, Dubois traveled to the Swiss town of Moillesulaz in the border area near Saint-Cergues and met with his superiors, Zürcher and Olgiati, to discuss the details and consequences of the incident. He also defended the involvement and actions of the two accused women (Näf and Hommel) and objected to their dismissal.[70]

Col. Remund, putting more credence into Kuesner's faulty allegations, labeled the versions told by Dubois and Mme Terrier as "largely incorrect." He requested Swiss ambassador Walter Stucki (in Vichy) to order the accused female staff members back to Switzerland. Because the border had been closed, Stucki decided to question Maurice Dubois, Germaine Hommel, and Rösli Näf at his office in Vichy. He interviewed Dubois and Hommel on January 11. Rösli Näf had missed her train and was interrogated the following day, also with Dubois present. On the first day Dubois had defended the role of Mlle Näf, withheld his knowledge of her collaboration with Renée Farny, and admitted that at least twenty-four teenagers had escaped from La Hille in the waning days of 1942.

The ambassador emphasized that Rösli Näf was neither entitled, nor capable, to judge the political situation nor the danger to the children under her care. According to records obtained by Antonia Schmidlin, Mlle Näf stated that she recognized that she had acted inappropriately and that she wished, for the sake of the Red Cross, to be recalled to Switzerland.[71]

It is interesting to note that the ambassador summoned Rösli Näf back to his office from her Vichy hotel after office hours that day and frankly told her that he was proud of her actions and wished that more Swiss citizens had the courage she had displayed. "His attitude was different from that morning. More than I had realized then, he understood the situation of our children. His remarks were like balm on my desperation and insecurity."[72]

Ambassador Stucki also wrote to Col. Remund as follows: "To you I need to emphasize that had Mlle Näf or Mr. Dubois asked my advice before Christmas (which he tried to do but failed to reach me), I would have had to answer truthfully that after November 11, 1942, [when the Germans occupied all of France] Mr. Laval [the French premier] is no longer capable of maintaining any assurance he might have given us. Personally I am convinced that these Jewish children, aged over 16, would have fallen into the hands of the Germans sooner or later, and actually will."[73]

Worried more about offending the Nazis than saving the Jewish children, Col. Remund felt obliged to inform, in ingratiating fashion, General Director Walther Georg Hartmann of the German Red Cross in Berlin "about the regrettable incidents which occurred recently in one of our children's homes in France" and that four Jewish children were arrested at the border by French and German authorities. He felt it was important that Hartmann learn of this first-hand from him before other reports would reach him and he assured the German that he had already taken the necessary measures to prevent any recurrence.[74] For good measure, Remund also notified the Swiss embassy in Berlin, in case there were German inquiries.

The management committee of the Secours Suisse discussed the border events and action to be taken at its meeting in Bern on January 26. Col. Remund criticized Rösli Näf severely during his review of the incidents and the result of Ambassador Stucki's interviews in Vichy. There was pro and con discussion about the dismissals of the three women (Näf, Hommel, and Farny) and it was decided that all three should be replaced, leaving it to Maurice Dubois to reassign or dismiss them.

During this meeting the fate of the ten La Hille refugees who had successfully crossed the border was also discussed. The week before, Edouard de Haller, the Swiss government official assigned to oversee the Swiss Red Cross, had requested that Col. Remund research their whereabouts with the help of the border police. Each had a Swiss godparent family that was ready to accept them in their homes. Typical of the attitudes of higher officials of that period, de Haller stated that "by escaping, these children have lost the protection of the Secours Suisse. It would lead to a dangerous outcome if we now rewarded them for their transgression." However, no action was taken.[75]

◇ **10** ◇

The Noose Tightens
and More Try to Escape

When the three La Hille teenagers were arrested at the Machilly border station and deported, theirs was already Transport No. 46 from France to Auschwitz. The members of the La Hille colony had feared for their lives ever since forty of their teenage and adult compatriots had been liberated from the Le Vernet camp in early September 1942. Since then, frequent police inquiries and visits at the château kept anxiety at a high level.

The stories that Kurt Moser, "Onze" Klein, Inge Joseph, and Walter Strauss told of their failed escapes and arrests at the Swiss border after they came back to La Hille only strengthened the other teenagers' fears and their determination to hide or escape. Little is known about what the younger children were told or what they may have noticed on their own. Yet, by then many of their parents and family members left behind in Nazi territories had already been driven from their homes or deported to murder camps.

"In January we learned that some of our good friends arrived safely in Switzerland," wrote Edith Goldapper (Rosenthal) in her diary. "That is truly good news! Several were caught but were lucky to make it back here. And unfortunately three, Dela Hochberger, Inge Helft and Manfred Vos were turned over to the Germans. That is a terrible misfortune. First they took them to Drancy. Now they've been sent elsewhere. But we don't know where. We are living in a very nervous and depressed mood."[1]

Alexander Frank, the former colony director now working on farms in the region, had come back to La Hille and urged the older boys and girls to head for the borders with him or on their own. Since there had already been personality and philosophical differences between him and his mother, Irène Frank, with the Swiss personnel, his interference was not welcomed by Rösli Näf and Maurice Dubois. On the night of December 24, 1942, Frank, his wife, Elka, Inge Berlin (then nineteen years old), Émile Dortort, and Gerard Kwaczkowski (Kovac) left La Hille for the Spanish border.[2]

The two boys were worried and returned to La Hille, Emile because he felt guilty about leaving his younger brother Joseph Dortort behind at the colony. Josef was a good friend of Inge's younger brother, Egon, and she and the Franks tried to persuade Emile that he and Inge were in greater danger than their under-sixteen-year-old siblings were, but without success. Emile turned back. He would be arrested later and was murdered in Poland.

Twice, during this and a later escape attempt, the Franks and Inge Berlin were arrested by the French police for traveling without permission and jailed briefly, the second time at the departmental capital of Foix, located seventy kilometers from the Spanish border. Alex, because he was of Belgian nationality, was released and he hired an attorney to free his wife and Inge. Inge Berlin recalls that all three then lived in an abandoned farmhouse and she and Alex worked as farmhands for two different nearby tenant farmers.[3] Elka Frank did household work for a widowed mill owner in the area.

Toward the end of March 1943 the trio again made plans to hike across the Pyrénées to Spain. The Germans had declared the border zone *verboten* (off limits) and were guarding all roads closely because Spain was a goal not only for the Jewish refugees, but also for suspected French resistance fighters and for Allied pilots downed in Western Europe.

With peaks rising from 6,500 to more than 8,000 feet in the area south of the Franks' departure point near St. Girons, the escape would have been hazardous in the summer. In late March the ascent on side roads and paths, mostly still under deep snow cover, was daunting. In one mountain village their supposedly experienced guide failed to arrive. They learned of another possible guide in a nearby village. Most of the guides were farmers' sons who herded cattle in the higher mountains in the summer and knew the more remote paths well. This time the young man did meet them at the prearranged spot in a barn where the trio received bread and milk. "Every place they tried to convince us to turn back. 'Especially with two women, you won't make it,' they said. But we told them: 'We simply can't go back'," recalled Alex Frank.[4]

One guide passed them to another, and yet a third one arrived after 9:00 p.m. and announced that he could accompany them only one hour further but he kept going until 1 a.m. "It was April 1 and we had no idea about these mountains. On many parts of the up-and-down trails we sank into the snow up to our hips. I literally had to push and lift my wife," Alex Frank recalled. For a day and-a-half they trudged up and down hillsides and valleys. Then at 11 p.m. the guide said: "Go down this hill and you'll be in Spain."[5]

Inge Berlin Vogelstein recalls that their first shelter in Spain was in a mountainside barn that looked like a small cavern and where a young couple lived with some goats. "They seemed to be used to such kinds of 'guests' and offered us the hayloft to sleep," Inge remembers. "We went out like so many lights and the next morning my muscles and bones were so sore that I could hardly get up."[6] Elka Frank became ill as a result of the arduous crossing and suffered from the after-effects all her life.[7] The trio was arrested by Spanish police but well treated and then reached Barcelona. There, Inge Berlin gained the support of the Jewish Joint Distribution Committee, received a US visa in February 1944, and came to New York via Portugal on the SS *Serpa Pinto*.[8]

Although they had destroyed all personal identification papers before starting their escape, the Frank couple, who were Belgian citizens, were able to prove their identities to the Belgian consul in Barcelona. After four months in Spain, they managed to get permission to leave for England by ship via Portugal and Gibraltar. Alex Frank, whose brothers were already there, volunteered for the Belgian Air Force operating from the UK, was trained as a gunner, and flew missions over the continent. He achieved the rank of second lieutenant.[9]

After World War II, the Franks moved back to Belgium and then to the East German Republic. Alex maintained contact with many of the La Hille colony survivors until his death in September 1998.

At La Hille the French police now came frequently. "There were roll calls and interrogation after interrogation," stated Margrit Tännler, a Swiss counselor who succeeded Rösli Näf in May 1943. "One had to be there to comprehend the fear and reaction of the children. One had to see it to know how they hold their breath whenever a car stops on the highway or turns into the road to the château."[10]

> On February 23 [1943] at noon a number of policemen suddenly appeared with a truck. They held a roll call and four boys and Mr. Schlesinger [husband of the cook, Flora Schlesinger] had to pack

26. Elka and Alex Frank after they escaped to England, where he joined the Belgian air force. From the author's personal collection.

their belongings and get on the truck. Some others on the list had
fled in January. It was a horrible day, especially for Mrs. Schlesinger.
Soon we learned that they were taken to the Le Vernet internment
camp and from there in handcuffs to Gurs [the notorious French
internment camp in southwestern France].

Thanks to the effort of Maurice Dubois, two of the boys under
eighteen [Henri Brunel and Manfred Kamlet] were freed from Gurs
and returned two weeks later. The others were deported. We were so
happy to get news from one of the boys from Lublin.[11]

The "others" were Bertrand Elkan (twenty), Walter Strauss (then
eighteen), and Ernst Schlesinger (forty-six). Elkan was deported on
Transport No. 51 from Drancy on March 6, the others on Transport
No. 50 on March 4. All were murdered in Majdanek, near Lublin.[12]
Just five weeks earlier, in Lyon, Ruth Schütz and Lixie Grabkowicz
had urged Bertrand and his friend Blumenfeld not to return to La
Hille and to stay "underground" at a farm. Unfortunately they did
not follow the girls' advice.

Margrit Tännler reported that things calmed down after the February 23 arrests. There was a gap in the colony caused by the departure of the older boys and girls but the younger teenagers took on
the work and those who remained interacted and assisted each other.
"There reigns a true camaraderie among the older youngsters."[13]

As a result of the uproar and decisions in Bern by the leaders of
the Red Cross and Secours Suisse, Rösli Näf left La Hille on May 6,
1943, exactly two years after she arrived as a stranger at Seyre. On the
same day Anne-Marie Piguet (Im Hof-Piguet), was transferred from
the Toulouse headquarters of the Secours Suisse to be a counselor-
helper at La Hille.

In her book, *La filière en France occupée, 1942–1944*, Anne-Marie
Im Hof-Piguet recalls that Mlle Näf brought her along that day on a
visit to a psychiatric clinic at St. Girons where Rösli Näf tried to place
Walter Kamlet to safeguard him from arrest and deportation. Neither
Kamlet nor the admitting doctor was willing to carry out her inten-
tions and Anne-Marie came to La Hille with Kamlet, while Rösli

Näf continued on to Switzerland. Just thirty-two years old, during her two years at La Hille she had been deeply involved in actions and traumatic events that most individuals would not face in a lifetime.[14] Young Anne-Marie would become a courageous initiator of escapes at La Hille and thereby violator of the hands-off orders from the Bern headquarters of the Secours Suisse.

Although the residents of La Hille were not aware that Adolf Hitler had already ordered the arrest and deportation of all Jews from France on December 10, 1942,[15] what had already happened to their companions and the Vichy government measures, such as the prohibition for Jews to move from their location without police permission, served to reinforce their desperation and the pressing urge to escape.

"Here at the colony we are very upset," writes Edith Goldapper in her personal diary. "Security lookouts are posted and whenever we sight a gendarme [policeman] someone yells 'court-circuit' ['short-circuit'] and all the older ones instantly disappear. It works perfectly and I must say it's well organized."[16]

"With all that we get a letter from Inge [Schragenheim] saying that she and her friend André had been arrested" in Nice, where she had moved after her rejection from Switzerland. "Mr. Lyrer [the Swiss teacher at La Hille] immediately gets on the train to Nice and manages to free her and bring her back to La Hille. I don't know how we will ever be able to repay his good deeds."[17]

With the departure of Rösli Näf, Edith reflects on how fast the past two years have passed and on the cascade of disturbing events, one after the other. "I think that the years 1942 and 1943 are the worst I have ever experienced and I hope fervently that the future will be more rosy."[18]

Edith reports in her diary that some of the older boys, now in the Restauration Paysanne [agricultural redevelopment] program, came back to La Hille for visits.[19] This is also reflected in the diary notes made by Kurt Moser and it probably led to plans by some of them to attempt an escape together across the Pyrénées into Spain.

By the end of May, Kurt Moser and his farm work companion Fritz Wertheimer (age nineteen) had begun to look for an experienced *passeur* (mountain guide) to make their escape across the Pyrénées. Mostly they searched in the nearby city of St. Girons, located about forty kilometers north of the Spanish border. The demands for payment were steep. On May 24 Moser writes, "found 3 possible guides; they're frightfully expensive. For 12,000 francs for 4 people I might get lucky."[20]

On May 31 one of the passeurs makes the demand of 28,000 to 30,000 francs for four persons. "Impossible[;] let's wait and hear from the others," Moser records. In the meantime he traveled back and forth to La Hille to meet with others seeking to escape. Their rendezvous point was at Borde Blanque, a farmhouse of friendly locals on the hill above the Château de La Hille.

On June 4 there's still no word from one passeur and Moser wonders whether he had been caught. That day Charles (Karl-Heinz) Blumenfeld requests by postcard that Moser notify him when "everything is arranged."[21] Three days pass and Moser wonders: "What will happen with Spain? Those born in 1920–21 and '22 are now inducted for forced labor in Germany. Because many try to escape, the border is guarded ever more closely. This can't last much longer. I'll probably land in Poland." On June 12 word comes that the guide would return from Portugal in two days and that he would make contact by June 15. Moser walks the thirty-plus kilometers to La Hille and meets with Werner Epstein and Charles Blumenfeld. That afternoon he also bicycled the ten kilometers over the hill to Mas d'Azil to meet with a Mr. Meyer, a refugee, who wanted to join them for the crossing. Moser notes that "even official sources have warned the Jews: [']Disappear in the next 3 weeks! There will be more deportations.['] Never before has there been such an outrageous injustice."[22]

Hurried notes end Kurt Moser's diary on June 15. He thinks that "30,000 francs for all 10" will do the trick and he names Werner Epstein, Edgar Chaim, Charles (Karl-Heinz) Blumenfeld, Addi Nussbaum, Fritz Wertheimer, Mr. Meyer, "and two young Frenchmen" as the participants. He and Wertheimer will travel from their farm location via St. Girons and La Bastide-de-Serou to the meeting point about sixty kilometers away.

Moser closes the diary by expressing his intention to deliver it for safekeeping to "Melanie" at Borde Blanque, which he did and that is why it survived. Under the date Sunday, June 20 he speculates: "By now perhaps already caught and off to Poland. But it had to be dared. One week earlier or later in Poland makes no difference." He then draws fat question marks on each remaining day of June and writes, firmly, at the end: "Hals und Beinbruch! Es wird schon schief gehen" (the whimsical German expression for "Good luck!" and "It will probably end in disaster").

On the following blank page, dated June 19, 1943, Walter Kamlet added the sad conclusion in his own handwriting: "Yes, my dear, dear Kurt, unfortunately it did end in disaster [*es ist leider schief gegangen*]. The terrible news arrived here last night and those few of us who learned it are with you with all of our thoughts. I hope with all my heart that we both will meet again, or at least that you will recover this little book one day, in happier times. As long as I am able to wish and to think, my best wishes and thoughts will accompany you. I thank you most deeply for your friendship. Will we be able, some day, to renew it? Stay well, dear Kurt. As long as I live, I shall remain your loyal friend Walter."[23]

Wertheimer too had speculated about the outcome, which resulted in his murder at Auschwitz. "Although we currently don't have any food or lodging difficulties, we are really concerned about survival because we don't yet know what tomorrow will bring," he had written to a Mrs. Schlesinger in Colombia, South America from La Hille in November 1942. "We don't know whether tomorrow we might have to share the fate of the thousands of coreligionists to whom it has already happened."[24]

An unsigned and undated typed document in the Archives du Centre de Documentation Juive Contemporaine in Paris recalls the tragic story of their failed escape.[25] It states that a Spanish wood-cutter near La Hille established the connection with a passeur who demanded 30,000 francs. The refugees were to meet at night in a small wood near the colony so that their farmer hosts would not detect their departure. Moser and Fritz Wertheimer never came, and the group learned later that they had been caught and arrested by German troops at St. Girons on the way to the meeting point.

After a lengthy wait it was decided to go on without them. The four La Hille boys were joined by the sixty-year-old Mr. Meyer from Mas d'Azil whose wife and children had been deported from Le Vernet in September 1942. That evening they walked to the Hotel Marinette in Varilhes, some fifteen kilometers away, where they met the guide two days later. He explained that he could not risk guiding a group through the heavily guarded city of Foix and that they would meet in a small wooded area beside the road at the village of Aurignac, eight kilometers south of Foix. He requested that they leave one at a time starting at 9:00 p.m. and at twenty to thirty-minute intervals in order not to attract attention.

The last one of the group left the hotel around midnight and noticed that something was not right. When he encountered the boy who had left before him, they concluded that something was very suspicious. This is how Edgar Chaim and Addi Nussbaum, both bright and alert by nature, turned back and returned to La Hille. The sixty-year-old Mr. Meyer could not keep up on foot and it is not known whether he turned back or was taken prisoner.

Charles Blumenfeld and Werner Epstein headed toward the mountains where their double-dealing guide turned them over to German troops. He had taken their money but collaborated with the Nazis.[26] Their captors took them to the St. Michel Gestapo jail in Toulouse where they encountered their friends Wertheimer and Moser. In his life history,[27] Werner Epstein recalls that the four were held in Toulouse for three weeks and then transported to the deportation center of Drancy near Paris. Somehow Blumenfeld managed to get a card sent back to La Hille, where their friends thought that they had escaped to Spain.

"We were sure that they had safely crossed into Spain," Edith Goldapper wrote in her diary.[28] "It's July 22 and it is awful, just horrible! Charles and Werner too were arrested trying to cross the border. We get a last postcard from Charles, which he apparently threw from the train window. Four nice comrades now are also in the place where so many of our coreligionists were sent. Yet I am still hopeful that we will see them again some day, as they are young and capable of enduring much."[29]

In fact all four were included in Transport No. 57 from Drancy to Auschwitz on July 18, 1943, along with about 1,000 other Jewish victims. Werner Epstein is one of only forty-three persons on that transport who survived from the Auschwitz camp. He and Kurt Moser endured hard labor at Birkenau and then "4 or 5 months in the coal mine 'Rudolf' in Javorzno, 50 kilometers from Krakow."

Epstein later wrote to Moser's sister Edith: "He became gravely ill and had severe diarrhea for 3 weeks. Even though visits were forbidden, I managed to see him. He was all bones and weighed only 25 kilos. He was happy that his suffering would soon be over. I won't ever forget what he said: 'Klein Eppelstein, you must endure and carry on. Visit and say hello to my little sister. But never tell Mutti [his mother] what happened. I will be gone.' Two days later they took him back to Auschwitz. I asked the doctor and he answered, '*Verbrennungsofen*' [crematorium]."[30]

Somehow, Werner Epstein survived the coal mine and also a brutal death march to the West when the Russians came near. At the Blechammer concentration camp, just before the Russians arrived, the survivors were herded into barracks that the Nazi guards set on fire, shooting anyone who tried to get out. Epstein and some Russian prisoners had previously managed to jump into a latrine where they hid in the muck until the Russian troops arrived. It was January 1945 and he was taken to Russia for three months. In July he returned to Paris.[31] The Nazis had marked his arm with Auschwitz No. 130581 and the events marked his life.

Historians have found that Premier Laval and others in Vichy resisted German demands for the arrest and deportation of French-born Jews in mid-1943, but those who had sought refuge in France from other countries were fair game.[32] This is why local French gendarmes in the La Hille area frequently came to the colony looking for individuals on their foreign Jews registration lists.

27. Werner Epstein at La Hille, 1943. Werner was arrested while trying to flee to Spain. He survived deportation to Auschwitz and lived in Paris and California. From Edith Goldapper collection, with permission from Joachim Rosenthal.

Meanwhile we hear that Rudi Oehlbaum, who is working on Mr. Roubichon's farm, was arrested and was probably taken to Le Vernet [the nearby internment camp]. [Indeed, Rudi Oehlbaum was arrested on September 8, 1943, by police from Varilhes as "the Jew Őhlbaum, Rudolph, aged 15, by administrative order," and delivered to Le Vernet].[33]

Word is sent immediately to Madame Authié (in Foix) that Rudi is under 17 years old and that he therefore should be released. A few days later, miraculously, Rudi returned to the château. He was released in the nick of time before they could deport him. Thank God that this worked out.[34]

[Mme Olga Authié was the cabinet secretary of the Ariège Department who maintained all the registration lists of foreigners, which the police used to arrest persons to be deported. There is convincing evidence, including Rudi's reversal and liberation, that she secretly helped prevent arrests, even though she was considered to have been a "collaborator" by some. (See chapter 11 for details.)]

Miss Tännler [the director who succeeded Rösli Näf] is very busy, as is Miss Anne-Marie [Im Hof-Piguet]. All day long they go searching everywhere in order to find suitable locations for the boys. And Mr. Lyrer too is busy with that task.[35]

Anne-Marie Im Hof-Piguet adds an interesting dimension to the events of that week in her book, *La filière en France occupée, 1942–1944:*[36]

On our return [from an excursion], by instinct, I stop by at the préfecture, where I am well acquainted because part of my job is food procurement. Madame Authié—who is well-disposed toward us—alerts me. She forewarns me that a new search of the château is imminent. I quickly grab a bicycle and rush back to La Hille to notify the director. We lead all who are endangered into the secret hiding place [the onion cellar]. The gendarmes arrive and thoroughly search the rooms. They were unable to find anyone. And they did not exactly look eager.

I should add that several days before we had 'bought' the goodwill of the gendarmes from Pailhès [the nearest gendarme station] who, by the way, were not all that nasty. They had heard a rumor that we had received a large shipment of potatoes. The Ariège region was suffering from drought and vegetables were in short supply. The gendarmes hinted to the director [Mlle Tännler] that a sack of potatoes would be most welcome. That night we ferried a full sack to the base of a large tree by the roadside outside the château. The next morning, as if by magic, the potatoes were gone. Out of sight, out of mind.

The sack of potatoes mellowed the gendarmes, but in spite of that, orders are orders. They continued to stand guard by a haystack 100 meters from La Hille, hoping to catch the boys when they returned from nearby farms. After two or three days they tired of waiting and disappeared.[37]

Both accounts shed light on the dangers, as well as the typical human aspects, of the La Hille youngsters' existence in a very hostile environment.

Ruth Schütz, who had fled from La Hille with Lixie Grabkowicz on the eve of 1943, had spent much of the spring months moving from farm to farm and in and about the city of Grenoble trying to find work, fleeing from persecution, and looking for a new place to stay whenever things became dangerous. Details are recounted graphically in her autobiography *Entrapped Adolescence*. Eventually she was recruited into Jewish youth organizations that performed clandestine rescue and hiding operations. By mid-year she was shepherding individual children and children's groups toward the Swiss border, always in danger of being caught.[38]

Her sister Betty Schütz, now age thirteen, had remained at La Hille, and was in far less danger than the older teenagers were. Worried about the future, Ruth decided to write a letter to Swiss teacher Eugen Lyrer, who played a quiet but determined role at La Hille in protecting the children and helping them escape.

She wrote, "his family is inviting Betty to be with her. We chose a place and a date to meet so that he could bring Betty to her 'relatives.' On the date we determined, we waited for him in a café in Annecy." (Fearing an intercept by the censors, she was used to camouflaging messages with hidden meanings.)[39]

Betty left La Hille with Eugen Lyrer on September 12. "Betty, whom I hadn't seen for a year, had not changed. She was still the same skinny and pale girl, and looked much younger than her age. We hugged with excitement and I felt my eyes filling with tears that I couldn't stop. Only then did I realize how much I had missed her."[40]

Their meeting place was in Annecy and Betty remembers being surprised and frightened by the large number of German military at the train station. Ruth took her to a safe house from which Betty was to pass the border that night with a boy, a girl, and their parents.

"It was very dark and the guide said he could take us only part of the way. He left and then we could not remember whether he had told

28. Siblings at La Hille, 1942. From left: Addi and Lotte Nussbaum, Ruth and Betty Schütz, Cilly Stückler and cousin Gerti Lind, and Norbert Stückler. From the author's personal collection.

us to go straight or to turn left. I told the adults that I thought it was straight ahead. We walked past three barbed wire fences and then we heard Germans. We turned back and went the other way. Then the Swiss guards met us and said, 'Yes, we saw you and heard you, and you were nearly in the hands of the Germans.'" The Swiss guards led them to their border post where they were interrogated, as were all who had crossed safely.[41] Betty and her companions apparently had the same problem with the border geography as Walter Strauss's group nine months earlier because they crossed near the same area, but they had better luck than Walter's group.

Next to attempt an escape—actually for the second time—was Addi (Eddie) Nussbaum, whose sister Lotte had been the second of the colony to cross safely into Switzerland one year before. Addi, a very bright and also cautious eighteen-year-old, had been one of the two young men who mistrusted the traitorous Spanish Pyrénées guide in June and thus avoided being caught and deported. His rescuer would be Anne-Marie Im Hof-Piguet, herself only twenty-seven years old and at La Hille since May 1943.

Anne-Marie tended to scoff at the attitudes and regulations advanced by the management of the Secours Suisse and by the higher Swiss authorities, especially those that forbade helping her protégés to escape. The several daring rescue activities that she was about to launch with Addi's escape violated the edict drafted by Col. Hugo Remund and Edouard de Haller in February 1943 and announced to all Swiss personnel in Vichy France. It demanded "strict adherence to French regulations and required the resignation of any Swiss staff member who was opposed to that host country's actions and would thus compromise the prestige of the Swiss Red Cross and of our country."[42]

The rescue of almost eighteen-year-old Addi Nussbaum would be only the first of several violations of this order by the courageous and somewhat insubordinate Anne-Marie (Im Hof) Piguet. The young Swiss woman had grown up near the French border in the hilly Jura region, some twenty miles north of Geneva, where her father was a forester. He knew every byway in the nearby wooded area known as the "Risoux." Anne-Marie collaborated with an anti-German twenty-four-year-old member of the French resistance movement named Victoria Cordier who helped dozens of refugees escape across this heavily guarded border terrain near her mother's home.[43]

In mid-September Anne-Marie and Addi left La Hille for the nearest train station at St. Jean-de-Verges for the ride to Toulouse. From there they continued to Lyon. Anne-Marie recalled that Addi had fake ID papers but she feared that Addi's accent, his features, and the not-so-professional fake papers might spell disaster if they were stopped. All went smoothly and she left Addi behind at a Secours Suisse children's colony in Montluel, not far from Lyon, where Anne-Marie had been a staff member before she came to La Hille. She would go ahead to the border by train and bus and telephone for him to follow if all was in order.[44]

"I telephone Addi and repeat the directions for getting to Champagnole. The bus arrives but Addi is not on it. Madeleine [Victoria Cordier's sister] promises to watch for the next arriving busses and

I leave with the others [Victoria's family members]," Anne-Marie recalls in her book. She describes the journey to the house of Victoria's mother, which was located in the forbidden travel zone not far from the Swiss border. After staying overnight, the group leaves at daybreak when Mme Cordier gives the all-clear signal—her imitation of a crowing cock—indicating that the German border patrol had just gone past.

Then came the climb up a steep cliff, the Gy de l'Echelle, where each traveler literally had to grasp the next rock or tree root to climb to the top. "But the ascent is not long and at the top it's freedom. We're in Switzerland."[45] They descend on the Swiss side of the Risoux to her parents' home. As planned, her father goes back up to the cliff at the border the next day to fetch the missing Addi. "But there is no Addi. Was he interrogated? Arrested? Deported? Did I commit an unpardonable stupidity? And what will be the consequences from the Secours Suisse? Then comes a mysterious telephone message from across the border: 'Your package has arrived.' My father doesn't hesitate and retraces his journey of the morning. Soon he returns with the precious human package."

It turned out that "in spite of the danger, our young man had gone to sleep at the Lyon train station, missed his train and Victoria's sisters Madeleine and Marie-Aimée had to bail him out. Monday noon our 'artist' arrived at the house in Champagnole [where the sisters lived]. Madeleine feeds him and takes him to her mother's house via a different route. Later Madeleine guides him across the same border path and he eventually arrives at Anne-Marie's father's house at Grandes Roches. The mystery of the strange phone call was solved. To make sure that our survivor did not go to sleep in another station, I accompany him to Zurich to Pastor Vogt's house."[46] In the customary Swiss border police interrogation, Addi stated that he crossed the border about 6:00 p.m. on September 22 near St. Cergue.[47] As happened with others, Addi's escape from La Hille succeeded only after several desperate tries.

In spite of the Swiss edict to refrain from rescue activities, Margrit Tännler, the La Hille director, did her part, as did Eugen Lyrer, to seek safe places and support the escapes of the teenagers who were liable to arrest. "Margrit, too, participated in the 'Grand Jeu' [the Big Scheme] in spite of the cautioning official orders," recalls Anne-Marie Im Hof-Piguet. "Following the supportive pronouncement of the Swiss Consul of Toulouse: 'One can do anything so long as one does not get caught,' Mlle Tännler found a producer of false ID's for her charges in a remote location. The real cards were buried in the La Hille garden."[48] Margrit Tännler returned to Switzerland in October 1943 and was replaced by Emma Ott who would manage the La Hille colony until it was closed in February 1945. On her journey home she succeeded in rescuing Inge Joseph, who would successfully cross the Swiss border to safety on her fourth attempt.

In August 1943, Mlle Tännler persuaded Inge to leave La Hille and go into hiding at a French family's home in a village some twenty-four kilometers away. After a ten-day stay Margrit Tännler reappeared and relocated her via a six-hour train ride to another host family at Jarnac, near Bordeaux. In mid-September, Inge would turn eighteen but she had already experienced more dangers than most might see in a lifetime.

On the way she stopped overnight in Toulouse where a young man supplied her with false ID documents. Inge Joseph would become "Irène Jérome," age seventeen (just below the critical eighteen-year-old category). For some weeks Inge, alias Irène, settled into daily activities with her host family and speculated whether she might remain hidden there until the war would end. In early October a letter from Margrit Tännler announced that she would arrive for a quick visit before returning to Switzerland. Her purpose actually was to persuade Inge to make another attempt at crossing the border, with Mlle Tännler's help. After a day's hesitation, Inge agreed and her rescuer outlined the plan of escape via the Cordier sisters' itinerary used by the other La Hille youngsters.[49]

Margrit Tännler carried a Swiss visa but Inge had only her fake ID. They rode the same train to Lyon but in different cars, and from there Inge made her way to Champagnole and the Cordier sisters' apartment, while Mlle Tännler went on the regular train into Switzerland.

Madeleine and Marie-Aimée Cordier took turns in shepherding Inge to their mother's house near the border. A freshly killed lamb was the main dish for dinner but Inge's appetite was ruined by the anticipation of her fourth attempt to sneak across the Swiss border the next morning.

It's October 10 when she follows the path up the cliff toward freedom. At the top Inge, too, had to conquer one more obstacle: the dash across the road that was next to the actual border. She crossed it on the run and on the other side she heard someone call her real name: "Inge? Inge Joseph?" It was the forester, the father of Anne-Marie, waiting for her.[50] At the Piguets' house a warm welcome was waiting and so was Margrit Tännler, who had arrived on the legitimate route but after a scary interrogation, which fortunately missed some incriminating documents that she was carrying.

Inge still had to move on beyond the fifteen-kilometer zone inside the border from which refugees were now returned if caught. With Margrit Tännler she went by bicycle to Yverdon and from there by train to the Bernese Oberland region.[51] All escapes of the La Hille children were daunting and some had to make several attempts, but Inge's efforts and success probably rank as the most remarkable and scary.

Because La Hille was so closely monitored by the police, it was advisable that the older boys and girls who wanted to escape first obtain permission to work and live at nearby farms or communities and try their luck from there. This is why Edith Goldapper was anxiously awaiting permission to be allowed to live at Pastor Garrigue's home in Les Bordes s/Arize and her friend Inge Schragenheim at Dr. Pic's at Fossat.[52] In vain they waited for the confirmation from Mme Authié and became desperate as the planned departure day of October 27 approached.

"Inge and I beseech Anne-Marie and Miss Ott to let us go without papers but Miss Ott is immovable. She insists that La Hille would be subject to police measures if we left without permission. Inge and I are deeply saddened. This would have been our great opportunity and we will miss out. It's just awful."[53] If they were not allowed to go, they begged Anne-Marie to allow at least Edith Moser (who was already lodged in a nearby village) to take their place. Anne-Marie gets on her bicycle to notify Edith Moser.[54]

The eighteen-year-old younger sister of Kurt Moser, Edith recorded the details in her diary a month after she arrived in Switzerland. She had left La Hille in the summer of 1943 and was in hiding, working at a nearby farm, possibly the same one as Rudi Oehlbaum, as the owner's name also was Roubichon at Varilhes.[55]

On October 27 Ilse Brünell, working as a housemaid at the home of Mme Authié in Foix, telephoned and requested that Edith (Moser) come to Foix right away to meet Manfred Kamlet (the eighteen-year-old brother of Walter Kamlet). Edith rode her bicycle there in pouring rain and learned that Manfred was being sought by the police, was out of money and ration cards, and needed a hiding place. She told Manfred that Mme Roubichon knew a tailor in Varilhes who needed a helper and Kamlet was skilled in that occupation.

Manfred agreed and Edith brought him secretly to her room at the farm, since the gendarmes were on his trail. She served him some food. Just as she cleared the dishes, Anne-Marie arrived and announced that it was time for Edith to attempt the flight to Switzerland. But she added that Walter Kamlet, who maintained a close friendship with Edith, was adamant that someone needed to accompany her. His brother Manfred volunteered to go with her to Toulouse and further if no one else were available.[56]

On the long train ride to Lyon the two shared a compartment with a uniformed member of the Garde Mobile, part of the Vichy French law enforcement units. Edith kept quiet in order not to expose her strong German accent but became very upset because Manfred chatted away, even about politics, "his favorite topic." So did the policeman, bragging about how he was fed up with his work and that he was treating black marketers and Jews leniently, as did many of his colleagues. He also bragged about having helped conscripted French laborers escape to Spain. Passengers heard him and applauded and shouted: "This guy has some nerve!" Edith writes in her diary.[57]

Though frightened, they managed to pass the German document control investigation on the train and after a long ride on an overcrowded bus arrived at the apartment of Madeleine Cordier in Champagnole. The next evening started with a short train ride two stations away. From there it would be ten kilometers hiking in increasingly tough terrain, with Madeleine leading the way.

As they got closer to the border, Madeleine asked them to wait under some pine trees while she scouted the terrain ahead for German patrols. When she gave the "all-clear," the two teenagers crawled, lying low, across wet terrain and eventually across a road. From there the path went uphill with the group halting often to listen for sounds of the feared patrols. After the almost six-hour hike in the dark, they arrived, exhausted, at the Cordier farmhouse. It was 4:00 a.m.

"The hills rose straight up behind that house and at the top was the border. Longingly we looked up that way," writes Edith Moser.[58] "Inside, Mother Cordier closed the curtains, lit a kerosene lamp and served us meat, vegetables and milk. I was so exhausted that I vomited it all."

When she awoke in the morning, the scenery looked magnificent but on the nearby road German patrols with dogs kept going past and she learned that they often checked the Cordier farmhouse. "How can we get past them in broad daylight," she worried. Anne-Marie's father was to meet them at 2:00 p.m. on the other side of the border. "Es wird schon schief gehen, dachte ich" ("I thought we were heading for disaster"), she writes.[59]

Edith then describes the frightening climb up the steep cliff, hands grasping roots, branches, and rocks, while worrying that the patrols might notice their ascent. They had separated and maintained a distance between themselves to avoid detection. She feared she was caught when a man climbed up behind her and passed her but did not stop or talk. The woods ended and she next had to move along a steep cliff and dare a scary long jump across a gap in the rocks. Eventually she reached the top and wondered which way to turn.

Just then voices called her name. It was Anne-Marie's father, waiting for her with Madeleine and Manfred who had arrived before her. The stranger who had passed her was also there. He had climbed the cliff to assist Madeleine with her charges but, just as Edith had feared him, he did not know them and was afraid she might denounce him and therefore passed her quickly.

The tired refugee pair was brought to his home by Mr. Piguet. Entering the Piguet residence proved to be a step into a normal home, something they had not experienced since they had left their own families. To their surprise, former La Hille director Margrit Tännler was waiting there. She had returned from escorting Inge Joseph and rode with them on bicycles lent by the Piguet family to catch a train to Zurich. As happened with all the illegal immigrants, they were interrogated and then interned.[60]

There was nervous tension at La Hille until word arrived that the two had safely crossed the Swiss border. "Naturally, Inge [Schragenheim] and I are elated to get the news but we can't forget that it could have been us," writes Edith Goldapper in her diary. Several weeks go by and their anxiety continues. On the evening of November 9 Anne-Marie asked Edith (Goldapper) to bring her friend Inge to her room right away. While Edith hoped they would leave within a day, she was shocked when Anne-Marie announced, "No, you're going tonight!" "We felt like we'd been struck by lightning," recalls Edith.

They receive detailed instructions from Anne-Marie who tells them to be ready to leave at 3:00 a.m. Eugen Lyrer walks with them part of the way to the train station, then returns to La Hille. In the bright moonlight they worry about drawing attention as they pass isolated farmhouses. Their fake identification papers are as troubling as reassuring. Edith had become "Eve Germain" and Inge was now "Danielle Pascal" and they rehearsed their new identities—in French, Edith recalls.

They traveled the same route as the earlier escaped comrades, the train to Toulouse, and another on to Lyon. Duly apprehensive about the expected ID check, they experienced no problems because their train compartment was shared by a German Air Force soldier who waved off the controller.[61] Their next train reached the provincial town of Lons-le-Saunier at midnight and they needed to catch a bus the next morning. They ended up shivering through the night in the

29. From left: Edith Goldapper and Inge Schragenheim at La Hille, 1942. Their attempted escape to Switzerland in 1943 was postponed, but each succeeded later. From Edith Goldapper collection, with permission from Joachim Rosenthal.

entrance hall of a building. The next morning they discover it was the town's police building.

And that morning was Edith's nineteenth birthday. "It's the first time that I experience it in such a depressing setting. Just a whispered 'Happy Birthday' from Inge. That's all. Where will I be this coming year? In Switzerland or in Poland?" They hit the train station restaurant for a warm beverage and take the bus to Champagnole at 9:00 a.m.[62]

There the Cordier sisters receive them warmly but they learn that the snow is already too deep to attempt the border crossing. If they were willing to wait, maybe the weather will change. It looks like they might have to wait until springtime. A telegram from Anne-Marie recommends that they go back to the Montluel colony. The Cordier sisters urge them to take on local household jobs until spring and Inge does find a job with the Girardet family. For Edith there's a job in a lovely villa, but the family needs a cook and Edith can't cook. "They're sorry and I'm sorry—but secretly I am glad; I hope that I still can get to Switzerland in 1943."[63]

In early December a man who crossed over from Switzerland visited the Cordier sisters and wanted to return there a few days later, recalls Edith. Victoria Cordier suggests that Edith could come along. "I am really excited. Ready to go today, any day and any night!" The date for the border crossing is December 12, 1943. It was decided that taking Inge would be one person too many and since she was well protected in her employment, she could follow in the spring.

So with the male friend of the sisters, a "Mr. A.," they take the train to near la Chapelle-des-Bois. Edith puts the photos of her parents in a coat pocket, for good luck. At the final train stop, Benoît, an uncle of Victoria bundles them into a donkey-drawn sled and they slide through the cold to his house in the countryside. Victoria Cordier skis to her mother's house in the forbidden zone to check on German patrols. When she gives the "all-clear," Edith and Mr. A. hike through the snow to the Cordier farmhouse near the border.[64]

At 10:00 p.m. on December 12 they start the journey, with Victoria in the lead. Edith was given snow boots several sizes too large, the same ones that Addi Nussbaum had worn for his border crossing. Soon Edith finds herself in snow up to her knees. Mr. A. treads a path through the snow for Edith, but for her the danger is minimal compared to the effort of slogging through the snow. And then came the steep cliff. Victoria had no problem climbing but came back to help Mr. A. and then Edith. "The woods looked the same, one tree is like any other, but I am in Switzerland," Edith exults.[65]

Victoria Cordier remembers the ascent in a somewhat different version.[66] Mr. A. actually was Roger, an underground member from Lyon. He had told Victoria, "I am a fugitive from Lyon, I'm in a hurry and no way will I cross the border with a Jewess. Not at this time." And Victoria answered: "Sorry, but you have no choice. Either you come with us or you try it alone. So he agreed because he had no other choice."

"The climb up the Risoux was no picnic. The slope was like a skating rink. She [Edith] just couldn't climb with her size 42 boots. I pulled and Roger pushed. It was hopeless. It took forever to get up there. As we got to the cliff, it was sheer ice. Edith refused to go on. She shivered and wanted to go back. I got angry. There was no way to go back to our house. The Germans had come that afternoon and interrogated my sister. They were on the lookout for any movement. It didn't help that Roger was furious. So I first took the backpack up the icy slope and had trouble getting back down."

"I tied myself to Roger's leather belt, took Edith on my back and, losing neither my courage nor my balance, with Roger pulling with all his might, we got up the slope conquering the steep drop and the blocks of ice. One more time we conquered the Gy de l'Echelle [name of the cliff]."[67] Descending cautiously, they arrived safely at the Piguet home. Victoria and Roger went on to Lausanne, and from there Victoria returned safely to Champagnole. The dramatic recollections poignantly portray the desperation and the incredible courage it took to save one's life and to escape from Germany's hate-filled madmen.

After a difficult hike through snow and ice, their first stop was at the house of Victoria's friends. Edith recalls that they arrived at 4:00 a.m. and "after 10 minutes' wait the door is opened and you can't even imagine the welcome! Immediately they bring all kinds of food and I can't believe my eyes . . . it's like paradise. I am deeply moved as Victoria says good-bye."[68] A daughter of the family led Edith to the Piguet home, just ten minutes further, where she received another warm welcome.

They had expected her a month earlier but not at this time of year and under these weather conditions. Early the next day—it was December 14—Mrs. Piguet leads Edith by train to Lausanne and then to Zurich to check in with Pastor Vogt.[69] The Anne-Marie/Cordier team had succeeded in the danger-fraught rescue of another threatened La Hille teenager.

For Edith the ordeal was not yet over. Now she had to undergo the customary detailed interrogation by the Zurich police. There is an interesting correlation between her diary and the official police interrogation record.[70] In her diary Edith recalls that she broke out in uncontrollable tears in front of the interrogators after Mme Piguet left the police station. As the interrogation begins, she reminds herself that "I must be careful not to mention anything about my guide [Victoria Cordier] or about La Hille."[71] Although she was upset and exhausted from the strenuous escape, Edith manufactured and stood by a completely fake story of her escape. Here is what she actually said, according to the transcript of the interrogation (signed by Edith):

> She credits a fictitious Jewish man in Lyon, who told her that his name was Charles (no family name) and who lived in a village near Lyon. When he warned that heavy snow made the escape difficult, Edith's companion [Inge Schragenheim] found work with a French family and Edith decided to go across the border without Inge.
>
> She and Charles left Lyon by train on December 13. She claimed not to remember the town where they left the train, even when four more policemen came to the interrogation room with detailed maps. After many hours of walking through snow and up hillsides they arrived at a Swiss train station and she could not remember its name or location either.
>
> She was not required to pay [the fictitious] Mr. Charles but believes that the woman who connected her with Charles was wealthy and may have paid him. When she arrived in Zurich, a stranger, who apparently recognized her as a refugee, volunteered to assist her and brought her to the refugee aid office.[72]

"Where did you get the false ID card with the name Eve Marie Germain?" the interrogator wanted to know. "At La Hille French Jews would come to visit us and one day a young Jewish man asked me whether I might need a false ID card. I gave him a photo and he brought me these fake papers. No, I don't know his name. It was a favor among coreligionists and I didn't have to pay him. I was never stopped to show this ID, but if necessary, I would have used it."

"Do you have relatives or acquaintances in Switzerland who might be able to care for you?" was the final question. She gave the name and address of Mme Goldschmidt-Brodsky in Basel (the former Belgian committee president). Except for her early childhood history, that was the only truthful answer given by Edith in the interview.[73]

It is evident that besides reaching and crossing the border secretly, hiding the real story and the identity of the rescuers was yet another necessity even after a successful crossing. (Edith had forgotten and was astounded to learn what she had said at the interrogation when I furnished her the official transcript sixty-four years later.) She too was interned for several months in various Swiss camps.[74]

At the Château de La Hille, there were other departures and arrivals in 1943. Irène Frank, the mother of Alex Frank, was asked to leave La Hille in January and moved to the Hotel Pons in nearby Pailhès, where her mother had been living. "She was asked to leave in January because of the endless controversies surrounding her."[75]

In January Gret Tobler, a young Swiss woman, came to replace Elka Frank as caregiver for the younger girls and Sebastian (Basti) Steiger, twenty-five years old, arrived from Switzerland in August, becoming the counselor for the younger boys and girls.

All during 1943 the mass murder of Jews in the gas chambers in Poland continued unabated. By the end of that year, the French Milice, a paramilitary force formed to enforce "the maintenance of order," became a willing and dedicated tool for the Nazis in the persecution and roundup of Jews. "With the Milice the Germans came closest to what they had always lacked in France . . . a parallel police force composed of men chosen for their ideological conviction rather than for professional competence, led by a chief [Joseph Darnand] outside the regular police and ready for anything."[76]

At La Hille the younger boys and girls were still leading a comparatively normal life, with local excursions, games, and school activity. In Sebastian Steiger they found a caring and creative counselor/ supervisor. Yet, they too began to feel the danger and they had, of course, grown three years older since their flight from Belgium and had seen firsthand the arrests and flight of their older comrades.

In early January another Swiss counselor had been assigned to La Hille. Since October, Gret Tobler had been working at the Secours Suisse nursery in Banyuls, located at the Mediterranean shore near the Spanish border. Maurice Dubois notified her that scarlet fever had broken out at La Hille and that her help was needed. When she arrived, she found out that the epidemic was just a ruse by Rösli Näf, but she easily assimilated to the new environment and quickly learned of the arrests and escapes already underway. Her diary, written in December 1943, sheds much light on the events at La Hille that year and on yet another narrow escape to Switzerland, which she organized.[77]

"We have scarlet fever here to keep the children out of the local school so that they can't reveal what's going on here," Rösli Näf informed her. "It's your task, Miss Tobler, to quell the anxieties of the little ones and to keep them occupied and cared for while they're out of school."

"I have 17 Mickeys [nickname for the group], aged 5 to 11. We do arithmetic, we write and we sing," she reports. "The 'grands' [the oldest boys and girls] work all day in the house and garden. In the evening they do math, compose music, write fiction and study languages. We're all together in the large hall with a fire in the fireplace. At 9:30 everyone goes to the dormitories. My Mickeys went to sleep earlier in the large dorm whose ceiling sometimes leaks from the rain."

Late in 1943 Gret Tobler was approached by Anne-Marie Piguet who whispers, "I've heard from Toulouse that Mlle Kündig [a staff member of that office] will not bring Inge Bernhard and Toni Rosenblatt to Switzerland illegally." "And if I help," she added, "directrice Emma Ott and I will be dismissed." "What to do?" writes Tobler. "The two girls have Swiss visas that expire on December 15 and today it's December 3."

"It's urgent," whispered Anne-Marie. "You're our best bet since you want to go home to Switzerland anyhow. But remember, I didn't talk to you," she added.

"It's Thursday and Mlle Ott went Christmas shopping in Toulouse," leaving the keys to her desk with Tobler. The two girls' Swiss visas were in that desk. "It's not easy to betray the confidence of a colleague, but sometimes that's the only way," Tobler writes.

"In the laundry I met Inge Bernhard [aged fifteen]. Want to come to Switzerland with me, on the sly?" It's a deal. In the evening she approached Toni Rosenblatt (age twelve), who also agreed to be part of the escape. They packed clothes and belongings into backpacks and destroyed incriminating papers and photos.

At 2:30 a.m. they left La Hille for the three-hour walk to the train station at St. Jean-de-Verges and took the train to Toulouse. There, instead of waiting for the express train to Lyon that evening, Tobler made a short connection to Carcassonne on a local train, afraid that the Swiss officials in Toulouse might have been alerted and gone to the station to stop the escaping trio. (Tobler notes that she learned later that the office personnel had indeed gone to look for them in the Toulouse station.)

In Carcassonne they took the tour of the ancient walled city with a small group that, by chance, included a German army officer and his interpreter. That evening they managed to get on the overcrowded train to Lyon and changed to another toward Annemasse. Delays and detours occurred because resistance fighters had blown up tracks, a new and frequent problem for the Germans by late 1943. At the station they see two German soldiers with rifles escorting a young man with his hands raised. "Will we make it across the border?" wonders Gret Tobler.

They hiked along the border to nearby Saint-Cergues and noticed that the Swiss had erected a new and more elaborate barbed wire. "They've done a quality job," she remarks. "Impossible to get across!" They were welcomed warmly at the Swiss children's colony. The next day, a Sunday, they explored the border, pretending to be out for a walk. There's a small creek flowing under the fence near a control station. Toni tries it, but shouts, "I can't get across!" "And suddenly a German guard appears but we get away. He must have been blind."

They continue on to the Machilly area (where the Walter Strauss group had been caught almost a year earlier), looking for a place to cross. Suddenly two human figures with a dog appear. Are they Germans? Fortunately they were French guards and the three refugees were taken in for an interrogation. Their luck continued because their Swiss visas and Tobler's money, hidden inside their clothes, were not discovered. They were freed with the warning not to reveal their liberation if they were arrested again.

Tobler sent the two girls back to Saint-Cergues and explored the border fence alone. Was there a gap somewhere in this Swiss-quality wire, erected just two weeks before? She did find a possible crossing point near Jussy and hurried back to the colony to fetch the two girls. Toni is afraid and worried about the dogs. Now it's nighttime and they have trouble locating the crossing spot. After what seems like an eternity, they find it, and Inge Bernhard manages to get across and calls out, "ça y est!" (I made it!). She was on the Swiss side.

Tobler returned to the Swiss colony for the night, worrying about how to cross in daylight. The next morning Toni was still hesitant but Tobler insisted. Now they had to find a different way from the night before. Dogs were barking and the German guards went past while the two hid by lying flat on the grass. Then they found a spot, Toni went under the wire and Tobler crawled through behind her.

The Swiss border guards who interviewed them were astounded that they had managed to cross without a guide. Tobler's coat is torn, her boots are in terrible shape. "But what do I care as long as my protégées made it to Switzerland, one missing her coat and the other in worn-out sandals."

"In Geneva Inge and Toni are assigned to internment, for quarantine. On December 15 we appear before the Territorial Command in Geneva. That day the two girls' visas expire. Everything worked out."[78]

For a while there was no border traffic from La Hille to Switzerland. Inge Schragenheim (then nineteen), who had stayed with the Girardet family at Champagnole when her friend Edith Goldapper was guided to safety by Victoria Cordier in November, followed the escape route across the Risoux with the help of the Cordiers on April 17, 1944.[79]

In Switzerland she was reunited with her ailing mother, Amalia Herz Schragenheim. Unlike her first attempt with Leo Lewin sixteen months earlier when she was returned to France, this time Inge was able to stay in Switzerland.

By April 1944 American troops, ships, and equipment had "invaded" England in preparation for the landings on the European mainland. But at La Hille fear of harassment and arrest prevailed as part of the daily life. On April 27 yet another order arrived, this time requesting that Walter Kamlet, the dedicated pianist, come to the police regarding an important matter about the Foreign Workers Battalion. Kamlet had already been weakened by typhoid fever from which he suffered during a temporary internment in 1942. Instead of reporting, Kamlet went into hiding on a farm in nearby Lacoste.[80]

The threatened arrest of Kamlet forced a quick decision. The final escape group to Switzerland is formed: Anne-Marie Piguet will lead Kamlet, Flora Schlesinger, the colony's cook, and her son Paul (age fourteen) to the border in the Jura Mountains. Teachers Henri Kägi and Sebastian (Basti) Steiger are accomplices for the otherwise secret getaway. But there were complications in forging a false identification card for Flora Schlesinger: born in Vienna, she speaks only Austrian-accented German, so the usual Alsatian fake card wouldn't work if she were stopped—and she doesn't speak French. Moreover, ever since her husband Ernst was deported in early 1943, Flora had become fearful and easily upset, even by minor mishaps. Eventually the two La Hille counselors collaborate in fixing her photo onto a Swiss immigrant's card.[81]

In pouring rain, Eugen Lyrer and Basti Steiger went to fetch Kamlet from his hideout at a friendly farm family and he spent the night at a La Hille outbuilding. The next morning Anne-Marie led them by train from Pamiers to Toulouse. They managed to go on toward Lyon without incident and Anne-Marie asked them to wait at the Swiss colony of Montluel (near Lyon), while she went on to the Jura Mountains area to check with the Cordier sisters whether the coast was clear. When she came back to Montluel, she told her protégés that the expected day of the escape would be May 17, the day before Ascension Day. The small group arrived by train in Champagnole without anyone questioning them.

A surprise visitor at the Cordier apartment startles the group. A tall uniformed French policeman knocks on the door, enters, and fakes surprise at finding a group of strangers. "They were obviously frightened and thought I'd surely lured them into a trap," recalled Victoria Cordier. The gendarme was the local police chief, coming to accept a

30. The Ernst Schlesinger family at La Hille, 1942. Ernst was arrested, deported, and murdered in Poland. Flora and son Paul escaped to Switzerland in 1943 with help from Resistance fighter Victoria Cordier. From Edith Goldapper collection, with permission from Joachim Rosenthal.

pack of cigarettes from Victoria. She had made the arrangement a few hours earlier and informed him of their plans. The gendarme quickly changed his demeanor and wished them a pleasant journey. "That's something I really shouldn't have done," Victoria wrote later.[82]

The incident poignantly demonstrates the refugees' fears of being caught, if that needed to be demonstrated. But it also documents that at least some French officials, including the police, could be sympathetic to the victims of their government.

At 6:00 p.m. they get underway, separately in groups of two, and buy the tramway tickets to the tiny town of Foncine-le-Bas up the hill. There the backpacks are loaded on the bicycles of Victoria and of her sister, Madeleine Cordier. Night has fallen and they start the more than three-hour climb across Mont-Noir (Black Mountain) toward its summit at 1,220 meters (4,000 feet).

Anne-Marie recalls that the Cordier sisters were laboring to push their overloaded bicycles uphill, followed by the fatigued refugees. She takes Flora Schlesinger by the hand. Every time a sapling snaps back at them or a bush is swayed by the wind, Flora winces, clings tighter to Anne-Marie and whispers: "A German!"[83] Eventually they come out of the woods and the sisters hide their bicycles in the bushes. Everyone now carries his or her own baggage. As they get closer to the forbidden border zone, the sisters scout the way ahead and the group follows.[84]

> Now we can't make a sound as we cross the road that marks the forbidden zone. If the Germans even saw a shadow move, they'd shoot. Finally we reached the back door of mother's house. I said quietly, "Maman!" A light sleeper, she jumped up immediately and said, "I expected you tomorrow." "This way," I said, "you didn't have to worry about us in advance." My mother put bowls on the table and heated milk and coffee for everybody. We didn't have much time to rest. In May the sun rises early up there and we needed to get over the cliff before 5:00 a.m. After all had some rest (a few even went to sleep), I insisted that it was time to get going.[85]
>
> On the way up the cliff the refugees faltered, the ascent taxed them beyond their abilities, but we urged them on: "It's your last chance! Go do it!"[86] The Gy [name of the cliff] is waiting. How will Mme Schlesinger get up on it? The path is steep and narrow and one's feet get caught in the tree roots, stones will get kicked down the hillside. Fear redoubles their energy. Luckily the stretch is not too long. Finally, finally we reach the border, and freedom.[87]

Once they reached the top, Anne-Marie announced that they would rest at the "Hotel d'Italie," a loggers' cabin in the woods with primitive furnishings. It was located barely inside the Swiss border and they needed to be just as cautious as on the French side because the Swiss guards would turn back anyone found within ten kilometers of the border. She would go ahead and notify her father and the group could rest in the cabin until they returned.

On the way through the woods, Anne-Marie worried that she was *not* carrying her Swiss passport and *was* carrying French money. This could be incriminating if she were stopped. Feeling smug about her shrewdness, she hid the money under a rock. After a happy reunion at her father's home he hurried off to the loggers' cabin, but no one was there. Her father came home and Anne-Marie was desperate. What could have happened to her fledglings whom she had guarded so zealously?

Her protégés were resting when a man in uniform entered the door of the cabin. "A German!" moaned Mme Schlesinger. But he was neither a German nor a Swiss border guard, just a local policeman from nearby Brassus, a small village. Proud of his catch, he played the official's role. Madeleine Cordier needed to come with him, he said, the others are to go back across the border. Orders are orders. Madeleine, brave and eloquent, pleaded their case. "Me, go to Switzerland? That's impossible[;] my mother is waiting for me. And sending these poor people back across the border who have come hundreds of kilometers trying to escape, whose lives are in danger and who are dead tired—they're counting on YOU. You just can't do that—it's inhuman."

The policeman vacillates and decides: "Okay, you can return to France and I'll take the others with me to Brassus [his village]. But listen, you're to tell no one that I found you this close to the border!" In return he demanded to get information about General Meillès, a famous French woman of the resistance who was gathering secret information, based in the Champagnole region. "An example of the dual roles of some border police," remarks Anne-Marie, "allowing illegal refugees in while also trafficking in vital secret information."[88]

From Brassus the three La Hille refugees followed the typical process of Swiss interrogation and internment. Anne-Marie was disappointed. She had intended to offer them a warm welcome at her father's house nearby and then lead them herself to Pastor Vogt in Zurich. She consoled herself realizing that then they would also have been interned.

Sheepishly Anne-Marie also explains the mysterious appearance of the Swiss policeman at the cabin: he had watched her hide the money while he was hiding behind a tree nearby, already suspicious of people at the loggers' cabin. She says that never had her money been in a safer place. The police returned it to her in full later on.

Flora Schlesinger tragically lost her husband to deportation but escaped safely with her young son Paul. Walter Kamlet survived

31. Many escaped; a few did not. From right to left (at La Hille, 1942): Ilse Wulff (Garfunkel) and Edith Moser escaped to Switzerland. Her brother, Kurt Moser (behind Edith), was caught fleeing toward Spain, was deported, and died in Auschwitz; Inge Helft and Dela Hochberger (first and second from left) were caught crossing into Switzerland, deported, and murdered in Poland; the two Kamlet brothers, Manfred and Walter (rear left and center), fled across the Swiss border and survived. From Edith Goldapper collection, with permission from Joachim Rosenthal.

internment and a fatal summons and was able to follow his brother, Manfred, to safety in Switzerland.

Altogether twenty-three refugees from La Hille managed to cross the Swiss border illegally and stayed in Switzerland until the end of the war. Six were caught and returned to France and two had to make repeated crossing attempts before they succeeded. This last crossing of La Hille escapees to safety in Switzerland occurred on May 18–19, 1944. The Allies landed in Normandy eighteen days later.[89]

◇ **11** ◇

Hidden and Surviving
in France until the End

E scaping the tightening Nazi deportation net by trying to get across the Spanish or Swiss borders on the sly was known to be very hazardous and therefore not the choice of all the older boys and girls of La Hille, especially after the stories of the failed crossings reached those who were left behind. For the younger children, the exertions required for such escapes were out of the question and the strict orders from Bern against illegal escape, following the dismissals of Rösli Näf, Germaine Hommel, and Renée Farny resulted in tighter control by Emma Ott, who was in charge at La Hille from 1943 until 1945.

The Nazi net was indeed drawing tighter. After the Wehrmacht occupied southern France in November 1942, German police forces were spread too thin to effectively round up Jews for deportation. Therefore the SS urged three steps on Vichy General Secretary of Police René Bousquet: evacuation of all Jews from the border and coastal departments, the internment of foreign-born Jews, and the concentration of French Jews in three or four centrally located departments.

Bousquet decreed the exclusion of Jews from the border departments and as of March 16, 1943, foreign Jews had to report to local police whenever they moved, even within a community. Their ID and ration cards were stamped with the telltale letter "J". And the Germans were eager to fill the deportation trains that departed frequently from Drancy to Poland.[1] Although the details of these measures had not penetrated to the colony at La Hille, the girls and boys had long been fully aware and afraid of the Nazis' intentions. Those who elected not to try and reach the borders were actively looking for hiding places. They found them in many ways and locations.

Ruth Herz, then twenty years old, was able to find work in another Swiss Red Cross facility in the spring of 1942. She moved to Praz-sur-Arly in the Hte. Savoie French alpine region, which was then under Italian Army control and therefore safer for Jews. With the help of Mme Barusseau, the colony's director, she was able to procure false identity papers. Later she transferred to another children's home near Castres, east of Toulouse, and remained there until 1947.[2]

Lixie Grabkowicz, who had fled from La Hille with Ruth Schütz on New Year's Eve 1942 (see chapter 9) found domestic employment and protection with the Fortrat family in Grenoble. "I lived with them, using a fake name, for 18 months. They warned me not to talk to strangers and they took me to church services," she recalled in an autobiography written years later. "I was required to eat in the kitchen and was not allowed to use their bathtub. Those are things you don't forget," she wrote.[3]

On the day after the American troops liberated Grenoble, she found her way back to Lyon, where she encountered La Hille companion Frieda Steinberg. When she returned to her host family, a son helped her find a position in a children's home in Villard-de-Lans, near Grenoble, where she took care of orphans whose parents had been executed by the Germans. One year later she returned to Lyon, again taking care of children, and took a course for dental technicians. Lixie met her husband there and they were married in 1947.[4]

Frieda Steinberg is another of the older girls (born in late 1924 in Vienna) who survived in France but had her share of near-miss adventures. She has excellent recall and shared her experiences in descriptive letters of recent years. When Eugen Lyrer assisted the older girls and boys with their escapes from La Hille in December 1942, Frieda paired with Helga Klein (age seventeen). Lyrer had provided them with money for the train and with canned food for the journey. Fanny Weinberg, one of the younger girls, recently arrived at the colony, urged Frieda to accept a pendant "for good luck." Mr. Lyrer advised them to catch a train to Toulouse at a remote station.

Unfamiliar with the region, the pair had still not reached the railroad when the curfew hour arrived and they were forced to seek shelter with a nearby family. They wandered all the next day, still unable to find the elusive train station and again sought shelter and food at a strange house. "The lady of the house arrived from evening prayers with an enormous cross ornating her ample bosom and a severe look in our direction," Frieda recalls. She had cautioned her companion Helga to remain silent because she spoke French poorly, and with a heavy German accent.

Suspicious of their fake story, the woman guessed they were Jewish and threatened to call the police. As she dialed, Frieda remembered the religious pendant. She showed her the pendant and invented a Catholic mother who had married a Jew and given it to her. She also confessed to being a refugee from Belgium and pointed to her Belgian Girl Scout belt (which she was wearing because it had a knife and whistle attached). "The belt and the pendant worked wonders," Frieda recalls. "From Belgium!" the woman exclaimed. "My mother was from Belgium." She allowed them to stay overnight and had her servant drive them to a train station on his cart in the morning, with a sandwich and "ersatz confiture" (substitute marmalade) for the road. The pendant had indeed brought them luck.

After the driver took off, the two girls faced a line of German soldiers checking passenger IDs at the station. Since they didn't have papers, it meant imminent detention. Just then a train whistle sounded and Frieda took Helga's hand and whispered, "Run with me!" Out loud she shouted in French, "our train is leaving, we'll miss it!" The trick worked and they were on their way to Toulouse. There they encountered the always cheerful "Onze" Klein who was returning from his unsuccessful crossing to Switzerland with Kurt Moser, and was heading back to La Hille.

The two girls managed the train ride to Lyon, but there they encountered the same surprise as other La Hille companions. The guide to the border recommended by Eugen Lyrer had been arrested by the Gestapo but his wife directed them to the Amitié Chrétienne (Christian fellowship), a cover organization for a resistance group.

There they were referred to a convent hiding place and from there to individual French families.

In Lyon Frieda happened upon other La Hille friends. Like Lixie she was referred to a family in Grenoble, "a refuge and hiding place in return for housework." Her hosts and rescuers were "the famous Mieg Family" (of the DMC—Dollfus, Mieg & Company, thread and yarn manufacturer). This family had fled to Grenoble from their home in the town of Mulhouse. Frieda says she "became the governess of their three children and I cooked in the morning." She recalls "spending the whole summer with this family and their relatives at their summer home in St. Jorioz on the shore of Lake Annecy. There I didn't even have to do the cooking as grandmother Mieg had brought her own cook." The local mayor provided Frieda with a real identity card and she became "Denise Soutout," born in Epinal. "It saved my life," she recalls.

By coincidence the new name proved to be a real danger for some time. The Gestapo was searching for a resistance fighter named "Soutout" and Frieda feared that she might be interrogated as a relative, especially since Grenoble was located near a hotbed of the French guerillas. She recalls other close encounters: "While I was ice-skating, the chief of the local Gestapo (who was just learning to skate with his French mistress) literally fell into my arms, looking for a hold. A very icy embrace for me! From that day on, whenever he saw me on the ski slopes, he would come up to me with a polite (German-accented) 'Bonnshoohr Mattemoisell.'"

With help from Ruth Herz and Mme Barusseau, Ruth's superior at the children's home, Frieda/Denise was able to obtain employment as a children's caretaker at the Centres Scolaires-Medicaux (Medical Education Centers) in the Mégève ski resort. With her authentic fake name credentials and her ability to speak French without foreign accent, her true identity was well camouflaged from her new French associates. And she was safe from detection by the Germans because she now was on the staff of a Vichy government facility.

Frieda recalls aiding resistance fighters whenever possible and that many of her colleagues were partisans. Following the liberation in the

32. Friedl Steinberg fled to the Annecy, France area and later hid in the Haute-Savoie region, then rejoined her surviving sister in Belgium after the war. She was one of the artists who left wall paintings at the "Barn" in Seyre. Photo from Alix Kowler collection, with permission.

summer of 1944, she returned to Lyon and did social work for the Jewish Committee, helping survivors who were returning from German concentration camps.[5]

Like so many others, Austrian-born Peter Hans Landesmann fled from the La Hille colony in the first days of January 1943 and headed for Lyon. The dark-haired lanky seventeen-year-old was somewhat of a loner and had aroused the anger of some older comrades who accused him of secretly raiding food supplies. In Belgium he had made outspoken comments to a host family. But his independence and resourcefulness served him well during several years of hiding and engaging in French resistance activities.

After he arrived in the Lyon region, Landesmann became connected with the Centre d'Accueil aux Jeunes Refugiés (Reception Center for Young Refugees) in suburban Villeurbanne. They furnished him a new name and fake credentials as Jean Pierre Bouché, born in Fourmies, a French town near the Belgian border. Bouché is the name he would retain until he died in the 1990s. Lyon was a dangerous place because the Gestapo was very active and they arrested Landesmann on January 28, not long after he arrived.

Peter may have been the son of a mixed marriage. Though his mother, Hilde, was Jewish, he was baptized in Vienna in late 1938, possibly as a protection. His father died before the war and he was identified in early documents as "Catholic." This might have helped him to be released a few weeks after his arrest in Lyon.

The director of the reception center then helped him get work as a warehouse packer in Lyon-St.Clair (at F 7.40 an hour, he noted). The sales manager of the firm knew his real identity but apparently protected him. Camouflaged as Pierre Bouché, he joined the young French resistance movement (often abbreviated "FUJ") in July 1943. A certificate issued in 1944 records that he had distributed clandestine leaflets and posters. This resulted in another arrest by French police on August 24 for "antinational behavior." A week later a judge freed him and put him on probation. By December 1943 Landesmann had become a translator and interpreter for the German Military Railway Authority at Lyon, probably a safe place to be for a Jewish refugee—as long as his identity was not discovered.

On August 15, 1944, he joined the Maquis (French partisans) in the countryside at Marcigny, northwest of Lyon, and then returned to Lyon. He enlisted "as a foreigner in the First Regiment (probably a battalion) of the Charolais" (which helped to liberate Villefranche-sur-Saône on September 3), became a sergeant, and was demobilized on September 19, 1945. In 1946 Landesmann became a French citizen and changed his name officially to Bouché. Later he would learn that his mother was deported from Vienna to Auschwitz in March 1942 and died there, supposedly of influenza, in November that year.[6]

Peter Landesmann would not be the only La Hille teenager who joined the ranks of the resistance and the Allied armed forces. When local gendarmes came looking for Henri Storosum at La Hille on February 7, 1943, he was able to hide at the farmhouse of Mme Emilie deGrenier in nearby Gabre. He stayed there until February 11. "She was a courageous and dedicated religious person," Storosum recalled.

During the night of February 11 Eugen Lyrer helped him get away and connected him with the Eclaireurs Israélites ("EIF," the Jewish Boy Scouts) at Lautrec in the countryside northeast of Toulouse. The

Vichy regime had disbanded the Jewish scout organization but it continued secretly as part of the resistance. (Many older members of EIF
joined the French resistance, forming their own units; they joined the
Organisation Juive de Combat in 1944. About 110 leaders of the EIF
were killed in action or deported to concentration camps.)[7]

Storosum was with the partisans who liberated nearby Castres and
the city of Albi (birthplace of painter Toulouse-Lautrec). He apparently had stayed in touch with Ilse Brünell of La Hille because she
eventually joined him at Castres and both were part of a group that
succeeded in an arduous crossing over the Pyrénées into Spain in
mid-1944.[8]

One of the most bizarre connections of the La Hille teenagers
befell Ilse Brünell, then already nineteen years old. She had been
arrested and interned with her companions at Le Vernet in August
1942. After they were freed, Rösli Näf sent Ilse to Foix where she
became the housemaid of Mme Olga Authié. This assignment probably was not by coincidence. Mme Authié was the official at the préfecture of the Ariège Department who compiled and kept the official
registration lists of foreigners and Jews, which was required by the
laws of the Vichy regime. It is from these lists that the deportation
roundups and deportations were carried out by local police forces. Ilse
disliked the work and Mme Authié intensely and complained bitterly
about her, and even about her young daughter, throughout her life.
She resented that she had to suffer so that, maybe, a few favors might
be obtained. The record shows that although Vichy law required the
shameful work being done by Mme Authié and her counterparts,
some of the officials, and certainly Mme Authié, played a double role,
apparently unbeknownst to Ilse.

La Hille colony counselor Anne-Marie Im Hof-Piguet recalled
that the maligned Mme Authié, "who looks out for our welfare,"
warned her that a new roundup was imminent at La Hille in August
1943. Anne-Marie rushed back to the Château and was able to send
those sought into hiding before the gendarmes arrived.[9]

Historical records in the local archives reveal that Mme Authié
actually was connected with the French resistance, especially after the

German fortunes were turning sour. She harbored resistance fighters sought by the police and by the Germans in her attic, apparently unbeknownst to her Jewish refugee maid. She also issued false identification papers and, at times, took endangered Jewish refugees off the arrest lists. It is likely, though not proven, that the older La Hille boys who were subject to being drafted into the foreign workers force were allowed to stay with local farmers instead, thanks to her manipulation of the lists.

After the liberation, honors were bestowed on Mme Authié by the de Gaulle government and by allied military commanders (because part of the resistance effort in which she was involved helped downed allied airmen to flee to nearby Spain). Confusion, deception, and intrigue were part of the daily life in Vichy France and it is not surprising that Rösli Näf and Anne-Marie were involved in protective schemes unknown to their protégés.[10]

Ilse Brünell became so frustrated that she contacted her friend Henri Storosum, who had already joined the Jewish Scouts, for help. "I was in written contact with him and even he noticed that I could no longer bear staying there. He sent a young woman from the resistance who brought me to Castres via Toulouse. My job was to knit socks and to do typing for an underground newspaper. My French was poor, so they urged me not to talk too much."[11]

Of all the La Hille teenagers who faced dangers and frightening experiences while trying to hide and escape from French and German pursuers, none came close to the chilling adventures, hardships, and daring of Ruth Schütz. Not yet eighteen years old when she fled to Lyon with Lixie Grabkowicz on New Year's Eve, 1942, she would spend the following eighteen months trying to survive with ever-changing false names and constantly on the move in the region around Grenoble. She described the details vividly in her autobiography, *Entrapped Adolescence*, published in 1997.

As "Renée Sorrel" she began her odyssey in early 1943 on a remote hardscrabble farm doing menial work for a taciturn, hapless owner who assigned her a primitive attic sleeping space. It was the first, but not the only, time that rats were running around her sleeping space. On her monthly day off she visited Lixie at her employer's home in Grenoble and decided to hunt for other employment. She found it with a fairly well-to-do family of Vichy France sympathizers who displayed odd behaviors. She had to wear three different maid uniforms each day, depending on the chore, and was given the scraps to eat after she served the family in the dining room.

Because she feared that her false identity might be discovered, she soon sought different employment and lodging at an employment bureau in town. There she was offered a new dress and lodging by a blonde woman who quickly turned out to be the front for a prostitution pimp. Ruth declined the lodging but was able to keep the dress.

She was next able to share a room at a convent and worked at a scarf factory. Always afraid of being discovered, Ruth kept changing from one dingy rented room to another. Finding enough to eat under the stringent rationing system occupied all of her spare time.[12]

On the street she repeatedly encountered a young woman whose name was Charlotte. She was also from Berlin and hiding out. Charlotte invited her to clandestine meetings of a Zionist youth movement group (Movement de Jeunesse Sioniste or MJS) who would gather in the countryside on weekends. These new connections with other young people led her to join the dangerous activities of the underground resistance movement and it would change her life.

Her first assignment was to deliver an elderly refugee to a nursing home. He only spoke German and they were almost caught by the Germans in a roundup on a streetcar. But she passed the test and learned the ropes quickly. Numerous deliveries of false ID papers and documents followed. Doing such illegal work in the Grenoble region was at first fairly safe because relatively benign Italian troops were the occupiers. This all changed when Italy signed an armistice with the Allies in September 1943 and withdrew its troops from France. German forces assisted by the French gendarmes now pursued Jews and resisters in that area with vicious zeal.

33. Ruth Schütz joined the Resistance and helped
to save younger sister Betty by arranging her escape
to Switzerland. In 1943 she walked over the Pyr-
enées to Spain. Photo from Alix Kowler collection,
with permission.

The following months brought varied assignments for Ruth, all of
them dangerous and risky. She had narrow escapes and used her wits
and good luck to fool interrogators and escape pursuit.

When her collaborators learned that the Gestapo was planning to
arrest a Jewish infant from a Grenoble children's home whose young
parents were already in custody, she insisted that the child had to be
saved. Since it was believed that "'the director will only give the child
to the Germans,' I said, 'in that case, I will be the German woman
to take Corinne [the infant].'"[13] Ruth disguised herself as a Gestapo
woman, with raincoat, hat and sunglasses and a falsified Gestapo
order for release of the infant Corinne. Faking a German accent and
rudely berating the staff and nursery director, she demanded the child
and hurried off with it via taxi and streetcar. With companions trail-
ing her on bicycles she delivered Corinne to underground associates.
(More than thirty years later, the now grown Corinne found Ruth at
her Kibbutz in Israel and thanked her for saving her life.)

Ruth was then barely nineteen years old and the Gestapo quickly
mobilized to arrest the child snatcher. Her underground leaders urged

her to escape and connected her with the so-called "Jewish Army" (Armée Juive), which was skilled at hiding and guiding refugees across the Pyrénées into Spain. By then, unauthorized travel across southern France was extremely dangerous and difficult.

In Toulouse and at other intermediate points, underground contacts using prearranged identification codes would give her directions and lodging. After Toulouse she embarked for the difficult hike across the rugged Pyrénées from Quillan (Aude Department), which is about sixty-five miles on foot from the border with Spain. A mountain guide assembled a group of eight fugitives and after a two-hour hike on narrow paths he ordered that all papers and identifications be destroyed. "The pile lit up with a big flame and he covered the ashes with earth. That was it, my identity certificate, which was so authentic, was gone, devoured by fire, and so were my last photos of my parents and sisters. Now I was a person without a past or a name."[14]

That evening the hikers reached an area controlled by the Maquis (French resistance guerillas). To her surprise, Ilse Brünell and Heinz Storosum, companions from La Hille, arrived that evening with another refugee group and joined hers for the hike to Andorra. It took several days of strenuous climbing on rugged mountain terrain before they reached the safety of the principality of Andorra. Food ran out, with only a limited supply of sugar cubes left. After the group crossed an icy mountain stream, they entered Andorra and then continued to Spain after a day's rest.[15]

For Ruth the heroic and hazardous actions and escapes, beginning with her flight with Lixie on New Year's Eve, 1942, ended successfully in Spain more than two years later. After several months she and others in her group obtained permission to emigrate to Palestine. Following a period of internment there she joined and helped to create a Kibbutz, where she has lived for many years and raised a family.

Although the younger children of La Hille had been spared during the roundup and internment of their forty older companions in August 1942, the continuing Nazi extermination campaign and the zeal of their local French collaborators in rounding up Jewish victims put all of the younger children in danger. As each month went by, they too were looking for places to hide or escape. Also, by then some were "aging" into the older teenage category.

In early 1942 four of these younger ones were still able to get away to the United States before the Germans occupied Vichy France. Their stories reveal narrow escapes and strokes of luck in the midst of chaos and misery. Their escapes were actively supported by Mme Lilly Felddegen from her office at the Hebrew Immigrant Aid Society (HIAS) organization in New York City.

Willy Wolpert's father had fled to the United States in January 1941 via England and Canada. Willy's mother and younger sister were left behind in Frankfurt, Germany but their necessary papers and affidavits were at the US consulate in Stuttgart in 1941.[16] The mother and sister apparently never were able to emigrate. On June 1, 1942, the eleven-year-old Willy left La Hille and sailed on the SS *Nyassa* from Marseille to Philadelphia via Casablanca. Father and son had a happy reunion there when the ship landed.

Arthur Kantor and his sister Eva were born in Vienna. Their father had died in 1934 and their mother Maria was able to escape with them to Belgium after the Germans invaded Austria. In the summer of 1939 Jack Blatt of Dayton, OH, a violinist and refugee from Austria, came to Brussels and married Maria.

As his spouse, Maria could accompany Blatt to the United States, but the children had to stay behind with friends of their mother until she was able to request their immigration from the United States. The German army invaded Belgium before the Kantor children could obtain US visas and they escaped to Seyre with our La Hille colony, probably because they had been placed in the care of the Belgian Rescue Committee by their mother's friends in Brussels.[17] Arthur, sixteen years old, Eva, fourteen, and Willy Wolpert traveled to the United States on the SS *Nyassa* with a group of thirty-eight other children who had received permission to immigrate through the efforts of the US Committee for the Care of European Children, Inc.[18]

The last La Hille child to escape to the United States was also the youngest. Toni Steuer, born in Essen, Germany on July 24, 1936, had a tragic family history and her experience was typical of the persecution that the Nazis inflicted on even the youngest of Jewish children. Little Toni had two older sisters and two Steuer cousins. Their father, of Polish origin, was interned in Dachau and the mother apparently was taken to a mental care facility. All five Steuer children were brought to Belgium. The boy cousins were briefly at Home Speyer in Anderlecht and the older sisters were placed with a Dutch family in Courtrai. Because Toni was only three years old, Belgian Committee Leader Mme Renée deBecker kept her in her own home.

Toni was somehow put on the refugee train to France with our children's group when the German army attacked Belgium in May 1940. At Seyre and at La Hille she became the "baby" and mascot of the colony. As an attractive child, and undoubtedly unaware of the events around her, there were plenty of girls eager to mother her. None of our campmates knew anything about her family and siblings.

34. Author Reed visiting Anne-Marie Im Hof-Piguet at her home in Bern, Switzerland, in 2004. From the author's personal collection.

Fortunately her sisters' caretaker family also fled to southern France when the Germans invaded and, because they were Dutch, managed to move on to one of that country's Caribbean colonies. But they were not allowed to bring Toni's sisters who were *apatrides* (stateless). They managed to place the sisters with Ottilie Moore, an American heiress who harbored more than a dozen young refugee children at her villa on the French Riviera. She succeeded in bringing them all to her home in New York City some time before little Toni Steuer arrived in the United States.[19]

On June 25, 1942, the SS *Serpa Pinto* brought one of the last groups of European refugee children (twenty-one girls and twenty-nine boys) from Lisbon to New York, via Casablanca and Bermuda. Among them was Toni Steuer, then still only five years old. A press release from the United States Committee for the Care of European Children, announcing the arrival of the SS *Serpa Pinto*, stated "the youngest, Antoinette Steuer, 5, is entirely alone in the world. Her mother is thought to be either dead or to have become insane, and her father was put in the concentration camp of Dachau, Germany, in 1939 and has never been heard from since. 'Toni' has been raised almost entirely in orphanages and children's colonies. She has blond curly hair, blue eyes and is an intelligent, active and affectionate child. In her short span of years she has seen more tragedy and more horror than is right for an adult, much less a child to have experienced."[20] The next day her photo appeared in the New York newspaper *PM* and in the *Herald Tribune* as part of a story about the fifty refugee children. It is through these newspaper photos that Mrs. Moore and Toni's sisters learned of her arrival and she became part of the Moore household.[21]

Gerhard Eckmann, born on August 7, 1929, in Burgpreppach, Germany, probably had one of the saddest and most heart-rending fates of all the La Hille children. On January 13, 1939, his uncle, Isidor Ganzman, had written to the Belgian rescue committee from New York, guaranteeing "to pay for his full upkeep" if the committee would accept him in Belgium until he could help to obtain a United States immigration visa for young Gerhard.[22]

On February 22, 1939, Gerhard did arrive at Home Speyer in Anderlecht and his American uncle, Isidor, stayed in touch with the Committee. However, on September 11, 1944, he wrote anxiously to Mme Lilly Felddegen at her home on Long Island, New York: "As you know, I obtained a visa for his migration to America and also deposited $520 with the HIAS [Hebrew Immigrant Aid Society] for his passage. Apparently it was too late, as I have never heard of him anymore. Do you know anything about those Belgium [*sic*] refugee children and do you know where they are? Is there anything that could be done at the present time?"[23]

Devoted research by German librarian and historian Cordula Kappner has recreated and illuminated the tragic fate of this innocent young boy. I remember Gerhard well as one of the meeker and shy young boys at Home Speyer who fled with us to France in May 1940. Through the efforts of his New York uncle, and with assistance from Mme Felddegen, the necessary affidavit and follow-up for a US immigration visa were procured. "The Department has given advisory approval to the appropriate American Officer at Marseille, France for the issuance of an immigration visa [for Gerd Eckmann]," wrote "H. K. Travers, Chief, Visa Division, Department of State, Washington," to "Mrs. Albert Felddegen" in New York on July 24, 1942.[24] Mrs. Felddegen happily notified Gerhard's uncle.

In all likelihood Gerhard Eckmann was brought to Marseille for the usual interview and formalities at the American consulate, but fate intervened. Historian Lucien Lazare explains what happened:

> In early November 1942, 500 children, gathered in Marseille by the OSE [Oeuvre de Secours aux Enfants] with the help of the Quakers, were finally ready to leave for Lisbon on a special train. They were provided with American visas and reservations on an ocean liner from Lisbon to New York.
>
> But the exit visas promised by Laval to the American chargé d'affaires, S. Pinkney Tuck, were revoked by order of René Bousquet, the secretary general of police in Vichy. Then on November 8, the American landing in Algeria and the breaking of relations

between Vichy and Washington definitively put an end to renewed efforts for emigration.[25]

Indications are that Gerhard Eckmann was one of the children who had visas but were refused exit permits from France. Instead of returning to La Hille, Gerhard apparently was taken to the nearby refugee children's colony of Grand Rabbi Zalman Schneerson in the outskirts of Marseille. Fervently orthodox, Rabbi Schneerson gathered threatened Jewish children from French internment camps and others whose families had already been arrested and deported.

On April 3, 1941, he had first moved the children to Marseille from an isolated village in central France, later to La Vieille Chapelle just outside that city. When the Marseille police chief warned him about imminent arrests, the Rabbi moved his colony again, in mid-November 1942, to a remote rural area 100 kilometers west of Toulouse. There is evidence that Gerhard Eckmann was among the seventy children of that colony. In her book about Rabbi Schneerson's colony, French author Delphine Deroo reports that Gerhard received a T-shirt there in a package from Marseille.[26]

When friendly employees of the Préfecture of Gers warned the rabbi that they could no longer guarantee the colony's safety, it was time to move again. On June 1, 1942, the colony left for a new refuge near Grenoble, and during the following year it was moved several more times and split into smaller groups to reduce the possibility of detection. Eventually Gerhard Eckmann and sixteen other children, plus one adult woman, were housed in a tiny hamlet, named La Martellière, near Voiron, about thirty kilometers north of Grenoble. In the fall of 1943 German troops and the Gestapo replaced the Italian occupation soldiers in that area and actively hunted the Jewish victims.

When Rabbi Schneerson hurried to the isolated house in La Martellière on March 23 to again move the threatened children, the Gestapo had already arrested them. They had knocked on the door at 3:00 a.m. looking for resistance fighters. Surprised, they shouted, "Da sind doch Juden!" ("They're Jews!"). The children were imprisoned in

Grenoble for two days and then taken to Drancy near Paris. Gerhard Eckmann, now fourteen years old, and a number of the other children were sent to Auschwitz in Convoy No. 71, on April 13, 1944.[27]

German researcher Frau Cordula Kappner has faithfully investigated and documented the final months of young Gerhard's brutal treatment by the Germans. At Auschwitz he and other young prisoners were trained as bricklayers in a special vocational program in Block 13a. As the SS moved surviving prisoners westward to escape advancing Russian forces, 356 young workers of the bricklayer program were put on a train bound for the Lieberose concentration camp near Cottbus, Germany. It was November 27, 1944, and there is a list of the prisoners. Gerhard was #118055.

It is worth noting that the Allied forces had invaded Normandy six months earlier and that most of France was already liberated. A little over two months before, Gerhard's worried uncle had inquired about his whereabouts in the letter to Mme Felddegen. No one, at that time, was yet aware of the Germans' final brutalities as they moved their captives back to Germany.

Frau Kappner describes the Lieberose camp, "which was in operation until February 2, 1945, and served as a forced labor construction facility," as "the largest and most brutal of the Sachsenhausen area subcamps containing mostly Jewish prisoners." While she states that the trail of Gerhard Eckmann at Lieberose is lost between December 1944 and February 1945, she cites eyewitness accounts of the brutal machine-gunning of young prisoners by the camp's guards in the final days before liberation. "Much of this action occurred on February 3 and 4," she writes.

Gerhard's father, Leopold, died in Bavaria in February 1940. His mother, Amalia, was deported from Berlin to Riga, the capital of Latvia, on September 5, 1942. Gerhard's uncle probably never learned of young Gerhard's terrible fate, as Frau Kappner did not start her research until the 1990s. Even with a US visa already granted, there sometimes was no salvation from the Nazis' brutal persecution.[28]

In 1997 the citizens of Voiron erected a memorial to honor the child victims of the 1943 Gestapo raid. Frau Kappner has organized exhibitions and lectures about Gerhard's tragic fate in schools and libraries of Gerhard's home area in northern Bavaria.

The cooperation and courage of farmers and other residents of the Ariège region were critical for the La Hille children of all ages who chose not to flee across the closely guarded Swiss or Spanish borders. There were plenty of French Vichy "collaborators," as they were called, and often it was difficult to recognize and differentiate them from the courageous sympathizers with refugees who were opponents of the Nazis and of the Vichy regime. The older boys and girls made their own connections with such friends but others were recruited and contacted by La Hille counselors like Eugen Lyrer, Anne-Marie Im Hof-Piguet, Mlle Ott, and others of the staff.

Edgar Chaim and Werner Epstein worked on the farm of the Swiss-born Schmutz couple near Escosse where Ruth Schütz had been arrested (a walk of several hours from La Hille). Georges Herz and Gerald Kwaszkowski spent more time at nearby farms than at La Hille. Rudi Oehlbaum, Joseph Dortort, and Egon Berlin were younger teenagers who forged close friendships with nearby farmers that lasted long into the postwar years. The farm home at nearby Borde Blanque was one of these friendly places for the youngsters of La Hille.

Henri Brunel recalls that he was given a train ticket to Pau, in the southwest corner of France, where a priest placed him with farmers for whom he worked until the end of the war. "Only my will to survive enabled me to endure this period of a very difficult existence," he recalls, "for the farmer, on whom I depended, learned quickly that I was a fugitive hiding with a false ID and I was regularly threatened with denunciation if I complained about their exploitation."[29]

By 1943 several of the younger girls had reached the age of sixteen and thus became more vulnerable to arrest and deportation. On the other hand, they were by then also old enough to leave the colony and be placed with families in the area. Pierre Tisseyre recalls coming to La Hille with his father in 1943 when they fetched Frieda Rosenfeld who came to live with his family in the tiny village of Villeneuve d'Olmes, about forty kilometers away.[30] Frieda recalls staying at the farm and later moved to the nearby city of Foix where she cared for a family's little girl until 1945. She was born in Vienna in 1927, her father was imprisoned in Dachau, then had to emigrate illegally to Israel, leaving his blind wife behind. She and other family members were deported, but Frieda and her older sister and their father were reunited in Australia after the war.[31]

In some cases members of the ever more active Résistance (the French Resistance or Maquis) played a role in moving and placing La Hille youngsters into rural hideouts. Cilly Stückler, barely fourteen years old, was taken by a resistance guide to a farm near Gaillac "where I was maid, babysitter and field worker, and of course with a fake name and false ID papers. Sometime in 1944 we watched the German retreat and then another Resistance member brought me back to Toulouse to a camp of child survivors, many from La Hille. I was so happy to find my sister Gerti there among them!"[32]

Fanny Kuhlberg, just fourteen years old, was also taken away by an unidentified young woman of the Resistance:

I don't remember where she took me, but on the way she gave me a new name, Françoise Colbert. I was now an orphan from Dunkerque and was to work on a farm. But I could say nothing about my real origin. This is how I lived with a farm family of Italian origin for three months. I cooked feed for the pigs, herded a cow and babysat a small child. On Sundays I walked 6 kilometers into some woods and met Cilly Stückler who was working on a farm about 12 kilometers from mine. [This indicates that Fanny must have been in the Gaillac area, about 140 kilometers from La Hille.]

The young woman from the Resistance came to visit me now and then to check on my well-being. She also asked whether I wanted to emigrate to Palestine and I agreed because my uncle was already there, the only family member who survived. When the war ended, I came to Toulouse and there I was reunited with my sister Rita. [Rita had also been at La Hille.]

More recently I discovered that it was the French Resistance that came to my aid.[33]

Insofar as possible, the staff of the Secours Suisse wanted to keep siblings together. This is how Guy (Günther) Haas was transferred (probably in late 1941) from La Hille to the Oeuvre de Secours aux Enfants (OSE) colony at Chabannes in the isolated Creuse region, where his two sisters were living. To balance the numbers, a child from Chabannes had to move to La Hille and Frances Weinberg agreed to the change. She was offered the chance to return to Chabannes if she did not like La Hille, "but I liked it and I stayed."[34]

For Guy Haas, then twelve years old, the Chabannes colony "was great fun, lots of sports, new friends and the reunion with my two sisters."[35] When the Wehrmacht occupied Vichy France in 1942, the colony was dispersed and Guy and his sisters were placed with farm families in the Haute-Savoie alpine region. "Cows, sheep and goats were my companions for 10 months," he recalls. Later the three Haas children escaped across the Swiss border.[36]

Every one of these stories of persecution, escape, and assistance while facing the threat of severe punishment testifies to the courage of these persecuted children and teenagers and of those who helped them.

◇ 12 ◇

New Faces at La Hille

When the Secours Suisse moved the colony from Seyre to the Château de La Hille in 1941, Maurice Dubois expressed his intention to add French children to the colony, probably to gain favor with the area's population and with the local government authorities. At that time the Jewish refugee children filled the château to capacity and there was no room for others.

As many of the threatened teenagers fled and went into hiding elsewhere in 1943, newcomers were added, some French and other young Jewish children whose families hoped that they would be safer in the Swiss-managed colony. Spanish refugee children also became part of the colony, including some adult family members. Their presence changed life at La Hille and the role of counselors and teachers became more important, as most of the older teenagers who had mentored the younger children had fled. "Our colony has changed much," wrote Edith Goldapper on September 23, 1943. "There are only a few older children left. No more concerts and that is very sad. With so few older youngsters, we each have to do more work. I am busy with doing laundry and I am also the librarian."[1]

The stories of the new arrivals illustrate the constant harassment, flight, and separation from their families endured by many of these younger children. The three Weinberg siblings, Robert, age eleven, Peggy, eight, and Percy, just four years old, arrived at La Hille a short time after the Germans occupied the Vichy zone in November 1942. The Weinberg family had fled from Vienna to Athens via Italy in 1938 (see chapter 1). They had moved to Paris in September 1938 and lived in primitive surroundings with father Viktor, the former attorney for

Austrian heads of government, lucky to find a job as a steel factory worker.[2]

On October 10, 1940, they managed to escape to Marseille, the temporary refuge for many Jewish families at that time. From Marseille Viktor Weinberg fled to Spain over the Pyrénées, and then made it to Portugal. "Miraculously," recalls oldest son Robert. "This I learned only later. At that time all I knew was that my father had disappeared."[3] He adds that "parents, being cautious, never told their children anything to prevent them from innocently revealing sensitive information. The less they knew, the better."

Young Peggy and Percy Weinberg were placed at La Hille, thanks to family contacts in Marseille who knew about La Hille. In the spring of 1943, mother Margaret Weinberg narrowly escaped arrest by the Gestapo and fled with Robert to Castelnaudary. There, she accidentally encountered a resistance member who provided her with lodging and local contacts. Robert recalls visiting his siblings at La Hille in the summer and for holidays, although other sources indicate that he spent most of his time there.[4] He vividly recalls scenes of the liberation at Castelnaudary (about fifty kilometers northeast of La Hille). The family was reunited after the liberation but it had lost many relatives.[5]

Though little Peggy was reunited with her family, she was killed six years after the liberation when a truck struck her on a narrow street of Castelnaudary.[6] Two other children who arrived at the colony in early 1943 had gone through hair-raising experiences after they fled with their parents from their native Holland to the Vichy French zone in October 1942. Fred (Samuel) Weinberg and his sister Gonda (Connie), then aged twelve and ten, and their parents were caught and interned at the Rivesaltes camp, where deportations were already in full swing. (Note: this family was not related to the other Weinberg family, mentioned above.)

After she heard stories that children of mixed marriages were being freed from Rivesaltes, their mother, Esther, pretended that she was not Jewish and was able to fool the camp authorities. Another requirement for their liberation was that close relatives would care for the children. Through the Red Cross, the Weinberg parents discovered distant relatives who had fled to Ax-les-Thermes, not far from the Pyrénées. A stranger helped Gonda and Fred escape from the Rivesaltes camp and took them to the Saphier family in that city. The price: Esther Weinberg paid with her wedding ring.

As in so many cases in Vichy France that year, French police and Germans hunted for hidden Jews and regularly checked all residents for identification papers. The Saphiers decided to flee across the Pyrénées to Spain and took the Weinberg siblings with them. They were stopped and imprisoned at the border of the principality of Andorra, where France borders Spain. The family was interned, but the Weinberg siblings were sent back to the city of Foix because their documents proved that they had been released legitimately from Rivesaltes.[7]

Gonda Weinberg (Van Praag) recalls, "because we had nowhere to go, we were temporarily housed at the Foix hospital." Their parents had been transferred to the Gurs internment camp where they encountered Mlle Emma Ott of the Secours Suisse. Through her intervention the two children were accepted at La Hille after a ten-week stay at the Foix hospital. "We were very grateful to go to the colony where we met so many children even though we could hardly speak any French," says Gonda Weinberg.

Their father was deported to Majdanek in March 1943 but the mother was freed from Gurs in September and was able to survive the war, staying temporarily at La Hille and in several other hiding places. Gonda and Fred remained at La Hille until September 1944 and returned to Holland in May 1945. They discovered that only five family members had survived, while eleven had been "transported to concentration camps, never to come back."[8]

The documents and recollections of another young latecomer to La Hille shed light on life at the colony after the older boys and girls had fled. Fernand (Fedja) Nohr was brought to La Hille by his mother in December 1943 and stayed there only until the spring of 1944. He was thirteen years old and had frequently been moved from one place to another since the defeat of France. His father was a union official in pre-Nazi Germany and his mother, native of Bialystok, then a Polish city, was a dedicated Communist. In danger because of their anti-Nazi activities, the family fled to Paris in 1933. Fernand's father was interned as a foreigner in 1940 and transferred to the French army supply forces in North Africa. His mother was able to escape from the Gurs internment camp in 1940 and joined underground groups in Vichy France.

Through her resistance connections she was able to place Fernand in various children's refugee camps, first in Moissac, then to the Swiss colony at Saint-Cergues, which served as the departure point for La Hille teenagers who attempted to cross the Swiss border. Fernand too was to have been sent across the border but by that time the Swiss had closed it completely.

After the Nazi takeover of southern France in November 1942 Fernand's mother spent some time in resistance activities at Montauban and placed him at the La Hille colony. "Although it was located in a scenic and isolated area, La Hille was for me just one of the many way stations since the defeat of France. The origins of the colony, the fate of the children and the dangers confronting the older ones actually were unknown to me until 50 years later because at La Hille these things were not discussed with the younger children," Nohr recalled in 2000.[9]

> For me it was a relatively happy time in a romantic château surrounded by a beautiful landscape and, compared with conditions elsewhere, there was enough to eat and I was well taken care of. I remember how the older ones took care of us, gave us lessons and that Walter Kamlet taught me Latin. I felt that we were like one big family.[10]
>
> We did kitchen duty and we carried water from the pump in a large kettle suspended from two long poles. Most of us wore wooden shoes like the local farmers. Each weekday from 1:30 to 5:30 p.m. we had classes at the château for French, English, German, arithmetic, geography, natural science and sports. We spoke mostly French, especially since many of the young ones had forgotten their German mother tongue, as did I.

France was liberated a few months after Fernand rejoined his mother in Montauban, "and we could again take up a normal life after the period of persecution and hiding. At the end of 1945 I returned to Germany with my parents." Nohr remained and worked in the East German Republic after the war.[11]

In November 1943 Emma Ott had become the director of the La Hille colony, appointed by the Secours Suisse. She had been a nurse at the internment camps of Rivesaltes and Gurs and in charge of several Swiss nurseries in France before coming to La Hille. She directed the colony until February 1945. Sebastian Steiger continued to care for the younger children and Eugen Lyrer remained as the teacher and devoted supporter for the older ones.

Poor health forced the retirement of Maurice Dubois as the director of the Secours Suisse in France in July 1943. He was succeeded by Richard Gilg, who had been Dubois's deputy director since the previous October. Gilg would remain as Secours Suisse director in France until March 1947.[12]

The story of Josette Mendes (Zylberstein) and her brother Daniel is typical of the new younger French children's arrivals at La Hille. Their father, Marcel Mendes, had been an astronomer and university faculty member at Besançon and Bordeaux. He lost his positions under the Vichy anti-Jewish laws in 1940 and the family, including Josette and her four brothers, were forced to move repeatedly to escape detention. Eventually the parents and children moved to Toulouse where the father taught mathematics at a Catholic institution. In December 1943, with the deportations of Jews in full swing, a policeman requested that Marcel Mendes report to his office for an "identity check." Suspecting the worst, Mme Mendes pretended that her husband was ill and due to visit a doctor but that he would report the next day.

The parents decided to flee immediately and placed Josette, then just six years old, and Daniel, age five, at La Hille. The two older brothers were hidden with farmers in the Isère region by the OSE and the parents managed to escape deportation by hiding and moving repeatedly. They kept the youngest child, born in 1941. Josette remembers that "at the Toulouse train station many people were crying as they turned their children over to the Red Cross. Only later in life did I realize why they were so upset."

"My stay at La Hille was not unpleasant," Josette recalled later. "I knew that there was a war going on but did not realize that we were in trouble. 'Les grands' [the older children] went into hiding when the police came but I had no idea why they were doing this. We had a Swiss teacher but my brother, who was handicapped, did not go to school. Thanks to Mr. Steiger [the Swiss counselor for the youngest children] I learned to read, write and do arithmetic."

Her immediate family survived, but fourteen of her Bordeaux relatives were murdered during the war years. Marcel Mendes came to fetch his two children at La Hille after the area was liberated in 1944.[13] Josette recalls that she did not recognize her mother when they were reunited.[14]

Paulette Abramowicz (Erpst) was born in Paris on March 14, 1933. Her parents were of Polish origin and her three older brothers were born in Poland. All became naturalized French citizens. After the French defeat she was able to flee Paris with her mother and an aunt but they were betrayed and interned at the Nexon camp and transferred to Rivesaltes. There her mother suffered severe diabetes attacks.

At first hesitant to leave her mother, she was persuaded by the Swiss Red Cross staff to leave Rivesaltes for a Catholic orphanage. She has forgotten her transfer to La Hille on November 18, 1942, but recalls that on her arrival she received treatment because she was covered with lice. Just nine years old, she too became part of the young group under the care of Sebastian Steiger. Paulette's father was arrested in the Corrèze region but managed to escape. One brother had joined the French resistance, and another the French army. Paulette remained at La Hille until July 1944 and, fortunately, was then reunited with her parents, her brothers, and all of her cousins.[15]

Little information exists about many of the other young French arrivals who filled the empty spaces at the colony in 1943 and 1944. Who placed them with the Secours Suisse and what happened to their families is not known, but their names are remembered by some of their companions and listed in the books written by Sebastian Steiger and Anne-Marie Im Hof-Piguet. They were Renate Treisler, Monique Evrard from Nice, Eva Fernanbuk (friends of Gonda Weinberg-Van

Praag); Renée Riemann, René Baumgardt, Rachel Borensztain, Marie-Jose Chenin, Daniel Reingold, Jean Pedrini (of Italian origin); Georges and his brother Pierre Costesèque, both from Pamiers; Raoul, Guy and Mireille Perry from nearby Foix; the Detchebery brothers, Pierette Schnee, Justin Souque, little Jojo, Lucien Cruc from Boulogne, and François Clément from Toulouse.

In the summer months of 1945 just over fifty younger children were still at La Hille, the majority non-Jewish French children who had been orphaned or displaced by the war and including a smaller group of Spanish refugee children, most with their parents.[16]

Among this younger group remained Isi Bravermann (Veleris) who had come to La Hille with the liberated teenagers from the Le Vernet internment camp in September 1942. His recollections in an interview on April 1, 1994, vividly describe his life history as well as life at La Hille for the youngsters of his age group. He recalls that when he arrived in 1942, just eight years old and separated from his mother who was deported from Le Vernet,

> I was taken to the bank of a creek where my head was shaved because apparently I had lice, scabies and sores. I stayed at the château two years and we went barefoot to the local school, not accompanied by anyone. Occasionally we were sent to work on nearby farms. I was assigned to herd cows, we made hay and collected potato bugs in tin cans.
>
> At the colony we also had non-Jewish French youngsters, some of whose parents also were taken away, so they were more or less orphaned. One day I had climbed up a cherry tree with 2 little friends. Someone came to get us and said we've got to leave right away.
>
> They led us away, the two boys older than I, and me, to a convent in a small village. There we acted like Christians. Although we were not baptized, we went to mass each day, we were taught the catechism and we were told to pray. If I prayed, my mother would come back, they said. My two companions fled. After two years in the countryside on our own, the convent and the old Sisters were too much for them. They left and I never saw them again. Both were Jewish.

> One day we heard airplanes flying over the village as I was pumping water at the well. My first American came down from the sky and landed in the village. That was the liberation.[17]

After the liberation, an aunt who had survived in Belgium searched for Isi and he returned to live with her for a time. Information about his mother, who undoubtedly was deported from Le Vernet in 1942, was unavailable.[18]

As mentioned in chapter 8, the Kokotek twin sisters, Irène and Guita, were brought to "the safety of La Hille" by their mother on the day before the arrests of August 26, 1942. They had already experienced frightening persecution, "which our new friends at La Hille couldn't believe," recalls Irène. The sisters were born in Chemnitz, Germany, and the family had fled to Paris in May 1933 when they were just three years old. The father was drafted into the French army supply service and returned to Paris in March 1941. Two months later he was arrested, taken to the Beaune la Rolande internment camp and deported to Auschwitz in June 1942. "Miraculously, we escaped the Big Roundup (of Jewish families) in Paris of July 16, 1942, with our mother and fled to the unoccupied zone," Irène recalls. From August 1942 until June 1944 they remained at La Hille and became part of the new contingent of younger children.[19]

Although the Allied forces had begun to turn the tide against the Germans by early 1944, the persecution and deportation of Jews remained in full swing in France and in other Western European countries. By June 1944, at the time of the landings in Normandy, a number of the younger La Hille children were no longer safe from arrest and it was in their best interest to leave La Hille.

"One evening in May 1944 Mlle Ott, the *directrice* [director of the colony], told me to prepare a bundle of clothes and the next morning four of us left the château, namely Guita and Irène Kokotek, Eva Fernanbuk and I, Edith," remembers Edith Jankielewicz (now Esther Hocherman).[20] She continues:

> A bus took us to Pamiers and in a public park Mlle Ott turned us over to a young woman, probably a member of the resistance. Seated

on a park bench she gave us our first instructions and new names. I became 'Edith Joncquet' from Strasbourg. The four of us were taken to a Catholic orphanage operated by the Franciscan sisters [in Pamiers]. The food there was even more limited and we spent our time sewing and praying.

A few weeks later a *tante* [aunt] came to fetch Eva and me and took us to Toulouse to Mme Gisèle where we encountered Peter Bergmann and Gustave and Manfred Manasse [three of the young boys from La Hille]. [The house of Mme Gisèle was a temporary hiding place for many young people who were brought there and then moved to other locations].[21]

We were taken from there to Perpignan to two French women who accompanied us by train to the Spanish border area. In a garden that evening they whistled like birds and two Basque men appeared. They marched us all night and we slept during the next day. The following night we arrived at the place of a Spanish family. It was a dangerous mountain crossing in the area of Andorra. Eventually we reached Barcelona and came to a villa managed by Mr. and Mrs. Rabinowitz, where we received a friendly welcome. For the first time in years we could select new clothes in a big department store.[22]

The Kokotek sisters were taken to a hiding place in the remote area near Castres in the Tarn region. A Protestant pastor hid them at the Château de la Barbazanié in the tiny village of Castelnau-de-Brassac, about seventy miles east of Toulouse.

A scary incident occurred while a young woman from the French underground transferred the girls to their new hiding place. It is so typical of the La Hille children's experiences that we should experience it in the rescuer's own words:[23]

One day we learned that the colony of the Secours Suisse near Pamiers [apparently La Hille] was closing its doors to Jewish children because the threat from the [German] occupiers became too imminent. We needed to place them with non-Jewish families whom I located with assistance from my friend Jeanne Tahou. At the end of

July 1944 I accompanied 2 or 3 young teenagers from the colony of the Secours Suisse near Pamiers to farmers in the Tarn region.

At the train station in Castres, the Germans on patrol, now more suspicious than ever, gathered the travelers in the waiting room for an identity paper check. I carried a briefcase filled with false ID cards, which I was supposed to deliver. What to do with this dangerous contraband? They'll surely ask me to open it.

Without thinking I told Irène, the smallest and most vivacious: "Lie down on the bench (on the briefcase) and pretend you're asleep." The Germans probably wouldn't wake a sleeping child. It was do or die. When one of the soldiers approached the "sleeping" Irène, the other one said, "Leave her alone—you can see that she's sleeping." From the corner I watched this scene, outwardly unconcerned but trembling inside. For the first time I risked the lives of these girls and possibly of others, too."

Of all my wartime experiences, this and one other were the most dangerous and they depended truly on God's help. When I met Irène 40 years later and she reminded me of the incident, I couldn't sleep all night.[24]

The two sisters stayed at the Château de la Barbazanié until the area was liberated in late August 1944. "Fortunately we were reunited with our mother and, after a year in various children's homes, we were able to return to our dwelling in Paris and to a normal life," recalls Irène, "but without our father, aunts, uncles and our grandmother who had arrived in France when we did, but disappeared in the Nazi death camps."[25]

Peter Bergmann and the Manasse boys had also been brought to a monastery in the village of Levignac, a few miles northwest of Toulouse, at that time. Perhaps a little more enterprising than the girls, they didn't like the restrictions there and fled but were apprehended by the police and put into a youth detention facility. They managed to flee again and reached the hideout at Mme Gisèle's. Sometime later they too found their way across the Pyrénées and to safety in Spain. At the time the Manasse boys were thirteen and nine years old.[26]

Since Maurice Dubois and his wife Eleanor and Rodolfo Olgiati, the general secretary of the Secours Suisse, had begun their humanitarian activities as members of the Service Civil aiding refugees of the civil war in Spain before the defeat of France, it was quite natural that they also would assist Spanish refugees in the Vichy France colonies of the Secours Suisse.

When the La Hille colony was established in 1941, the carpenter Mr. Salvide was the first Spaniard to work with the youngsters. Starting in 1943 and until the closing of La Hille in 1947 some twenty Spanish refugees, most of them children, were added to the population. The carpenter, M. Nadal, and his wife followed Salvide and in 1943 several families with young children became part of the very mixed La Hille population.

In 1939 José and Carmen Marimon had to flee from Spain as republican refugees with their daughter Rosa, born in 1937. José Marimon had been in the textile business, but, like many thousands of their countrymen, they were interned in camps like Argelès, St. Cyprien, and Barcarès. The father managed to leave the camps by working as a farmhand and when Carmen and Rosa became ill, they found refuge at the Secours Suisse nursery at Elne.

In July 1943 the family was able to transfer to La Hille and Carmen was put in charge of the laundry. José became a gardener and Rosa was one of the youngsters under the care of Sebastian Steiger. The family remained there until the closing of La Hille after the liberation. "My early childhood was spent first [in the camps] with other Spanish refugee children and then with Jewish refugee children and with non-Jewish French children who were separated from their families," recalls Rosa Marimon (Moreau).[27]

While they were not Jewish, the Jaime Palau family of Borriol, Spain, underwent upsetting displacement and experiences similar to those of the refugees from Nazi persecution. Father Jaime fought against General Franco's forces in Spain. He urged his wife Maria to take their two young children to France where his mother was living in the Hérault Department. Together with a cousin, her two children, and the newborn Pépito, Maria Palau made her way, mostly on foot, over the Pyrénées to the French border. From there they were transported by cattle car to Rennes, in Brittany. Nine months later they managed to move in with her French mother-in-law in southern France, where husband Jaime was also able to join them. Pregnant again, Maria was invited to come to the Elne nursery in 1941 by Elisabeth Eidenbenz, a Secours Suisse nurse who brought pregnant mothers to the facility from various internment camps. In 1943 the whole family was transferred to La Hille, including father Jaime. The children quickly became part of the younger group, now of mixed nationalities, origins, and religion. "We were finally in a peaceful shelter, protected from the external events," remembers then six-year-old Conchita Palau (Romeo). "I had a Swiss teacher, Mr. Sebastian Steiger, who taught me to read, write and sing."[28]

It appears that Maria and Grégoire Villas, Sinda Losada, and the Olivo brothers were other Spanish refugee children who came to La Hille during the final year or two.

With the liberation of France the La Hille children left the colony, some to be reunited with surviving parents or relatives, others transferred temporarily to various children's homes. The colony was closed in November 1945.[29]

◇ 13 ◇

Those Who Helped
and Those Who Hindered

That twelve members of our La Hille colony (eleven children and one adult) were caught and sent to their deaths in Poland is a lamentable tragedy. On the other hand, the fact that more than 100 of the La Hille children, though persecuted and hunted, survived the savagery of the Nazis and their cohorts, is an unusually fortunate outcome for any Holocaust group. Their survival was possible only because caring human beings and organizations were willing to risk their own safety to protect and save innocent lives while the bestiality raged around them. In addition to the important task of preserving the history of the La Hille children's fates, it is compelling to illuminate the behavior and actions of those, supporting and opposing, who played a role in determining their survival.

To properly tell this story it is vital to factor in the psychological and daily life attitudes of the populations of the European countries during the time of World War II. Young Germans and Austrians and many women of both countries soon became enthusiastic participants in the Nazi agenda. Before long, any citizen who appeared to be opposed or hesitant—or who dared to remain friendly with the Nazis' declared enemies—risked being denounced by neighbors and punished severely, usually under new and discriminatory laws. Dachau and the many other newly established concentration camps became much-feared places where non-followers and perceived enemies were "concentrated" and punished.

In Vichy France (the southern zone not occupied by the Germans until November 11, 1942), the government of Maréchal Philippe Pétain and Prime Minister Pierre Laval ruled without a parliament and imposed a new patriotism and collaboration with the Germans who, it was believed, would soon rule all of Europe. Denouncing dissenters and assisting with the roundup of the Jews (whom the Pétain regime blamed for the defeat of France) became logical for at least some of the Vichy French population. To gain advantages in finding work and to advance their businesses motivated other French citizens to become collaborators.

It should be emphasized, however, that even beginning in 1940 and more so as the Allied forces began to defeat the Germans, resistance by the French population soon matched and counterbalanced the actions of those who collaborated. The children of La Hille benefitted importantly from the assistance of these rebelling French citizens, especially after 1942.

Equally important, but much different, were the attitudes and actions of Swiss leaders and citizens of that era. The decisions and actions of Swiss officials had a direct and critical influence on the fates of the children of La Hille. Priding themselves on their self-reliance and their country's historical practice of neutrality in modern European history, the Swiss authorities were, above all, determined to preserve this neutrality in order to prevent a German takeover.

The quest for normal commercial activities, as their homeland became sandwiched between German-related countries on all sides, also made it desirable to maintain favorable relations with both sides of the raging war conflict. These concerns appeared to dominate Swiss government mentality and decisions, including those of the Swiss Red Cross, which was part of the Swiss army medical system (the Secours Suisse became a subsidiary of the Red Cross in 1942). At the same time, the ordinary people of Switzerland had an enviable history of assisting needy persons abroad as well as at home and acting as a refuge and caretaker of people who required help.

So, who were the helpers and who were the "hinderers" (to use a perhaps too generous term) of the children of La Hille? As this story has already established, many individuals and organizations performed large and small deeds to support and safeguard the children of La Hille.

One result of the Kristallnacht brutalities in November 1938 was the sudden awareness of Jewish parents that their very lives were now threatened. The nationwide acts of aggression, even in small villages, persuaded caring Jewish parents to send their children away to foreign countries in order to save their lives. It is bizarre to think that, in this fashion, the Nazi thugs contributed importantly, if unintentionally, toward the survival of the La Hille children.

Belgium was the first way station of the La Hille children and that country's officials, led by Justice Minister Joseph Pholien, authorized their immigration and temporary stay. Although probably more symbolic than material, the gift of 5,000 Belgian francs from Queen Elisabeth of Belgium is an example of the attitude and cooperation of Belgian families who acted as foster parents for many of the Jewish refugee children from Germany and Austria. Their willingness to help was exceeded by the devoted members of the Belgian Comité d'Assistance aux Enfants Juifs Réfugiés (CAEJR, or the Jewish Refugee Children Help Committee), who had lobbied for the immigration of nearly 1,000 Jewish children and funded and supervised their care.

Elka and Alex Frank, the young couple in charge of the Général Bernheim girls' home at Zuen, did their best to make young children separated from their parents feel at home and played a vital role in leading the colony after the children's arrival in Seyre, France during the summer and fall of 1940. The letters written by Alex to members of the Belgian Committee from Seyre[1] underscore the hardships and desperation of the living conditions at Seyre, as well as the Franks' complete devotion to the safety and well-being of the children in their care.

Many of the La Hille survivors retain unpleasant memories of Gaspard DeWaay and his harsh-discipline personality. Yet he and his spouse, Lucienne, both not yet thirty years old, worked hard to keep order and supervise some forty boys at Home Speyer from early 1939 to May 1940. When the German army invaded Belgium, the DeWaays

(Lucienne six months pregnant with their second child) led ninety-three of us in escaping by freight train to southern France on May 14. Belgian nationals who were not Jewish, the DeWaays were not in personal danger from the Germans, yet they helped to save our lives by leading us to safety and Gaspard headed up the colony in Seyre under difficult circumstances until Alex Frank replaced him in September 1940.

After our group arrived in the hamlet of Seyre, we soon became potential targets of the anti-Semitic laws and measures enacted by the Pétain government as well as of "collaborators" who surfaced throughout Vichy France and were happy to "finger" Jewish refugees. The farm population of the area surrounding Seyre welcomed the new young residents, employed the older boys on their farms, and willingly provided scarce foodstuffs when Alex Frank came calling, although there is little to no documentation of this generosity apart from the memoirs and records of the La Hille survivors themselves.

The owner of much of the farmland surrounding our colony, Mr. Gaston de Capèle d'Hautpoul, harbored us at his large barn and in several other buildings of Seyre until the spring of 1941. As mayor of the tiny village, he probably was instrumental in accepting and protecting the Grossmann brothers, Leo and Willy, when they returned to hide and work on nearby farms in late 1942 until the liberation. Mr. de Capèle's actions risked denunciation and negative consequences at a time when the Vichy government intensified its persecution of Jewish refugees.

The benevolent attitudes of Mr. de Capèle and nearby residents were duplicated and exceeded by the population of the Ariège Department in which the Château de La Hille is located. Their involvement covered the longer period from 1941 to 1944. While government officials, the gendarmerie (local police) and the Le Vernet camp authorities continuously pursued and arrested the children as required by Vichy law and directives, many of the local population and some officials acted to support and harbor La Hille children from 1941 until the closing of the colony. This can be illustrated with specific examples.

In his report at a Secours Suisse meeting in Toulouse on February 20, 1941, La Hille staff member Max Schächtele stated that "Maurice [Dubois] had the good fortune of finding the Préfet in Foix [chief regional official] very cooperative. Besides 100 beds [real iron beds with springs] he provided us with 500 kilos of horsehair mattress stuffing, 100 straw blankets and bolsters."[2] Not mentioned is the fact that the préfet also must undoubtedly have given permission for our colony to move from Seyre to La Hille. In a report signed by Rösli Näf she states, "like other vacation colonies, the préfecture has provided us with extra ration coupons for bread, meat, sugar and fats."[3]

On December 2, 1941, a new teacher-in-training, Mr. René Vigneau, was hired at the nearby village of Montégut-Plantaurel so that nineteen of our under-fourteen-age La Hille children could get a regular education in the local school.[4] Not only did this new teacher dedicate himself to instructing the La Hille children, his daughter-in-law, Mme Annick Vigneau, has enthusiastically devoted herself to preserving the history of the colony and educating present-day students about it through her support of recent survivors' reunions and by leading the creation of a museum about the La Hille colony in the village in 2007.

In spite of these examples of tolerance and support by local and departmental authorities, they were also expected to carry out government laws and edicts, and they usually did. Thus all the La Hille children were registered and added to the lists of foreign Jewish refugees that were maintained at the préfecture in Foix. These lists were used when the forty teenagers were arrested in the summer of 1942 and also in later individual searches and arrests by local police.

An unusual example of who helped and hindered in the destiny of our La Hille colony is that of Mme Olga Authié, the cabinet secretary at the Ariège Préfecture in Foix. She was in charge of creating and maintaining the voluminous registration lists of Jewish foreigners ordered by the Vichy regime. Many of these lists[5] include all the La Hille children and are in her handwriting. Nearly all carry the heading *"rédigé par Authié"* (compiled by Authié). In some postwar comments and writings, Mme Authié is vilified as culpable and anti-Semitic. (Especially in statements by La Hille survivor Ilse Brünell Domke and in their quotation on page 340 of *Les Enfants du Château de La Hille* by Sebastian Steiger.) Like many others during that era, Mme Authié apparently played a dual role, unknown at the time. After the liberation she was honored by President Charles de Gaulle and by British and American military officials for secretly harboring resistance fighters in her attic and providing false papers for resistance fighters who were fleeing toward Spain, as well as cooperating with resistance leaders.[6]

Mme Authié later stated that she removed certain Jewish families and individuals from the deportation lists and she also protected older La Hille boys from the Vichy government's forced labor draft.[7]

Apparently Mme Authié had a behind-the-scenes friendly relationship with La Hille directrice Rösli Näf. Like other French officials of her time, Mme Authié had both an official negative role and a secret private one that only came to light after the war.

A similar mixed outcome resulted from the activities of the so-called *passeurs* (smuggler guides) whose help was essential if one wanted to flee across the Pyrénées to Spain and the Jura mountains to Switzerland. These guides took great risks since the border was closely guarded on both sides and being caught brought severe consequences. While some were paid, others were members of mountain shepherd or farm families who passed escaping refugees from one to the other up the daunting mountain paths. Alex Frank and his group, and later Ruth Schütz and her companions, received the help of such compassionate mountain dwellers. On the other hand, the passeur paid by Kurt Moser and his group delivered them to the German guards and they were arrested and deported to Auschwitz. The traitor's identity has not been established.

There were a number of local farmers and residents whose support of the La Hille children—and especially of the endangered teenagers—deserves mention and commendation. Foremost among these was the Swiss-born Schmutz family whose remotely located farm, Le Tambouret at Escosse, became a workplace and refuge for

Ruth Schütz, Edgar Chaim, and Werner Epstein. Staff members like Eugen Lyrer, Sebastian Steiger, and Margrit Tännler were welcomed as visitors.

Similarly, the farm of Mme Melanie Saurat at Borde Blanque, up the hillside from La Hille, was a workplace, home and refuge for a number of the boys, including Rudi Oehlbaum, Kurt "Onze" Klein, and others. These and other area farmers employed La Hille youngsters even though they risked criticism and retaliation for befriending young Jews. Fritz Wertheimer wrote that in September 1942 (apparently soon after their liberation from the Le Vernet internment camp) he and eleven other La Hille boys were employed by farmers for the grape harvest in the Tarn-et-Garonne Department and paid ten francs a day.[8]

After the war, and even now, many of the surviving La Hille children maintained contact with their local area French supporters and some returned regularly for visits. For Inge Berlin Vogelstein of Rochester, New York, an emotional get-together with her "farmer's daughter" Julienne (Dejean) Eychenne in 2000 brought back emotional memories of shared experiences when they were young girls. A number of the La Hille children have returned regularly to visit the Soula family, whose farmstead is located next to the château. During the war the now elderly family members had been schoolmates and playmates with the colony's younger children.

These acts of kindness and support are in stark contrast to the official policies and actions of the Vichy regime. The Pétain government not only passed hostile laws and regulations against Jewish citizens, and especially against those of foreign origin, but its leaders also enacted and announced their anti-Semitic attitudes in many other ways.

The senile Maréchal Pétain tolerated and supported the actions of his associates, and Premier Pierre Laval shamelessly bartered Jewish refugee lives for those of French Jews and non-Jewish forced laborers. Their enthusiastic collaborators were the successive commissioners-general for Jewish affairs Xavier Vallat and Darquier de Pellepoix, and national police chief René Bousquet.[9]

The prefects and other government bureaucrats, local police forces, and internment camp leaders and guards, for the most part, carried out orders handed down from their superiors. There were exceptions, but not many.

The La Hille children were, most of all, benefitting from the positive actions and protection of their Swiss caretakers, but also subject to the often negative attitudes and decisions of their superiors in Switzerland and of Swiss government leaders. It is appropriate to illuminate the starkly divergent attitudes and feelings of the Swiss caretakers and supporters versus those of the leaders of the Swiss Red Cross and the Swiss government authorities of that era. This divergence produced open conflicts and animosities and directly affected the fate of the La Hille children.

One of the little known components of this conflict is the enthusiastic and generous contribution of ordinary Swiss citizens who were recruited as our *parrains* (godparent sponsors) through the efforts of Maurice Dubois and the Toulouse office of the Secours Suisse. The dedication and actions of these *parrains* and *marraines* (male and female godparents) were the direct opposite of their country's official behavior and decisions. Virtually every La Hille child had such a sponsoring family in Switzerland.

"Meanwhile many of us now have a godfather or a godmother in Switzerland who care for us," states a letter penned by Lotte Nussbaum on January 30, 1941, to Mmes Felddegen and deBecker in the United States.[10] "Some of us have already corresponded with them by mail. Some are families, also employee groups, teachers and entire classes who write us nice letters or send packages and even money. A few days ago some 50 packages arrived, which created a lot of happiness. They were shared with everyone and we realized with how much affection they were sent to us."[11]

In addition to leaders and special heroes among the staff of the Secours Suisse in France, numerous other staff members played a vital role in the welfare and protection of the La Hille children. Among them were Renée Farny, who helped with the border crossings near Saint-Cergues, La Hille teacher and aide Henri and Annelies Kägi,

Margrit Tännler, Emma Ott (who succeeded Tännler as directrice), to name just a few of the caring Swiss staff.

Mme Germaine Hommel, directrice of the Saint-Cergues children's home, was not officially implicated in the illegal border crossings but probably played a courageous role by harboring several of the fleeing La Hille teenagers who were attempting to cross the nearby Franco-Swiss border.

Attitudes directly opposite those of the devoted Swiss staff were common among Swiss government authorities and Swiss Red Cross leaders who controlled the Secours Suisse as of January 1, 1942. The latter were usually concerned only about their own agenda and displayed little direct interest in the welfare and survival of the La Hille children. They regarded aid to the children of war-torn Europe as a positive factor that could ameliorate views on both sides of the battlefield that Switzerland merely maintained a "do-nothing neutrality," but this protective impulse did not necessarily extend to assisting Jewish children.[12]

Because the leaders of the Secours Suisse came largely from the pacifist-leaning Service Civil volunteer organization, there was mistrust and controversy from the beginning on the part of the conservative leadership of the Red Cross and the pertinent Swiss government officials. "The authorities in Bern were always suspicious of Toulouse [where the Secours Suisse leadership in Vichy France was headquartered]. The membership in the Service Civil of Maurice Dubois, my predecessor, was one of the stumbling blocks," wrote Richard Gilg to Dr. Theo Tschuy on January 27, 2003.[13]

"That Col. Remund did not trust the Service Civil is evidenced by the fact that although Mr. Olgiati was allowed to continue as general secretary [of the Secours Suisse] upon the takeover by the Swiss Red Cross in January 1942, he was forced to resign as general secretary of the Service Civil at the end of his term. The numerous Spanish [refugee] colleagues at the Toulouse office also were a 'red flag' for Bern. They considered them as Communists. The fact is that our most valuable staff member, Mr. Parera was a Socialist Party member and had to flee from [General] Franco with his family."[14]

218 | THE CHILDREN OF LA HILLE

It is thought that Rodolfo Olgiati, the Bern-based chief of the Secours Suisse and Maurice Dubois welcomed the fusion with the Swiss Red Cross because it would alleviate the existing lack of funding and increase the availability of food and other supplies.[15]

The fateful clashes between Red Cross leaders at home and key Secours Suisse staff members in France, which led to several dismissals, arose within a year of the organizations' union. Rösli Näf and Maurice Dubois, who were shocked by the August 1942 arrests of the La Hille teenagers and saved them from deportation, understood and helped their attempts to flee illegally to Switzerland and Spain at the end of that year and in early 1943.

Col. Hugo Remund, the Red Cross official in charge of the Secours Suisse, de Haller, and others in Switzerland, on the other hand, cared much less about the fate of the Jewish children than about the reaction of the Nazis. Thus, when five of the fleeing teenagers were arrested at the Franco-Swiss border in early January 1943, word reached the authorities in Bern immediately and caused a panic nearly equal to that of the fleeing youngsters. There is considerable documentation of the hurriedly convened meetings, the urgent communications between Col. Remund and Swiss Ambassador Walter Stucki in Vichy and the ambassador's interrogations of Rösli Näf, Maurice Dubois, and Mme Hommel.

After interviewing Maurice Dubois at Moillesulaz near the Franco-Swiss border on January 9, 1942, his superior, Max O. Zürcher, and R. Olgiati stated in their report of January 21, 1943:

"We attempted to explain to M. Dubois that the decisions made in Switzerland (and telegraphed to Vichy) should not be interpreted as measures against his colleagues or as definite condemnation of their actions but rather they should be understood as measures 'aimed at the outside': We wanted to have a tangible token of evidence in hand, i.e., we want to be able to explain that in advance of definite action we have launched a thorough investigation to make sure that there will be no repetition."[16]

Setting a bad precedent and upsetting the Nazi regime and the Vichy authorities, rather than the fate of the fleeing Jewish children, also were the principal worries of the Secours Suisse bosses in Bern at a meeting on January 26, 1943.[17] "Col. Remund continues to feel that Frl. [Miss] Näf, Mme Hommel and Frl. [Miss] Farny need to be removed. . . . [T]he children who were arrested by the Germans undoubtedly confessed everything. Therefore Col. Remund informed Mr. Hartmann [chief of foreign affairs of the German Red Cross in Berlin] in order to distance himself from what happened because he is certain that the news would reach Berlin."[18] "[Although] the accused persons should not be judged, as they had rendered us outstanding service, they should be dismissed, though not as punishment," stated Mr. de Haller, the Bundesrat (Swiss Council of Ministers) representative. "As to the children who succeeded in getting into Switzerland, he warned about the effect if they now would be accepted into their foster families' homes. It would result in a dangerous consequence if they would now be rewarded for their [illegal] flight."[19]

Not all participants at this meeting shared the extreme views cited here. However, the group concluded officially to remove all three of the accused Swiss staff members from their positions and to give them the choice of returning to Switzerland or change to subsidiary positions in France without management authority.[20]

In order to understand the actions and behaviors of Swiss officialdom, it is revealing to review the exchanges between Col. Remund and Ambassador Stucki, who had offered to interview Dubois, Näf, and Hommel in Vichy since the Germans had closed the Franco-Swiss border and they could not immediately return to Bern. "For someone who has learned about what happened in the past few weeks only from newspapers it is impossible to get a real understanding of the chaotic feelings and viewpoints that reign," Stucki wrote to Remund on January 13, 1943.[21]

That the Jews are especially seized by a frantic panic is a fact and is totally understandable. Therefore I can well comprehend the mentality, not to say psychosis, which has sprung up, had to occur, in our colony at the Château de la Hille. If one is aware that in the newly occupied zone of France hundreds of Aryan family heads are forcibly transported to Germany every day and that thousands of Jews disappear every day to an unknown destination, then one can understand the extreme agitation of these children.

To you I want to underscore that had Miss Näf or Mr. Dubois asked me just before Christmas, I would have had to answer truthfully that Mr. Laval [the French prime minister] is no longer in a position since November 11, 1942 [when the Germans occupied all of France], to fulfill the assurances that he had previously given us [regarding the safety of the La Hille children]. Personally I am convinced that sooner or later all of these Jewish youngsters would have fallen into German hands, or will in the future.[22]

From this and other evidence Ambassador Stucki emerges as a skilled diplomat who dutifully executed his government's policy but displayed a comprehending and moderating humanity in a time of constant turmoil and clashing viewpoints.

Rösli Näf summed it up succinctly in her recollection in 1989:[23] "There was a deep chasm between Switzerland and France, between the officials residing in a safe country and the co-workers on the firing line. In Bern they know nothing whatsoever about the real situation."

A closer look at the attitudes and actions of those who helped and those who either persecuted or remained indifferent illuminates the persistent turmoil under which the children of La Hille and, for that matter, all the intended victims of the German oppressors lived throughout the war.

◇ 14 ◇

The Heroes of La Hille

W ere it not for heroic action by several groups and many individuals, the history of the Children of La Hille would be a
relatively brief obituary of yet another group of innocent victims murdered by the Nazis during the Holocaust. This is why their story is
not complete without a detailed account of the heroes of this history.
They are reported here partly by chronology and partly by category,
rather than in any order of importance. The readers can and may draw
their own ranking, though none is needed nor desired.

Foremost among these heroes were the desperate Jewish parents
in Germany and Austria who did what even a few years earlier would
have been unthinkable—sending their young children away to a foreign country where their well-being and safety would be up to the
benevolence of strangers and where most of them did not even speak
or understand the language. In 1938–39, these parents already had
anxious forebodings that they might never see their children again.
Had they lacked the courage of sending their youngsters away, many
of the Children of La Hille would have perished with their families in
the gas chambers in Poland a few years later.

"The act of giving up one's child, of surrendering one's own
daughter or son, of recognizing that one no longer could protect and
shelter that small person to whom one had given life, was the first and
most radical step in the chain of rescue. It was a paradox: to save one's
child one had to accept that one was unable to protect and defend the
child," wrote Prof. Debórah Dwork in *Children with a Star.*[1] She concludes, "it would be a mistake to say that these people alone [persons
and organizations who accepted the children] however estimable, just,

kind, considerate, or accommodating they may have been, saved the children. It was the parents who took the first and most terrifying step of all."[2]

Crediting the La Hille children's parents above all else diminishes in no way the crucial role and contribution of their Belgian rescuers. It was the Belgian attorney and Jewish leader Max Gottschalk who initiated the creation of the Comité d'Assistance aux Enfants Juifs Réfugiés (CAEJR) in December 1938, immediately after Kristallnacht. Active since 1933 in assisting Jewish refugees from Germany, Gottschalk helped the committee members to lobby the Belgian government toward its decision to grant the refugee children a temporary stay in Belgium. After he escaped to New York City in 1940, he rendered valuable assistance to Mme Felddegen and her colleagues in procuring the guarantee from exiled Belgian prime minister Paul-Henri Spaak to allow the La Hille refugee children to return to Belgium after the war if the United States would allow them entry. His readiness to use his excellent connections in high places contributed importantly to the children's safety, though none ever knew his name or about his involvement.

Mere words cannot describe the devotion and selfless actions of the members of the Belgian women's committee (CAEJR). The value of their influence, caring involvement, and total devotion to "*nos pauvres enfants*" (our poor children), as they often referred to us, did not surface until the discovery, a few years ago, of the personal archive of Mme Lilly Felddegen and the correspondence of Marguérite (Guétia) Goldschmidt-Brodsky, leaders of the Belgian committee.

While we had been sent away by our birth parents, the women of the committee acted as though we were indeed their own children when we were in Belgium and throughout our stay in Vichy France. Besides these two leaders, the other committee members who were most active are Mme Renée deBecker-Remy and Mme Alfred Wolff.

During our stay in Belgium, the Committee women were fully occupied with raising and contributing the funds for our upkeep, finding host families for many, staffing the several boys' and girls' homes, and facilitating the safe emigration of at least several dozen children from Belgium to other countries. The women of the committee not only assured our admission to Belgium, they also guaranteed our care and maintenance, including medical and dental services, which the Belgian government had required as a condition of our admission.

When the German invasion in 1940 threatened to catch up with the children under their care, Mme Goldschmidt-Brodsky quickly returned from a visit to Paris and probably played an important role in deciding our flight to France (no direct documentation or proof has been discovered on this subject, however).

Immediately after our arrival in Seyre, France in late May 1940, Mme Felddegen and Mr. Gottschalk undertook steps with the US government from New York to try to bring all of us to the United States. Mme Goldschmidt-Brodsky, who had fled with her husband to Cahors, north of Toulouse, soon was in touch with Gaspard deWaay, the director of the colony at Seyre, and in September personally negotiated our colony's takeover by the Secours Suisse, another action that contributed directly to the survival of most of our children.

Although the effort to bring the entire colony to the United States did not succeed, Mme Felddegen continued to work day-in, day-out from the offices of the Hebrew Immigrant Aid Society (HIAS) in New York to find other means of rescuing the La Hille children. By allying herself with the leaders of a New York-based rescue committee, of which Mrs. Eleanor Roosevelt was an honorary member, she succeeded in having seventeen La Hille children included in that committee's rescue of 100 children by special permission of the US government.

Mme Felddegen continued her support and rescue efforts until nothing more could be done in 1943 and Mme Goldschmidt-Brodsky made determined efforts from Basel, Switzerland, after she and her husband had escaped there from Cahors, including requests for help from the US chargé d'affaires S. Pinkney Tuck in Vichy, whose wife she had met in Brussels, as well as with Walter H. Sholes, the US consul in Basel.[3]

While Alexander Frank played a lesser role than his wife Elka Frank (who was the directrice at the girls' home in Belgium) before we fled from Brussels, his total commitment, energy, and leadership were essential to our survival at Seyre during the fall and the severe winter of 1940. He had replaced Gaspard deWaay as leader of the colony in the summer of 1940.

Only those who endured those difficult months of shortages of food, clothing, and everything else needed by the children, as well as the illnesses and apprehensions, can comprehend the important role played by Alex Frank during that period. Describing the desperate food situation in the area's stores, he stated that "because our special efforts were successful, we have been able to provide for our children at Seyre a privileged situation[,] but I am worried about the future."[4] In the same letter he sought instructions in case the Secours Suisse decided to abandon the children or if other major problems occurred. He obviously took his responsibilities very seriously and was largely responsible for our well-being and survival from the fall of 1940 to the spring of 1941.

A separate book should be written about the stewardship, devoted management, and diplomatic skills of Maurice Dubois, the délégué (administrator) of the Secours Suisse for all of Vichy France, with headquarters in Toulouse. Ably assisted by his wife Eleanor Dubois, he had the authority for decisions regarding the colony at La Hille, appointed and supervised the staff, and provided the liaison with the often critical and disinterested authorities of the Swiss Red Cross and the Swiss government in Bern.

His diplomatic skills were valuable in that he had to deal constantly with the Vichy French bureaucracy, which was hostile to foreigners and to Jews. In the face of shortages of funds, food, clothing, and other necessities, he played the role of guardian angel for the children of La Hille and expressed his interest and concern by regular visits to Seyre and to La Hille. In August 1942 he intervened personally in Vichy and enlisted the help of the Swiss embassy to prevent the deportation of the forty teenagers and adult Jewish staff members who had been interned at Le Vernet. He literally saved their lives.

A few months later he found himself in the delicate situation of defending La Hille colony director Rösli Näf and several other colleagues, as well as his own role, because the authorities in Bern became upset over the assistance given to the older La Hille teenagers who attempted to cross illegally into Switzerland and Spain. More than any other individual, Maurice Dubois can be credited with achieving the survival of the La Hille children. It was certainly appropriate that Maurice Dubois was honored as one of the "Righteous among the Nations" at Yad Vashem in Israel in May 1995.

Equally important and praiseworthy are the actions and contributions to the children's survival of Rösli Näf, who was in charge at La Hille from the spring of 1941 until she was dismissed and left this post on May 6, 1943. She volunteered to come to France and work for the Secours Suisse and was appointed by Dubois to replace Alexander Frank primarily so that the colony would have a non-Jewish Swiss leader in dealings with hostile French authorities.

Rösli Näf accomplished these relationships with dedication and success, especially in connection with Mme Authié, the refugee lists manager of the Ariège Préfecture. Though she was not always successful in relating to the older teenagers, Rösli Näf took personal charge to protect the members of the colony when hostile gendarmes invaded La Hille and arrested forty teenagers and several Jewish staff members in August 1942. Just thirty-one years old, she joined them voluntarily at the Le Vernet internment camp and was instrumental in dealing with the authorities toward their liberation.

Totally devoted to the children, she then tried, unsuccessfully, to lobby in Bern for their admission to Switzerland. When this attempt failed, she actively assisted the older boys and girls with their plans to flee across the Swiss and Spanish borders. She provided them with maps, food, and funds and traveled to the Swiss border area when the group of five La Hille teenagers was caught as they tried to escape into Switzerland.

Her actions drew the ire and criticism of the higher-ups in Switzerland and resulted in her interrogation by Ambassador Stucki and dismissal from her post by Secours Suisse chief Colonel Remund. Rösli Näf was directly responsible or related to the rescue of almost thirty of the La Hille boys and girls who escaped across the borders in 1942–43, not to mention the safekeeping and hiding of many of the younger children who had remained at La Hille. Castigated and humiliated for her heroic actions at that time by her Swiss superiors (but not by Dubois or Ambassador Stucki), Rösli Näf, too, was appropriately designated as "Righteous among the Nations" at Yad Vashem on May 7, 1989.

Anne-Marie Im Hof-Piguet is another of the Swiss La Hille caretakers who was honored at Yad Vashem (on July 16, 1990), and rightly so. Only twenty-seven years old when she arrived at La Hille on May 6, 1943, her independent, almost rebellious spirit caused her to disregard the Swiss authorities' prohibitions against helping our children to escape. Her determination and courageous actions saved several of the La Hille colony members from the escalating Nazi persecution. Daringly, she first guided Addi Nussbaum across the Swiss border near her father's home area. She played a role in the illegal Swiss border crossing of Edith Moser and Manfred Kamlet, and then accompanied Edith Goldapper and later Walter Kamlet and Flora Schlesinger and her son Paul on their difficult journeys to safety.

It was Anne-Marie who made the connection with the Cordier sisters, who guided a number of the La Hille refugees across the Swiss border. It is noteworthy that most of her rescue operations were carried out after her Swiss superiors had issued a strong edict that specifically prohibited such actions by the Secours Suisse staff members.

Another, perhaps more "laid-back," Swiss hero of La Hille was Eugen Lyrer. Functioning as teacher of the middle and older children, he contributed immeasurably to the educational and cultural advancement of his charges. They recall that he exposed them to European literature and led extended discussions, all during an epoch when they were unable to receive regular formal schooling.

Eugen Lyrer also played an important role by misleading and misinforming the frequent police patrols who came looking for La Hille teenagers. When particular fleeing teenagers were secretly leaving La Hille in the middle of the night, Eugen Lyrer would accompany them for several miles through the countryside to help assure a safe start of

35. Toni Steuer at Seyre (late 1940) in front of powdered milk barrel provided by the Secours Suisse. From the author's personal collection.

their hazardous journey. Many of the older colony members remember him fondly as a solid and valued supporter and protector.

The same can be said of Sebastian Steiger, another young Swiss counselor/teacher who was fully occupied, between 1943 and 1944, with caring for the youngest boys and girls. He not only conducted classes for these children, he also was in charge of their recreation activities, took care of frequent medical and psychological problems and, in short, was truly a substitute parent, which was a special need of the younger children. Many of them remained closely related to him in later life. Steiger also was honored at Yad Vashem for his actions in 1993 and is described as "more than a teacher" in a Swiss anthology of Yad Vashem honorees.[5] Steiger and Im Hof-Piguet both have written very useful books recounting their recollections as La Hille staff members.

A listing of the Swiss "heroes" of La Hille must include Gret Tobler, who accompanied Inge Bernhard and Toni Rosenblatt to safety in Switzerland under dangerous circumstances, Margrit Tän-nler who helped bring Inge Joseph across the Swiss border, and Emma Ott, who, as director of the colony, had to navigate carefully between the German-French persecutors and her Swiss superiors' instructions of strict neutrality during the colony's final year.

Although they played a lesser role, Henri ("Heiri") and Anneliese Kägi also served loyally as teacher and caretaker, respectively. Their wedding near La Hille in March 1944 was a special occasion for the younger children.

Outstanding among the French persons who played an important role in the survival of the La Hille people is Victoria Cordier, the courageous then twenty-four-year-old activist of the resistance move-ment. Connected to La Hille through Anne-Marie Im Hof-Piguet, whose home area is not far across the Swiss border from Victoria's mother's home, the young Frenchwoman guided nine members of the colony across the heavily guarded border cliff near her mother's isolated house in the hilly Jura mountain area north of Geneva.

With assistance from her sisters Madeleine and Marie-Aimée, Vic-toria Cordier led the following La Hille refugees across the dangerous border, with great risk to her own life and in very difficult terrain: Addi Nussbaum, Inge Joseph, Edith Moser, Manfred Kamlet, Edith Goldapper, Inge Schragenheim, Walter Kamlet, and Flora Schlesinger and her son Paul. Her rescues took place over a period of months while she did the same for dozens of others fleeing from the Nazis and French police. She also acted as information courier for French and Swiss intelligence organizations. Victoria Cordier is another of the La Hille heroes who was honored as one of the "Righteous among the Nations." She recorded her actions in the publication "Ce que je n'oublierai jamais . . ." (I shall never forget this . . .).[6]

After all is said and done, by far the most noteworthy "heroes of La Hille" are the teenagers and children of the colony themselves. In the history of the Holocaust few examples exceed their survival instinct, their endurance, and the gritty determination to escape and survive in the face of the ever mounting threats and danger under which they had to live.

The prime example of their spirit and determination is the story of the four teenagers, each about sixteen years old, who joined the Franc-Tireurs et Partisans (FTP) French resistance forces in the late spring of 1944. Georges Herz, Egon Berlin, Joseph Dortort, and Kurt "Onze" Klein had recently left the château to establish themselves in a hideout in the countryside not far from La Hille in order to escape the repeated searches by the police authorities.

An Alsatian named Schnee engaged them to cut trees in the nearby woods. When German forces killed several young Maquis resistance fighters and civilians in an engagement near Vira (about twenty-five kilometers east of La Hille) on June 9, 1944, word of the tragedy spread and reached the La Hille youngsters in their hideout. Egon Berlin is said to have exclaimed, "If we don't act, who will? Let's go fight the Germans, let's join the Maquis. . . ."[7]

Egon, Kurt, and Joseph contacted their friend Rudi Oehlbaum at a nearby farm and headed in the direction of Vira. At first they fell into the hands of Spanish guerilla fighters, but then were accepted by "Daniel," a French Maquis leader. They were now ready to fight the French *milice* (Vichy militia) and the German occupation troops.

"Onze" was seventeen, and the other three were each just sixteen years old. Their French Maquis fellow fighters, for the most part, were under twenty years old and their objective was to waylay and harass German troops and French militia soldiers in preparation for the expected Allied landings on the Mediterranean coast. They had to adopt new names, in case they were captured.

Egon Berlin became "Paul Berdin" and soon was nicknamed "Petit Paul."[8] He was one of the youngest *maquisards* (Maquis members) of their group. Capturing arms, providing food for the group, committing sabotage, and punishing French collaborators were their main activities.

On July 1, almost a month after the June 6 invasion in Normandy, the group of young fighters moved into the hilly area near the hamlet of Roquefixade, about thirteen kilometers east of Foix. Five days later French militia forces arrived in the area to hunt down the partisans. In the ensuing battle on the hillside, seventeen of the young fighters were killed, including the sixteen-year-old Egon Berlin of La Hille. A monument on the site draws veterans for a commemoration service every year. Egon Berlin is buried beneath a monument to the fallen in the cemetery at Pamiers, along with several of the other victims.[9] In March 2003 the entrance hall of a Pamiers high school in the Ariège region was named "Salle Egon Berlin" in his honor.[10]

"Onze" Klein was taken prisoner by French police forces during this battle and detained in Toulouse until liberation. Joseph Dortort and Rudi Oehlbaum were able to escape and Rudi later joined the French Foreign Legion.

At least six members of the La Hille population became allied soldiers and thus were able to participate in the efforts to defeat their German persecutors—another remarkable aspect of the colony which is unusual in the history of the Holocaust, especially regarding teenagers.

36. Three of the La Hille sixteen-year-olds who joined the Maquis Resistance fighters in 1944. From left: Rudi Oehlbaum, Egon Berlin, and Joseph Dortort. Egon was killed in a battle near Roquefixade at age sixteen. From the author's personal collection.

Former colony director Alexander Frank and his wife Elka, who had escaped across the Spanish border in 1943, managed to reach England in September of that year. "There I was transferred to the Belgian military authorities and volunteered to be an air gunner in the Royal Air Force," he recalled in a letter written in 1997. "In the last month of the war I was posted to participate in operations over Germany. Our planes were USA-made 'Mitchells.' Until February 1946 I was stationed with the RAF [Royal Air Force] near Osnabrück [Germany]."[11]

Joseph Dortort, the teenage member of the Maquis, participated in the liberation of Foix and Pamiers, the main towns in the region near La Hille. "By the end of 1944 we were asked to sign up [with the French army] for the duration or go home," he recalls.

"After training on the Riviera, equipped with American arms, we were part of the First French Army that had come out of North Africa. Then we went to Alsace, Germany and finally Austria, where I found myself in Kitzbühel, mainly translating. By October 1945 all foreigners were discharged."[12]

Lucien Wolfgang was another La Hille teenager who became an allied soldier at age eighteen. He had fled on foot across the Pyrénées in 1942 and arrived in Casablanca with 1,000 other refugees from France. He volunteered for the Free French Army that landed in southern France jointly with the American forces in September 1944. As a tank driver in the 5th French Armored Division, he participated in the liberation of numerous cities, including Marseille, Avignon, Lyon, Belfort, Colmar, Stuttgart, Singen, and, finally Sigmaringen in the Alpine foothills. After the German defeat he was part of the French military government in Vienna, where he was reunited with his mother.[13]

Edgar Chaim had worked on farms near La Hille even before the August 1942 arrests and continued that activity after he and the other thirty-nine teenagers were freed from Le Vernet. In January 1945 he joined the French 11th Infantry regiment and, after training near Dijon, was assigned to the 4th Moroccan Division. When the Germans surrendered in May 1945, his unit had advanced to Bregenz on Lake Constance. Until 1947 he served with the French occupation forces in the Austrian cities of Bregenz and Innsbruck. During a furlough in France he was able to bring La Hille friend Cilly Stückler back to Vienna to reunite her with her mother. Chaim returned to France when he was discharged in February 1947.[14]

Still named Werner Rindsberg, I was able to emigrate from La Hille to New York in the summer of 1941, was drafted into the US Army at age nineteen in 1943, became a US citizen that year and changed my name to Walter Reed. I was shipped to England in early 1944 and landed at Utah Beach one week after the Normandy invasion.

Later I was transferred, as a German prisoner interrogator, to the 95th Infantry Division, which advanced from Metz, France, to Belgium and Germany. After the German defeat I served as a counter-intelligence agent with the US military government, assigned to help with the denazification of local governments and the faculty of Marburg University. I served in the US Army for three years and became a staff sergeant.

Three other La Hille teenagers distinguished themselves in the dangerous activities of the resistance, foremost among them Ruth Schütz (Usrad). The others so engaged were Heinz (Chaim) Storosum and Peter Landesmann, who received high commendations for his actions after the German defeat.

The ranks of the La Hille colony heroes include all of the teenagers (and three adults) who made their way across the closely guarded borders of Switzerland and Spain under the most trying circumstances, risking their lives and their safety in order to seize the alternative to an even worse outcome—probable shipment to the gas chambers in Poland.

Those who escaped to Switzerland include: Almuth Königshöfer, Lotte Nussbaum, Peter Salz, Regina Rosenblatt, Margot Kern, Jacques Roth, Hans Garfunkel, Leo Lewin, Else Rosenblatt, Ruth Klonower, Ilse Wulff, Betty Schütz, Addi Nussbaum, Edith Moser, Manfred Kamlet, Edith Goldapper, Inge Schragenheim, Inge Joseph, Inge Bernhard, Toni Rosenblatt, Walter Kamlet, and Mme Flora Schlesinger and her son Paul.

Those who crossed the Pyrénées into Spain include: Lucien Wolfgang, Norbert Stückler, Alex and Elka Frank, Inge Berlin, Ruth Schütz, Ilse Brünell, Heinz Storosum, Eva Fernanbuk, Edith Jankielewicz, Gustave and Fred Manasse, and Peter Bergmann.

Except for the eleven boys and girls and Ernst Schlesinger who were caught, deported and murdered, all of the other original members of the colony succeeded in hiding and surviving either at La Hille or in different sections of Vichy France. Among these were Friedl Steinberg, Ruth Herz, Henri Brunell, Rita Leistner, Lixie Grabkowicz, Cilly Stückler, Gerti Lind, Georges Herz, Gerard Kwaczkowski, Frieda Rosenfeld, Gertrude Dessauer, Fanny and Rita Kuhlberg, Henri Vos, and Leo and Willy Grossmann.

One would expect that the liberation of the Ariège was cause for celebration. Unfortunately the final stage of the Château de La Hille was marred by tragedy. The successor of Emma Ott, a Mr. Claude, was using the Croix Rouge (Swiss Red Cross) truck to transport supplies from Pamiers to La Hille and had taken some of the children with him. Apparently overloaded, the old vehicle overturned in the village and Mr. Claude and Jaime Palau, the Spanish refugee and father of several of the La Hille children, were killed.

That all but twelve of the La Hille children and staff were able to escape the persecution by the Nazis and the Vichy French government is probably unique in the annals of the Holocaust. This outcome required true heroism among the rescuers and supporters, as well as among the girls and boys of La Hille themselves.

◇ 15 ◇

After the Liberation

Although the gradual liberation of European countries brought relief and joy to the local population of each area retaken from the Nazis, the massive destruction caused by the military actions, the displacement of people, and the utter shortages of the necessities of life created havoc everywhere and for a long time after the hostilities had ended. Many displaced persons camps were filled to capacity with survivors who had no place to go.[1]

By the time the Germans surrendered in May 1945, the children of La Hille also were scattered in many places and countries. Altogether twenty-three boys and girls had reached the United States by 1943 and were placed with relatives or foster families in different locations. The majority of us never saw our parents again, though some went to live with siblings and other relatives.

A large contingent of those who crossed the border illegally had been interned by Switzerland and now had to contemplate where to turn for their future. Some were able to rediscover a parent or relatives in England and in the United States but many would soon find out that their loved ones had been murdered in the death camps. For many the logical place for relocation was Palestine, which soon would be embroiled in the war for independence and become the homeland which many of the young refugees of La Hille would then help to build. Palestine already had been the destination for some who had illegally fled across the Pyrénées to Spain in 1943 and 1944. A number of others eventually found their way to Paris, with some reuniting there and staying for a time, and others moving on—literally—across the world.

Here is an account of the postwar readjustment and experiences of at least some of the La Hille colony girls and boys:

The most painful experiences of those who survived were suffered by Werner Epstein who was deported to Auschwitz from Drancy near Paris as a nineteen-year-old and was subjected to horrendous treatment and situations. He survived a westbound death march and was freed by the pursuing Soviet forces in January 1945, followed by a three-month stay in Russia.

The news of Werner's survival spread quickly and Peter Salz (who had escaped to Switzerland) reported to Alex Frank, "I would like to share wonderful news with you. Werner E. [Epstein] has written from Poland to Mr. Schmutz [the farmer at Escosse where Epstein had worked]. He is safe and sound and will return as soon as possible."[2] By July 1945, Epstein managed to get back to Paris and was reunited with his favorite La Hille companion, Gertie Lind. They were married there five months later and lived in Paris until 1963.[3] Friedl Steinberg was an official witness at the ceremony which was attended by several other La Hille friends.[4] In 1963 the Epstein family emigrated to California, supported by an immigration affidavit provided by Edith Moser of La Hille, who had married and then also lived in California.

Friedl Steinberg witnessed the departure of the German forces in Lyon and participated in the care and rehabilitation of displaced persons there, including children. While accompanying a group of these children to Paris, she chanced upon several La Hille companions. "The paths of the La Hillers always had a way to cross!!" she recalls.[5] Among these were Edgar Chaim, still a French soldier, Peter Landesmann, Lucien Wolfgang, and Gertie Lind's sister, Cilly Stückler.

About that time, Friedl rediscovered her older sister who had survived internment in Belgium. "My only dream was to see her again, her being, with me, the only survivor of my family. I succeeded to smuggle myself into Belgium. My sister urged me to return for good and that's what I did in the end."[6]

The dilemma facing the uprooted young La Hille survivors is poignantly described by Lotte Nussbaum in a letter to Alex Frank:[7] "As a stateless person [all Jews had lost their German citizenship], I now need to decide where I want to go. Definitely I am not interested in learning Russian. It goes against my grain, as does any negotiating with the Americans. [A devoted Communist, Alex Frank was at that time returning to live in the new East Germany.] I have decided to definitely not accept the US affidavit."

"The decision is agonizing for me. Addi [her younger brother] and my relatives want me to join them in America. My conscience and the crying needs for help are calling me to serve humanity in Europe."[8]

In fact, Lotte Nussbaum underwent training for social work in Zurich and then worked with refugee children and persons with disabilities. After two years' further training and study in Basel and London to prepare for social work in Africa, Lotte spent seven months in Lisbon to learn to speak Portuguese. Then followed twenty years in Angola where she founded and directed a school for native girls. Shaken by the 1967 Six-Day War in Israel, she felt compelled to return to her "Jewishness," moved to Israel, and devoted her life to the rehabilitation and vocational training of blind persons.[9]

Among others who became citizens of Israel, Else Rosenblatt had obtained her nursing education in Neuchâtel and Geneva, then practiced the nursing profession in a kibbutz and later in hospitals and as a nursing teacher in Israel. Her sister Regina moved from Switzerland to Paris. She was incapacitated by a tragic 1975 automobile accident. Another sister, Toni Rosenblatt, remained in Switzerland. Ruth, the youngest of the four sisters, had stayed in Belgium and then returned to her parents in Germany where all were deported and murdered.[10]

Fanny Kuhlberg returned to Toulouse when the hostilities ended and was reunited there with her sister Rita. "Later I learned that this reunion was brought about by the French resistance organization. We spent the time from early 1945 to September in a girls' home in St. Cloud, near Paris, where we underwent training and arrived in Palestine on a British transport ship."[11]

After fleeing to Spain in the summer of 1944 at age thirteen, Edith Jankielewicz (Esther Hocherman) was able to leave for Palestine in November. Edith lived on a Kibbutz and attended an agricultural training school. Later she served in the Israeli army. Beginning at age thirty-two, she pursued a career as a tourist guide.[12]

Margot Kern, who had fled to Switzerland, first was assigned to a refugee labor camp. With help from Rösli Näf, who had by then returned to Switzerland, Margot found work at a children's refugee camp, where her friend Else Rosenblatt was also employed. "We stayed there until the war's end in 1945. Having no news whatsoever about my parents, I decided to leave Europe and join my relatives in Palestine. I was in the Kibbutz Sdot Jam and during the War of Independence in 1948 I served in the Palmach [the Jewish liberation army]." Later Margot became a book editor and translator.[13]

Peter Salz is another La Hille youngster who had escaped to Switzerland and decided to start a new life in Palestine. After internment he lived with his Swiss godparents for two years and completed his high school education. After a year of university study in Geneva, Peter also made the move to Palestine—as an army volunteer. During eighteen months of service he participated in battles on the road to Jerusalem and in the Negev area. After demobilization he began life at the northern area Kibbutz Lehavoth Habashan where Ruth Schütz and Peter's future wife, Marion, were already settled.[14]

Ruth Schütz, who had fled across the Pyrénées to Spain, was able to board a ship to Palestine in Cadiz in November 1944 and, because of her German origin, was promptly put into an internment camp by the British authorities. In 1945 she became a founder of the Kibbutz Lehavoth Habashan in the Galilee region where she would live and raise a family.[15]

While many of the La Hille children emigrated to Palestine, others were scattered in many countries. Ruth's sister Betty Schütz was able to leave Switzerland to join their mother in England. "My objective was to learn the language as quickly as possible, to learn a profession and to be able to assist my mother," she recalls. "I became a secretary and occasionally did French translations. Beginning in 1948 I worked for various Jewish organizations and that is where I met my future husband."[16]

After the liberation in 1944, Cilly Stückler was brought from her rural hideout to a displaced Jewish children's camp in Toulouse. "To my great joy my sister Gerti was also there and so were some other La Hille friends. Some time later we were taken to various children's homes in Paris which were funded by the American Joint [Distribution Committee]." In late 1945, La Hille friend Edgar Chaim, who was then a French soldier on leave, brought Cilly home to Vienna where she was reunited with her mother. For many years she worked as a secretary in Vienna's French embassy.[17]

Jacques Roth also was one of several who, having escaped to Switzerland, moved to Paris in the postwar years. He wanted to study medicine and did night work to earn money, helping the "American Joint" organization to process refugees. Lack of money forced him to abandon his medical studies and he then worked full time doing communications work for the Marshall Plan and then for UNESCO. Later he had a successful career in advertising and went on to write novels. In the 1990's Roth was instrumental in proposing Maurice Dubois and Rösli Näf for the "Righteous among the Nations" designation by Yad Vashem.[18]

Inge Schragenheim had to make two attempts to arrive illegally in Switzerland (she was turned back the first time). There she was reunited with her mother and did office work in Montreux until 1945. After the German defeat, both moved to Italy and Inge worked for the United Nations Relief and Rehabilitation Administration (UNRRA) and for the Allied Control Commission (ACC). There she met her future husband, a Polish soldier attached to the British forces. She followed him, as did her mother, when he was transferred to England in September 1946.[19]

Ruth Herz, using false identity papers, had survived the war as a caretaker at a Secours Suisse children's home in Savoy, and later near Castres, close to Toulouse. When this home was closed in 1947, she was transferred to another children's home in Pau, near the Pyrénées. Through Alex Frank she was connected with relatives in England and, through them, with others in New York. The latter provided the needed affidavit and she was able to emigrate to New York in late

1947. She earned a degree in nursing and practiced that profession in New York area hospitals for thirty years.[20]

After the German defeat, Edith Goldapper, who had fled to Switzerland, discovered that one uncle in Vienna and an aunt in Italy were her family's only suvivors. From 1947 until 1953 she found work in Zurich. In 1953 the Bulova Watch Company was providing the needed affidavits for European refugees to come to the United States and Edith was one of these immigrants. In New York she worked for a rare stamp dealer and then as bookkeeper for a branch of the Israeli Bank Hapoalim, where she stayed twenty-six years. In 1982 Edith and her husband moved to Florida.[21]

After internment and then schooling in Switzerland, Hans Garfunkel migrated to Sao Paulo, Brazil in October 1947 where he worked as a translator. One year later he came to the United States and pursued a career as an executive in the steel industry. In 1948 he married Ilse Wulff, one of the La Hille companions who had also fled to Switzerland.[22]

Leo Lewin was another La Hille teenager who left Switzerland for South America after the war. His parents had emigrated to Buenos Aires from Berlin in 1941 and Leo was able to join his mother there in 1948 (his father had died there in 1944). In Argentina Leo conducted a wood products import business and married Renée, who had also escaped from a French children's home to Switzerland and then emigrated to Argentina.[23]

Addi Nussbaum also was interned after he crossed illegally into Switzerland in October 1943, but then was able to begin university studies in mathematics. In February 1947 he obtained a US immigration visa, continued his studies to earn a PhD at Columbia University, and then launched an academic career that included work at the Princeton University's Institute for Advanced Study and long-time tenure at Washington University in St. Louis, Missouri.

Hanni Schlimmer was among those who could leave Vichy France in 1941. Because her parents were able to emigrate from Berlin in May 1941, she joined them in Spain for the crossing to New York. Unfortunately her father was infected with typhus on the ship and died soon after their arrival in New York. She worked while finishing high school and married in 1947, moving with her husband to northern California a year later. In 1979 she earned a master's degree in science literature and worked as a teacher and translator. From 1957 to 1961 her husband's career caused them to live in Paris.[24]

Several of the younger children who were brought to the United States in 1941 through the efforts of Mme Felddegen quickly lost contact with each other and with their erstwhile companions of La Hille for many years.

The Findling brothers were placed with families and pursued law degrees. At least one also remained in touch with Max Krolik because both lived in the Detroit area. Krolik's sister Rosa studied nursing and practiced that profession, living in the Philadelphia area.

Herbert Kammer, who was placed in a Milwaukee children's home, was reunited with his mother in April 1948 when she arrived in Milwaukee from England. She was able to ecape from their native Vienna to England and worked there in a dress factory. Her husband, Georg, and young son Herbert escaped to Belgium. The father was deported from France and murdered.[25]

Herbert Kammer earned a PhD in bacteriology from the University of Wisconsin and in a twenty-four-year career with United Vaccines, Inc. developed specialized vaccines for fur animals.[26]

Alfred Eschwege, another of the younger La Hille boys who arrived in the United States in the summer of 1941, survived traumatic stays in several foster homes, eventually joined the US Army, and later became a machinist. He raised a family on Long Island, New York.

Over the five decades after World War II a number of the former La Hille teenagers stayed in touch and developed lifelong bonds even though they lived in different parts of the world and were busy with careers or raising families. As they became older, had more leisure time, and were financially secure, they organized a number of reunions. The first took place at the Kibbutz Lehavoth Habashan in Israel in May 1985, with participants coming from Israel, Europe, and the United States. Ruth Schütz Usrad and Peter Salz were living there, so it was a logical site.

Another get-together was arranged by Alex Frank June 1–4, 1993, in Seyre and at the Ariège Department sites related to the colony when a West German television network wanted to film a story about the La Hille colony. Thirteen of the colony survivors participated, as did Rösli Näf, Anne-Marie Im Hof-Piguet, and Sebastian Steiger.[27]

The next gathering, in Chicago in mid-July 1998, brought together a dozen of the La Hille survivors and their family members from the United States and Alex Frank, who came from Berlin. He would die of cancer at age eighty-four later that year. Still fit and eager to reminisce, he proclaimed that "once you were my children, but now you are my brothers and sisters." The reunion was filmed by the Discovery Channel cable system and broadcast repeatedly in North American cities.

At this gathering, as at the next one, several of the participants who were only eight to eleven years old during World War II had little recollection of the Belgian and French sites or of their refugee companions. Thus the experience literally helped them to recreate a time of their youth that had become mysterious or largely blurred. "Considering I started off knowing no one until less than a year ago," wrote Alfred Eschwege, "if it weren't for this Reunion in Chicago, I would never have met anyone from our original children's group again. I would not have found out more about my past. I would not have gotten any photos of my brother, Heinz. I also found out (for the first time) that my brother Heinz was put to death just months before his camp was liberated by the allies."[28]

My wife, Jeanne and I had organized the Chicago reunion and there were enthusiastic requests for a repeat. This took place at the original sites in southern France in September 2000. This time thirty of the then known fifty-five survivors came from all over the world with family members and were joined with enthusiastic participation by local French citizens, school children, and government represen-tatives. A memorial plaque and stone were unveiled on the grounds of the Château de La Hille and visits included all the relevant sites, such as the barn at Seyre, the monument at Roquefixade, the Pamiers cemetery, and the memorial deportation rail car near the Le Vernet internment camp. The group was also welcomed at the city hall of Toulouse.

Zvi Paz (originally Henri Vos) was deeply touched by his participation, as were his wife and family members. Only six years old when he arrived in Brussels, he had been searching for his past without success when I rediscovered him in Israel in 1999 during preparations for the reunion of 2000. "It hasn't been easy for a 67-year-old man to relive childhood experiences, which to him were partly unknown until now," commented his wife Rivka Paz. "It was difficult for Zvi," she added, "to hear the stories of fellow travelers and the traumatic events of the long days and nights that occurred those many years ago. No less difficult was it to attempt to learn of the fate of a long-lost brother who was swallowed up in the tragic events of those terrible years." (Zvi's brother, Manfred Vos, was caught at the Swiss border with Inge Helft and Dela Hochberger and all were murdered at Auschwitz in early 1943.)[29]

"Zvi has raised a family who had no knowledge of their father's childhood and family. Now with the gaps of this saga filled in, it is having a profound effect not only on us, but also on our children and grandchildren," Rivka added.[30] No words could better describe the harm and trauma inflicted upon innocent children by the Nazi hoodlums, trauma that for many would last for a lifetime.

Another smaller survivor reunion, but with extensive community and school participation, was held in connection with the inauguration of a museum about the Children of La Hille at the library of the nearby village of Montégut-Plantaurel in June 2007.

Even sixty-five years later the experiences that the Children of La Hille were forced to endure as targets of the Nazis' anti-Semitic murder machine have marked their lives and influenced their attitudes and behaviors. These experiences also forged a lifelong bond which still binds many of the survivors in friendship and meaningful recollection today. "Basically, ever since Seyre and La Hille I have remained a *chef de groupe* [a group leader]!" wrote Lotte Nussbaum. "Our communal life of those war years and the support of the Swiss Red Cross and its staff members will always remain unforgettable."[31]

Joseph and Martin Findling remembered the positive influence of their teacher, Irène Frank: "Our parents were not there. The responsibility for the two younger brothers fell on Joe [Joseph Findling]. But he was still a child himself. Irène Frank had a strong influence on us because she motivated us to always reach for educational advancement. Each of us did well. We have achieved success in our professions and with our families and we are sharing this history with our children."[32]

Similarly, Hanni Schlimmer Schild wrote, "About those who, unfortunately, perished in such tragic circumstances I think with great sadness and about those of you who survive with a warm heart and great nostalgia. Those years of 1939–1941 certainly were the most impressive and moving years of my whole life."[33]

And Henri Brunel wrote, "These experiences have enabled me to maintain the will and the hope for a better life and to eventually reach the feeling of happiness of which I was so cruelly deprived during those six years."[34]

Betty Schütz Bloom sums it up as follows: "When I now think back from time to time to the years at La Hille, I think less of all that bothered me so much at the time (especially the cold and the lice), than of the camaraderie and of the readiness to help each other on the part of both the older and the younger ones, and especially of the music, the history and literature thanks to Blibla [Irène Frank's nickname] and the many great books (thanks to Mr. Lyrer) which helped to broaden my horizon—and which helped me to overcome all else— but 'topinambour' [Jerusalem artichokes], I cannot eat even today!"[35]

Acknowledgments

◇

Appendix

◇

Historical Timeline

◇

Notes

◇

Index

Acknowledgments

The content of this book is based on a veritable treasury of original letters, documents, diaries, private archives, reports, and citations from professional historical publications gathered on-site in Belgium, Germany, France, Switzerland, and the United States, with virtually no recourse to present-day reminiscences or survivor interviews. The majority of these records and materials are written in French and German and were translated by the author.

Deep gratitude is due to many individuals and institutions through whose willing assistance and cooperation illuminating and much previously unknown information was discovered. It has made this book and the pleasure of working on it far more meaningful than I expected when the project began in 2004.

Several sources and collaborators stand out among these: Foremost, the ideas and inspiration of the late Dr. Theo Tschuy who conceived and intended to write this book. The many footnotes crediting the material that he discovered and deposited at the Archiv für Zeitgeschichte, Eidgenössische Technische Hochschule Zürich (ETH) Zentrum, Zurich, are testimony to his skills and dedication. Through them he lives in this history.

Special thanks are due to his widow, Ruth Tschuy, and her family for permitting full access and use of his research, and to Dr. Uriel Gast and the staff at ETH in Zurich for their assistance. Credit is due also to the late Dr. Ben Nachman of Omaha for originating the author's connection with Dr. Tschuy.

The rich and factual documentation of this story would be impossible without the discovery of the personal archive and papers of Mme

Lilly Felddegen, the outstanding heroine of this history. Because her granddaughter Susan Johnson provided this hitherto unknown collection of more than 1,000 letters and reports—including copies of virtually every letter her grandmother wrote or received—and authorized their utilization, the authenticity of this story was enriched beyond measure. Thanks are due to Valery Bazarov of the New York Hebrew Immigrant Aid Society (HIAS) staff for bringing us together and for assisting with the research at the YIVO Institute for Jewish Research in New York.

In addition to these two most important collections, many must be mentioned and recognized with sincere gratitude. Readers will appreciate the rich drama and feeling of the quotations from the autobiography of Ruth Schütz Usrad's *Entrapped Adolescence*; the personal diaries of Edith Goldapper Rosenthal; of Irène Frank, provided by David Gumpert; of Kurt Moser, graciously furnished by his brother-in-law, Warren Lefort; of Edith Moser; and of Gret Tobler, provided by her niece Ursula Cummins; the life story of Helga Schwarz Assier, "Le prix de la vie"; and the collection of reminiscences of the erstwhile Secours Suisse staff members provided by the late Richard Gilg.

The vivid recollections and documents of Frieda Steinberg Urman and her willingness to share them, as well as the treasure trove of documents about Peter Landesmann, shared by his grandson Damien Landesmann Bouché, are gratefully acknowledged. All are invaluable first-hand threads woven through this historical carpet and add immeasurably to its texture and dimension.

Many others deserve and are owed sincere expression of appreciation. Because there are so many, it is best to offer these attributions in chronological and geographic sequence. In Belgium the excellent "Mémoire" study of the Belgian Committee by Simon Collignon provided inspiration and further sources of information, augmented by Simon's assistance at the Université Libre de Bruxelles Jewish History Department archive, and also the guidance of Prof. Jean-Philippe Schreiber of that department.

Pierre Goldschmidt and his family members graciously pursued and made available the correspondence of his grandmother, Mme

Goldschmidt-Brodsky, thereby providing valuable insight and under-standing of her dedication and vital role in the children's survival in France.

The late Mr. Gaston de Capèle d'Hautpoul shared valued input about the colony at Seyre, as did his son-in-law René de LaPortalière, especially about the history of Seyre and of that village's "arsenal" building.

Special thanks are due Regina Illmann and Vera Friedländer, who permitted the study and copying of the meaningful personal archive left in their care by Alexandre Frank (now deposited at the United States Holocaust Memorial Museum in Washington, DC). His volu-minous correspondence from Seyre and other papers provide a reveal-ing insight beyond the recollections of the colony members.

The extensive examination of the attitudes and behind-the-scenes interactions of the Swiss authorities, the Swiss Red Cross, and the Secours Suisse personalities, as revealed in *Eine andere Schweiz* by Antonia Schmidlin, and in "Croix-Rouge Suisse, Secours aux Enfants en France 1942–1945, (sa formation, son activité, ses relations avec le Gouvernement Suisse, son rôle)," by Esther Schärer, were crucial to the evaluation and description of how the actions of Swiss officials influenced the fate of the children. Dr. Ruth Fivaz-Silbermann also made available useful information in that regard.

Special thanks are due Mme Christine Rouaix of the departmen-tal archives of the Ariège Préfecture in Foix for her invaluable assis-tance in procuring extensive documentation about wartime Vichy government regulations and the "dossiers" concerning the La Hille children. Additional documents retrieved from these archives and furnished by the dedicated La Hille survivor Rosa Marimon Moreau added insight and valuable information, especially about the Spanish refugee children.

The devotion and emotional caring of Ariège area residents and officials have earned our special gratitude and affection. In addition to the indefatigable La Hille colony history "guardian" Mme Annick Vigneau, who is the Montégut-Plantaurel community's sparkplug behind the village's recently opened La Hille colony museum, special thanks are due to Jean-Jacques Pétris for his valuable assistance at the Foix archives and for making the connection with Mme Lucette (Authié) Franco. To Mme Franco thanks are due for shedding light on the official and clandestine wartime roles played by her late mother as cabinet secretary of the Ariège Préfecture.

At the Mémorial de la Shoah Museum in Paris, Mmes Diane Afoumado and Lior Smadja provided access to and advice about useful material from their Holocaust archive.

The devoted work accomplished by Frau Cordula Kappner to retrace the disappearance and heartbreaking fate of Gerhard Eckmann and her willingness to share the results deserve recognition and special thanks.

The vast archive of the United States Holocaust Memorial Museum yielded insightful information about the actual involvement and role of the American Friends Service Committee (Quakers) and transcripts of the Swiss border interrogations of many La Hille children who escaped across the Franco-Swiss border, plus other valuable information. The expertise and friendly guidance of Peter Lande, Genya Markon, Judith Cohen, and other United States Holocaust Memorial Museum staff members are remembered with profound gratitude.

The enthusiastic support and services of the very competent professional staff members of Syracuse University Press and the thorough professional input of copy editor Bruce Volbeda have earned my sincere appreciation and respect. They have contributed importantly to the completion of my undertaking.

To all who helped with information and encouragement well-deserved thanks are due. There are so many that all are not named individually. Above all, however, loving thanks are due to my wife, Jeanne Dupuis Reed, for her unselfish patience with the process, her continuous encouragement, and her valuable assistance and support every step of the way.

List of Twelve Who Were Deported and Murdered

Eleven La Hille teenagers and one adult were arrested, deported to Poland, and murdered. They are remembered with sadness and with love:

Karl-Heinz Blumenfeld, age nineteen, Transport No. 57 to Auschwitz, July 18, 1943.

Émile Dortort, eighteen, Transport No. 51 to Majdanek, March 6, 1943.

Gerhard Eckmann, fourteen, Transport No. 71 to Auschwitz, April 13, 1944. (Gerhard survived Auschwitz but was murdered in Germany in early 1945.)

Berthold Elkan, twenty, Transport No. 51 to Majdanek, March 6, 1943.

Inge Helft, sixteen, Transport No. 46 to Auschwitz, February 9, 1943.

Dela Hochberger, sixteen, Transport No. 46 to Auschwitz, February 9, 1943.

Kurt Moser, twenty-two, Transport No. 57 to Auschwitz, July 18, 1943.

Ernst Schlesinger, forty-six, Transport No. 50 to Majdanek, March 4, 1943.

Walter Strauss, eighteen, Transport No. 50 to Majdanek, March 4, 1943.

Manfred Vos, eighteen, Transport No. 46 to Auschwitz, February 9, 1943.

Fritz Wertheimer, nineteen, Transport No. 57 to Auschwitz, July 18, 1943.

Norbert Winter, nineteen, Transport No. 51 to Majdanek, March 6, 1943.

Historical Timeline

January 30, 1933	The Nazi party comes to power in Germany
March 12, 1938	Germany takes over Austria
Nov. 9/10, 1938	The Kristallnacht Pogrom in Germany and Austria
December 1938	Formation of the CAEJR Belgian Rescue Committee
June 15, 1939	Last group of children arrives in Brussels
September 1, 1939	Germany invades Poland; start of World War II
May 10, 1940	Germany invades Belgium, Holland, France, and Luxembourg
May 14, 1940	The La Hille children flee to France
June 22, 1940	France signs armistice with Germany
September 1,1940	Alex Frank replaces Gaspard DeWaay as Seyre colony director
October 1, 1940	Secours Suisse aux Enfants assumes responsibility for the Seyre colony
October 3, 1940	The Vichy government issues the Statut des Juifs (definition of who is a Jew)
February 12, 1941	Advance work group of teenagers arrives at Château de La Hille
May 6, 1941	Rösli Näf arrives at Seyre
June 1, 1941	Main group of children moves to La Hille
June 22, 1941	Germany invades Russia
Summer of 1941	Two children's groups, totaling seventeen La Hille youngsters, are brought to the United States
January 20, 1942	Wannsee Conference, near Berlin, finalizes plans for mass murder of European Jews

August 26, 1942	French gendarmes arrest and intern forty La Hille teenagers and several adults at Le Vernet for deportation
September 2, 1942	La Hille teenagers and adults are liberated from Le Vernet
September 12, 1942	Almuth Königshöfer is first La Hille teenager to cross the Swiss border illegally
November 8, 1942	US troops invade North Africa
November 11, 1942	Germans occupy Vichy France unoccupied zone
Late December to Early January 1943	Numerous La Hille teenagers attempt illegal flight to Switzerland and Spain
January 2, 1943	Group of five La Hille teenagers arrested near Swiss border
May 6, 1943	Rösli Näf leaves La Hille
June 6, 1944	Allies invade Normandy
July 6, 1944	Egon Berlin is killed in the battle at Roquefixade
May 7, 1945	Germany surrenders

Notes

Prologue

1. Leopold Tauber, letter to Comité d'Assistance aux Enfants Juifs Réfugiés (CAEJR), 23 December 1938, CAEJR files, Centre National des Hautes Études Juives (CNHEJ), Université Libre de Bruxelles, Brussels, passage translated from German by Walter Reed (all subsequent translations also by Reed, unless indicated otherwise).

2. Ruth Strauss, letter to Comité d'Assistance aux Enfants Juifs Réfugiés (CAEJR), 8 March 1939, CAEJR files, Centre National des Hautes Études Juives (CNHEJ), Université Libre de Bruxelles, Brussels, passage translated from German by Walter Reed.

1. Please Take My Children

1. Lucy S. Dawidowicz, *The War against the Jews 1933–1945* (New York: Bantam, 1975), 51–52.

2. Ibid., 58–59.

3. Ruth Herz Goldschmidt, autobiography, Dr. Theo Tschuy archive, Archiv für Zeitgeschichte (AFZ), Eidgenössische Technische Hochschule Zürich Zentrum, Zurich.

4. Ruth Schütz Usrad, *Entrapped Adolescence* [in Hebrew: "Neurim be-malkodet"] (Tel Aviv: Miśrad ha-biṭaḥon, 1997), 7, this passage and all subsequent quotations translated by Brenda Weitzberg.

5. Ibid.

6. Helga Schwarz Assier, *Le Prix de la Vie* [The Value of My Life] (unpublished autobiography), courtesy of Helga Schwarz Assier, passage translated by Walter W. Reed.

7. Robert Weinberg, letter of family's history written to Emilie Pin, 16–17 March 2002, Tschuy archive, AFZ, translated by Walter Reed.

8. Jean-Percy Weinberg, interview by the author, September 27, 2003 in Annecy, France.

9. Schütz Usrad, *Entrapped Adolescence*, 13.

10. Dawidowicz, *The War against the Jews 1933–1945*, 97.

11. Ibid., 97–98.

12. Ibid.

13. Inge Berlin Vogelstein, e-mail message to the author, 30 March 2003.

14. Inge Berlin, statement by Inge Berlin, Alex Frank archive, United States Holocaust Memorial Museum, Washington, DC, translated from German by Walter Reed.

15. Dawidowicz, *The War against the Jews 1933–1945*, 100–103.

16. Ibid., 102.

2. Refuge in Belgium, 1938–1940

1. Julie Rosenthal, handwritten letter in German with photo of smiling girl (age approx. five years old) to Belgian Comité d'Assistance aux Enfants Juifs Réfugiés (CAEJR), 3 December 1938, CAEJR archive, Centre National des Hautes Études Juives (CNHEJ), Brussels, translated by Walter Reed (unless indicated otherwise, all translations from any source are by Walter Reed).

2. Arnold Schelansky, letter to CAEJR, 19 December 1938, CNHEJ archive, Brussels, translated by Walter Reed.

3. Iakar Reiter, letter to CAEJR, 16 March 1939, CNHEJ archive, Brussels, translated by Walter Reed.

4. Jean-Philippe Schreiber, *Dictionnaire biographique des Juifs de Belgique: Figures du judaïsme belge XIXe–XXe siècles* (Brussels: Editions De Boeck Université, 2002), 139–40.

5. Ibid., 132.

6. Rosemarie Cosmann file, 7 December 1938, Sureté Publique record 37 C I/3: "The Government has authorized, awaiting their emigration, the entry and temporary stay in Belgium of 250 Jewish children from Germany"; Justice Minister Joseph Pholien, letter to Prime Minister Paul-Henri Spaak, 11 January 1939, E61, 214, p. 2, Archive of the Office of Queen Elisabeth, Archives of the Royal Palace, Brussels.

7. Correspondence, CAEJR archive, CNHEJ, Brussels.

8. Joseph Pholien, "Pholien to Spaak," 11 January 1939, E61, 214, p. 2, Archive of the Office of Queen Elisabeth, Archives of the Royal Palace, Brussels.

9. "Liste des Enfants Prévus Pour le Prochain Transport le 15 Juin 1939," CNHEJ archive, Brussels.

10. CAEJR, report to Lilly Felddegen signed by CAEJR Brussels staff members, 10 December 1939, Felddegen private archive, United States Holocaust Memorial Museum (USHMM), translated by Walter Reed.

11. List of the June 15 Transport, Felddegen private archive, USHMM, translated by Walter Reed.

12. Joseph Pholien, letter from Justice Minister Joseph Pholien to Prime Minister Paul-Henri Spaak, 9 January 1939, 219, Archive of the Office of Queen Elisabeth, Archives of the Royal Palace, Brussels.

13. Joseph Pholien, letter from Justice Minister Joseph Pholien to Prime Minister Paul-Henri Spaak, 11 January 1939, E61, 214, p. 2, Archive of the Office of Queen Elisabeth, Archives of the Royal Palace, Brussels.

14. Ibid.

15. Ilse Wulff Garfunkel, e-mail message to Theo Tschuy, 10 July 2003, Dr. Theo Tschuy archive, Archiv für Zeitgeschichte (AFZ), Eidgenössische Technische Hochschule Zürich Zentrum, Zurich.

16. Susie Davids Shipman, letter to the author, 10 October 2006.

17. Handwritten transcript [in French] of Channel 34 German TV documentary interview in France with Lucien Wolfgang during first La Hille reunion, 1993, Alex Frank archive, USHMM, translated by Walter Reed.

18. Undated interview of hidden children in Palm Beach County, FL, furnished by Herbert Kammer to the author.

19. Friedl Steinberg Urman, e-mail message to the author, 30 May 2005.

20. Lilly Felddegen, letter to A. Willis, 7 February 1941, Felddegen archive, USHMM.

21. Fanny Findling Labin, e-mail messages to the author, September 2007; Joseph Findling, conversation with the author, 29 February 2008.

22. Alfred Manasse, letters to CAEJR, 5 May 1939 and 22 June 1939, Felddegen archive, USHMM; Fred Manasse, affidavit, 26 December 1944, YIVO Institute for Jewish Research archives, New York.

23. Letters, 20 April 1941, 22 May 1941, Felddegen archive; Steinhardt Family History, 1 October 1972, provided by descendant Marc Zaller; American Friends Service Committee immigration documents for Jules and Kurt Steinhardt, 5 May 1941, YIVO Institute for Jewish Research archives, New York.

24. Edith Goldapper Rosenthal, unpublished private diary, translated from German by Walter Reed, 3–6.

25. Alix Grabkowicz Kowler, letter to the author, 28 June 2005.

26. Werner Epstein, personal biography furnished to the author via letter, summer 2005.

27. Inge Joseph Bleier and David E. Gumpert, *Inge: A Girl's Journey through Nazi Europe* (Grand Rapids, MI: William B. Eerdmans, 2004), 23.

28. Ruth Schütz Usrad, *Entrapped Adolescence* [in Hebrew: "Neurim be-malkodet"] (Tel Aviv: Miśrad ha-biṭaḥon, 1997), 23–26, passage translated by Brenda Weitzberg.

29. Henri Brunel, response to questionnaire from Dr. Theo Tschuy, 10 July 2003, Tschuy archive, AFZ.

30. From the author's Dinslaken visit and interviews with Dinslaken Stadtarchiv staff members. In 1993, the citizens of Dinslaken erected a memorial sculpture of the hay wagon by sculptor Alfred Grimm.

31. Inge Berlin Vogelstein, e-mail messages to the author, 16 December 2003, 26 March 2006, and 27 March 2006.

32. Betty Garfinkels, *Belgique, terre d'accueil: problème du refugié 1933–1940* (Brussels: Editions Labor, 1974), 178.

33. CAEJR, committee report, 31 March 1940, Felddegen private archive, USHMM.

34. Simon Collignon, "Le Comité d'Assistance aux Enfants Juifs Réfugiés: les homes Général Bernheim et Herbert Speyer, Bruxelles, 1938-1940" (thesis, Université Libre de Bruxelles, Faculté de Philosophie et Lettres, 2004), 54–55; Marguérite Goldschmidt-Brodsky, letter to Queen Elisabeth, 13 May 1939, copy in the author's files.

35. Ibid., 57–58.

36. Ibid., 9 April 1940, Felddegen private archive, USHMM.

37. CAEJR, report to Lilly Felddegen in New York, 10 December 1939, Felddegen archive, USHMM.

38. Helga Schwarz Assier, "Le prix de la vie," unpublished private autobiography, 7–8, translated from French by Walter Reed.

39. Collignon, "Le Comité d'Assistance," 61, translated from French by Walter Reed.

40. Various letters in Felddegen archive, USHMM.

41. Various letters, Foyer des Orphelins archives, Brussels, furnished to the author.

42. Gen. Bernheim (1861–1931) was a Belgian officer and funds were contributed to the establishment of the home by the Bernheim department store family. See also Collignon, "Le Comité d'Assistance," 66.

43. Collignon, "Le Comité d'Assistance," 63–64.

44. Various letters, Foyer des Orphelins archives, Brussels; Frida Ajzenberg, telephone conversation with the author, February 2008. Ajzenberg survived the war at the Foyer.

45. Alex Frank, letter to the author, 18 October 1997.

46. Employment contract and records, Foyer des Orphelins archive, Brussels; Collignon, "Le Comité d'Assistance," 83–84.

47. DeWaay employment documents, Foyer des Orphelins archives, Brussels.

48. Jean-Philippe Schreiber, "L'accueil des réfugiés juifs du Reich en Belgique, mars 1933–septembre 1939: le Comité d'Aide et d'Assistance aux Victimes de l'Antisémitisme en Allemagne," *Les Cahiers de la Mémoire Contemporaine* 3 (2001): 26–28.

49. CAEJR, report to Lilly Felddegen in New York, 25 October 1939, 2, Felddegen archive, USHMM.

50. Letters from and to Willy B. Cox Therapy Office and (CAEJR) committee members Renée deBecker and Louise Wolff, 22 July 1939, 24 July 1939, 21 September 1939, 22 September 1939, and 29 November 1939, CNHEJ archive, translated by Walter Reed.

51. Handwritten transcript [in French] of Channel 34 German TV documentary interview in France with Lucien Wolfgang during first La Hille reunion, 1993, Alex Frank archive, USHMM, translated by Walter Reed.

52. Ruth Herz Goldschmidt, autobiography, provided to Theo Tschuy in 2003, Tchuy Archive, AFZ.

53. Author's recollection.

54. CAEJR, staff report to Lilly Felddegen in New York, 10 December 1939, Felddegen archive, USHMM, translated from German by Walter Reed.

55. CAEJR, staff letter to Lilly Felddegen in New York, 14 February 1940, 1, Felddegen archive, USHMM.

56. CAEJR, letter to Lilly Felddegen, 10 December 1939, Felddegen archive.

57. Collignon, "Le Comité d'Assistance," 84–85.

58. CAEJR, letter to Auswanderungsabteilung, der Israelitischen Religionsgemeinde Leipzig, 8 June 1939, CAEJR archive at CNHEJ.

59. Undated list of names and countries, Felddegen archive, USHMM.

60. CAEJR, various committee lists, CAEJR archive, CNHEJ; and Felddegen archive, USHMM.

61. Ibid.

62. Susie Davids Shipman, letter to the author, 10 October 2006.

3. Second Escape, May 14, 1940

1. Ruth Schütz Usrad, *Entrapped Adolescence* [in Hebrew: "Neurim be-malkodet"] (Tel Aviv: Miśrad ha-biṭaḥon, 1997), 33, passage translated by Brenda Weitzberg.

2. Edith Goldapper Rosenthal, private diary, 22–23, passage translated by Walter Reed.

3. *Le Soir*, 12 May 1940, front page story, translated by Walter Reed.

4. Michael R. Marrus and Robert O. Paxton, *Vichy France and the Jews* (New York: Basic, 1981), 15.

5. Comment by Ruth Herz Goldschmidt to the author regarding herself and Trude Dessauer; Inge Berlin Vogelstein also joined her brother Egon of Home Speyer.

6. Edith Kurzweil, *Full Circle: A Memoir* (New Brunswick, NJ: Transaction, 2007), 39–41.

7. Louise Wolff, interview conducted by Jacques Déon, "Enfants réfugiés 1938–1940," Fondation de la Mémoire Contemporaine de Bruxelles series, "CNHEJ Histoire Orale des Juifs en Belgique," Brussels (1980–1981), Dr. Theo Tschuy archive, Archiv für Zeitgeschichte (AFZ), Eidgenössische Technische Hochschule Zürich Zentrum, Zurich, translated from French by Walter Reed.

8. Gaspard DeWaay, letter to Foyer des Orphelins General Secretary DeGronckel, 23 July 1940, in Foyer des Orphelins archive, Brussels, translated by Walter Reed.

9. Marguérite Goldschmidt-Brodsky, letter to Lilly Felddegen, 14 November 1939, Felddegen archive, United States Holocaust Memorial Museum (USHMM), Washington, DC.

10. Marguérite Goldschmidt-Brodsky, letter to Joint Distribution Committee (the "Joint"), New York, 16 July 1940, JDC–AR 33/44 #450, Joint archive, New York.

11. Ibid.

12. Goldapper Rosenthal, private diary, 24.

13. Ibid.

14. Schütz Usrad, *Entrapped Adolescence*, 34.

15. Alphonse Danis, "Seyre de l'ancien régime à nos jours" [Seyre from the old days until now], April 1995, 16 and 96, (an unpublished history of the Village of Seyre graciously furnished to the author by René de LaPortalière), translated by Walter Reed.

16. Gaston de Capèle d'Hautpoul, interview with the author in Seyre, France, 1997; René de LaPortalière (the owner's son-in-law), e-mail message to the author, 26 October 2005, and conversations with the author, 2007.

17. Ibid.

18. Jean Estèbe, *Toulouse 1940–1944* (Paris: Librairie Académique Perrin, 1966), 12.

19. Rodolfo Olgiati, "Bericht des Sekretärs über seine Informationsreise nach dem unbesetzten Frankreich 16. bis 28. Juli 1940" [Report of the Secretary about his research trip to unoccupied France, July 16–28, 1940], 2, Olgiati private archive, Social Service Library, Zurich.

20. Annie Charnay, "Rapport de police du 6 juin 1940, 1960/88," *Annales du Midi* 104, no. 199–200 (July–December 1992): 483–99, Archive of the Department of Haute-Garonne, Toulouse, France.

4. Life at Seyre, 1940

1. Herman Dons (Foyer des Orphelins president), employment letter to Gaspard DeWaay, 20 January 1939, Foyer des Orphelins archives, Brussels.

2. Ruth Schütz Usrad, *Entrapped Adolescence* [in Hebrew: "Neurim be-malkodet"] (Tel Aviv: Miśrad ha-biṭaḥon, 1997), 37, all passages translated by Brenda Weitzberg.

3. Rodolfo Olgiati, "Bericht des Sekretärs über seine Informationsreise nach dem unbesetzten Frankreich 16. bis 28. Juli 1940" [Report of the Secretary about his research trip to unoccupied France, July 16–28, 1940], 3, Olgiati private archive, Social Service Library, Zurich.

4. Marguérite Goldschmidt-Brodsky, letter to Joint Distribution Committee of New York (often abbreviated "the Joint"), 16 July 1940, Joint archive, JDC-AR 33/44 #450; Marguérite Goldschmidt, letter to Lilly Felddegen, 14 November 1939, Goldschmidt private archive.

5. Edith Ditta Weisz Kurzweil, letter to parents, 26 July 1940, Kurzweil private records, translated from French by Walter Reed.

6. Michael R. Marrus and Robert O. Paxton, *Vichy France and the Jews* (New York: Basic, 1981), xii.

7. Jean Estèbe, *Les Juifs à Toulouse et en Midi toulousain au temps de Vichy* (Toulouse, France: Presses Universitaires du Mirail, 1996), 52–53; Marrus and Paxton, *Vichy France and the Jews*, 4.

8. Lucienne DeWaay, interview by Dr. Theo Tschuy, Waterloo, Belgium, 11 May 2003, cited in e-mail message from Dr. Theo Tschuy to Walter Reed, 19 May 2003.

9. Belgian Red Cross, minutes of meetings at Cahors chaired by Alfred Goldschmidt, summer/fall 1940, Belgian Red Cross archives, Malines, Belgium.

10. Marguérite Goldschmidt-Brodsky, general employer commendation letter written at Cahors, 4 September 1940, archives of the Musée Juif de Belgique, Brussels (letter may have been donated by Lucienne DeWaay in the 1990s).

11. Werner Rindsberg (Walter Reed), letter to Marguérite Goldschmidt-Brodsky, 26 July 1940, files of the Secours Suisse, J2.15 (-) 1969/7, Boîte 320–22, 97 C.1, Archives Fédérales Suisses, Berne, Switzerland.

12. Alex Frank, interview by Marion Rager, "Alltag und Widerstand im NS-Regime-Erinnerungen Berliner Antifaschisten," 23 March 1998, 2–3, Alex Frank archive, United States Holocaust Memorial Museum (USHMM), Washington, DC.

13. Lotte Nussbaum, letter to Lilly Felddegen, from Seyre, France, 18 December 1940, Felddegen private archive, USHMM, translated by Walter Reed.

14. Ibid.

15. Inge Berlin Vogelstein biography, Alex Frank private archive, USHMM.

16. Irène Frank, private diary, 71, translated from German by Walter Reed.

17. Ruth Herz Goldschmidt, letter to Regina Illmann, 18 February 2002, Alex Frank private archive, USHMM.

18. Werner Epstein, personal autobiography, 2, furnished to author; Alex Frank, letter to Lilly Felddegen, 30 January 1941, Felddegen private archive, USHMM; Alex Frank, letter to Renée deBecker, 26 October 1940, Felddegen private archive, USHMM; Alex Frank, letter to Marguérite Goldschmidt-Brodsky, 26 September

1941, Goldschmidt-Brodsky private archive; Alex Frank, interview by Marion Rager, 8, Alex Frank private archive, USHMM.

19. Alex Frank, letter to Renée deBecker, 26 October 1940, 1, Alex Frank private archive, USHMM.

20. Ibid.

21. Ibid.

22. Ibid.

5. The "Secours Suisse aux Enfants" and a Tough Winter

1. The German name was "Schweizerische Arbeitsgemeinschaft für kriegsgeschädigte Kinder," or "SAK."

2. Secours Suisse, meeting minutes, 23 September 1940, Felddegen private archive, United States Holocaust Memorial Museum (USHMM), Washington DC.

3. Marguérite Goldschmidt-Brodsky, letter to American Joint Distribution Committee (often abbreviated "the Joint"), New York, 16 July 1940, Joint archive, JDC—AR 33/44, no. 450.

4. Joseph J. Schwartz, letter to Max Gottschalk, 19 October 1940, Lisbon, Portugal, Felddegen private archive, USHMM.

5. Maurice Dubois, letter to Lilly Felddegen, 19 March 1941, 2, Felddegen private archive, USHMM.

6. Antonia Schmidlin, *Eine andere Schweiz: Helferinnen, Kriegskinder und humanitäre Politik (1933–1942)* (Zurich: Chronos Verlag, 1999), 149.

7. Renée deBecker, letter to Marguérite Goldschmidt-Brodsky, 2 December 1940, 1–2, Goldschmidt private archive.

8. Alex Frank, letter to Renée deBecker in New York, 26 October 1940, Felddegen private archive, USHMM.

9. Schmidlin, *Eine andere Schweiz*, 146.

10. Ibid.

11. Author's recollection and Irène Frank private diary, 53, translated from German by Walter Reed.

12. Irène Frank, private diary, 57, translation by Walter Reed.

13. Ibid., 58.

14. Inge Berlin Vogelstein, e-mail message to the author, 6 August 2007.

15. Edith Weisz Kurzweil, letter to the author, 8 January 2006; John Weiss, letter to the author, 6 February 2006.

16. Helga Schwarz Assier, "Le prix de la vie," (unpublished autobiography), 6.

17. Ibid., 9.

18. Ibid., 14.

19. Ibid.

20. Maurice Dubois, letter to Marguérite Goldschmidt-Brodsky in Basel, 21 October 1941, Goldschmidt-Brodsky archive.

21. Manfred Tidor, e-mail message to the author, 16 November 2007.

22. Alex Frank, letter to Renée deBecker and Lilly Felddegen, 30 January 1941, Felddegen private archive, USHMM.

23. Ruth Schütz Usrad, *Entrapped Adolescence* [in Hebrew: "Neurim be-mal-kodet"] (Tel Aviv: Miśrad ha-biṭaḥon, 1997), 40, all passages translated by Brenda Weitzberg.

24. Ibid.

25. Irène Frank, private diary, 57.

26. Schütz Usrad, *Entrapped Adolescence*, 35.

27. Alex Frank, letter to Renée deBecker, Lilly Felddegen, and Max Gottschalk, 3 November 1940, Felddegen private archive, USHMM.

28. Alex Frank, letter to Lilly Felddegen, 24 February 1941, Felddegen private archive, USHMM.

29. Alex Frank, letter to Lilly Felddegen, 30 January 1941, Felddegen private archive, USHMM, translated from French by Walter Reed.

30. Schütz Usrad, *Entrapped Adolescence*, 35–36.

31. Inge Berlin Vogelstein, autobiography, Alex Frank private archive, USHMM.

32. Inge Berlin Vogelstein, letter to the author, 16 November 1998.

33. Herbert Kammer, handwritten letter to his father, Georg Kammer, at Camp Recebedou near Toulouse, 2 March 1941, Herbert Kammer private records, translated from German by Walter Reed.

34. Georg Kammer, letters dated 2 March and 30 May 1941 to Herbert Kammer, Herbert Kammer private records.

35. Irène Frank, private diary, 69–70, passage translated by Walter Reed.

36. Ibid., 70–71.

37. Ibid., 71.

38. Maurice Dubois, memorandum, 27 December 1940, Dubois private archive, La Chaux-de-Fonds, Switzerland, copied by Dr. Theo Tschuy upon examining the original document, copy archived at Dr. Theo Tschuy archive, Archiv für Zeitge-schichte (AFZ), Eidgenössische Technische Hochschule Zürich Zentrum, Zurich, translated by Walter Reed.

39. Ibid.

40. Rodolfo Olgiati, General Secretary of the Cartel Suisse de Secours aux Enfants Victimes de la Guerre, "Rapport du Secrétaire sur son second voyage en France" [Report of the Secretary regarding his second trip to France], 22 February 1941, 12, Olgiati archive, Social Service Library, Zurich, translated by Walter Reed.

41. Ibid.

42. Alex Frank, letter to Renée deBecker and Lilly Felddegen, 30 January 1941, Felddegen private archive, USHMM, translated by Walter Reed.

43. Ibid.

44. Elka Frank, "Globke, Kinder klagen Dich an!" [Globke, Children Accuse You], "Für's Wochenende" [For the Weekend] section, *Freiheit* (newspaper published in Halle a. d. Saale, Germany), 20 July 1963, 11, translated from German by Walter Reed. This article takes up a full feature page and shows photographs of four La Hille teenagers who were deported and murdered.

6. The Belgian Angels' Rescue Effort from across the Atlantic

1. Evident from various letters and reports in Felddegen private archive, United States Holocaust Memorial Museum (USHMM), Washington, DC.

2. Based on information gathered by the author from various historians' reports about the "Kindertransports" to England. See, for example, Holocaust Education and Archive Research Team (HEART), "The Kindertransports," http://www.holocaust researchproject.org/holoprelude/kindertransport.html; Debórah Dwork, *Children with a Star—Jewish Youth in Nazi Europe* (New Haven, CT: 1993); and archives of the United States Holocaust Memorial Museum (USHMM), Washington, DC.

3. Max Gottschalk, letter to Monsieur le Ministre Paul-Henri Spaak, London, 3 December 1940, Felddegen private archive, USHMM.

4. Count van der Straten-Ponthoz (Belgian ambassador in Washington), letter to Max Gottschalk, 19 February 1941, copy of letter in Felddegen private archive, USHMM.

5. Max Gottschalk, letter to Ambassador Count van der Straten-Ponthoz, 24 February 1941, copy in Felddegen private archive, USHMM.

6. US State Department, unsigned copy of letter from US State Department to Belgian Ambassador Count van der Straten-Ponthoz, 31 March 1941, copy in Felddegen private archive, USHMM.

7. Lilly Felddegen, letter to Marguérite Goldschmidt-Brodsky, 5 December 1940, Felddegen private archive, USHMM.

8. Ibid.

9. Lilly Felddegen, letter to Maurice and Eleanor Dubois, 26 February 1941, Felddegen private archive, USHMM.

10. David S. Wyman, *The Abandonment of the Jews: America and the Holocaust, 1941–1945* (New York: Pantheon, 1984), 124.

11. Ibid., 124–25.

12. Valery Bazarov, "Out of the Trap: HIAS French files," *Avotaynu* 21, no. 3 (Fall 2005): 18–19.

13. Wyman, *The Abandonment of the Jews*, 191.

14. Lilly Felddegen, letter to Marguérite Goldschmidt-Brodsky in Basel, 17 March 1941, Felddegen private archive, USHMM.

15. Ibid.

16. Nightletter telegram from "AFSERCO" [American Friends Service Committee] to "Quakers Marseille (France)," 11 March 1941, Doc 187, American Friends Service Committee archive, USHMM; and duplicate follow-up letter titled, "Communication No. 240" by John F. Rich, Associate Secretary [American Friends Service Committee] in Philadelphia to Howard E. Kershner, American Friends Service Committee in Marseille, 12 March 1941, Doc 29 #185, American Friends Service Committee archive, USHMM.

17. Information based on extensive collection of correspondence in Felddegen private archive, USHMM.

18. Ibid.

19. Lilly Felddegen, letter to Marguérite Goldschmidt-Brodsky, 27 January 1941, Felddegen private archive, USHMM.

20. Information from American Friends Service Committee lists of 100 USCOM children (United States Committee for the Care of European Children), and various other sources in USHMM archive.

21. Various letters in Felddegen private archive, USHMM.

7. Life at the Château de La Hille, 1941–1942

1. Dr. Theo Tschuy archive, Archiv für Zeitgeschichte (AFZ), Eidgenössische Technische Hochschule Zürich Zentrum, Zurich, Switzerland.

2. Information researched by Patrick Raluy, son-in-law of the present owner of "Château de La Hille."

3. Ibid.

4. Maurice Dubois, letter to Rodolfo Olgiati, 21 February 1941, described in notes taken by Dr. Theo Tschuy upon visiting the Maurice Dubois personal archive at La Chaux-de-Fonds, Switzerland, Dr. Theo Tschuy archive, Archiv für Zeitgeschichte (AFZ), Eidgenössische Technische Hochschule Zürich Zentrum, Zurich, Switzerland.

5. List is based on photographs of the period in the author's collection, and an entry in Kurt Moser's private diary of 12 February 1943 in which he notes "the 2-year anniversary of our arrival." Kurt Moser, private diary, copy provided to the author by Warren LeFort.

6. Secours Suisse, meeting minutes, 20 February 1941, 3–6, Felddegen archive, USHMM.

7. Ilse Wulff Garfunkel, e-mail to the author, 20 June 2008.

8. Irène Frank, private diary, unnumbered pages.

9. Maurice Dubois, letter to Rodolfo Olgiati, 27 December 1940, from notes taken by Dr. Theo Tschuy from Maurice Dubois personal archive at La Chaux-de-Fonds, Switzerland, Tschuy archive, AFZ.

10. Richard Gilg, ed., "Die Schweizer Kinderhilfe in Frankreich 1939/40–1947" [The Swiss Childen's Aid Society 1939/40–1947], Dok. 4426, SRK, 27.7.94, Tschuy archive, AFZ.

11. Ibid.

12. Ibid.

13. Rösli Näf, undated report to Secours Suisse [late summer 1941?], Secours Suisse files, copied by Dr. Theo Tschuy, Tschuy archive, AFZ.

14. Irène Frank, private diary, 49.

15. Ibid., 50.

16. Rösli Näf, undated report to Secours Suisse [late summer 1941?], Tschuy archive, AFZ.

17. Ibid.

18. Rösli Näf ("Rosa" Näf), report, 13 December 1941, 1, Secours Suisse files, Tschuy archive, AFZ.

19. Ibid.

20. Ibid.

21. Ibid.

22. Ibid.

23. Elka Frank, letter to Marguérite Goldschmidt-Brodsky in Basel, 11 October 1941, Goldschmidt-Brodsky private archive.

24. Alex Frank, letter to Marguérite Goldschmidt-Brodsky, 28 January 1942, Goldschmidt-Brodsky private archive.

25. Maurice Dubois, letter to Lilly Felddegen, 19 March 1941, 3, Felddegen private archive, USHMM.

26. Alex Frank, letter to Marguérite Goldschmidt-Brodsky, 22 June 1941, 1, Goldschmidt-Brodsky private archive.

27. Alex Frank, letter to Marguérite Goldschmidt-Brodsky, 28 January 1942, 1, Goldschmidt-Brodsky private archive.

28. Ibid., 2.

29. Ruth Schütz Usrad, *Entrapped Adolescence* [in Hebrew: "Neurim be-malkodet"] (Tel Aviv: Miśrad ha-biṭaḥon, 1997), 45, passage translated by Brenda Weitzberg.

30. Ibid., 51.

31. Lixie Grabkowicz (Kowler), letter from La Hille to her parents in Vienna, 16 July 1941. The letter was forwarded by her parents to an uncle in Italy and returned to Grabkowicz upon his death; copy furnished by her to the author in 2006; translation by Walter Reed.

32. Maurice Dubois, report, 15 December 1941, Secours Suisse files, Tschuy archive, AFZ.

33. Ibid.

34. Alex Frank, letter to Marguérite Goldschmidt-Brodsky, 22 June 1941, 2, Goldschmidt-Brodsky private archive.

35. Rösli Näf, undated report to Secours Suisse [late summer 1941?], Tschuy archive, AFZ.

36. Edith Goldapper Rosenthal, private diary, 32–33, translated by Walter Reed.

37. Peter Wertheimer (grandson of Julius and Klara Wertheimer), e-mail message to the author, 28 October 2009.

38. Irène Frank, private diary, 57, passage translated by Walter Reed.

39. Ibid.

40. Goldapper Rosenthal, private diary, 35.

41. Maurice Dubois, letter to Marguérite Goldschmidt-Brodsky, 10 September 1941, 2, Goldschmidt-Brodsky private archive.

42. Elka Frank, letter to Marguérite Goldschmidt-Brodsky in Basel, 23 September 1941, Goldschmidt-Brodsky private archive.

43. Irène Frank, private diary, 57.

44. Ibid.

45. Rösli Näf ("Rosa" Näf), report, 13 December 1941, 3, Tschuy archive, AFZ.

46. Flora Schlesinger to Rolf Weinmann, 17 November 1941, 1, Felddegen private archive, USHMM.

47. Secours Suisse, meeting minutes, 14 September 1941, 1, Secours Suisse archives copied by Dr. Theo Tschuy, Tschuy archive, AFZ.

48. Ibid.

49. Herbert R. Lottman, *Pétain, Hero or Traitor: The Untold Story* (New York: William Morrow, 1985), 187.

50. Ibid., 192.

51. Susan Zuccotti, *The Holocaust, the French, and the Jews* (New York: Basic, 1993), 56.

52. Ibid., 56-57.

53. Ibid., 60.

54. Michael R. Marrus and Robert O. Paxton, *Vichy France and the Jews* (New York: Basic, 1981), 100.

55. Zuccotti, *The Holocaust, the French, and the Jews*, 61-62.

56. Schütz Usrad, *Entrapped Adolescence*, 50.

57. Antonia Schmidlin, *Eine andere Schweiz: Helferinnen, Kriegskinder und humanitäre Politik (1933–1942)* (Zurich: Chronos Verlag, 1999), 129.

58. Ibid.

59. Ibid., 202.

60. Ibid., 214.

61. Ibid., 215.

62. Ibid., 381n120.

63. Ibid.

64. Maurice Dubois, letter to Lilly Felddegen in New York, 21 July 1941, Felddegen private archive, USHMM.

65. Alex Frank, letter to Marguérite Goldschmidt-Brodsky, 28 January 1942, Goldschmidt-Brodsky private archive.

66. Ibid.

67. Lilly Felddegen, list of thirty-one children, Felddegen private archive, USHMM.

68. Lilly Felddegen, letter to Maurice Dubois, 22 May 1941, Felddegen private archive, USHMM.

8. Internment and Liberation

1. Raul Hilberg, *The Destruction of the European Jews* (New York: New Viewpoints, 1973), 32.

2. Pierre Pucheu (Vichy interior minister), order no. 76, pol. 8,9, and 4, circ. from archive of Département de l'Ariège, Foix, France.

3. See departmental archive of the Ariège, Foix, France, document file no. SWII2.

4. Michael R. Marrus and Robert O. Paxton, *Vichy France and the Jews* (New York: Basic, 1981), 219.

5. Ibid., 220.

6. Irène Kokotek Nathan, e-mail message to the author, 20 July 2008.

7. Hans Garfunkel, telephone conversation with the author, 7 July 2008.

8. Rösli Näf, report to Secours Suisse [in German], 15 September 1942, copied by Dr. Theo Tschuy, Dr. Theo Tschuy archive, Archiv für Zeitgeschichte (AFZ), Eidgenössische Technische Hochschule Zürich Zentrum, Zurich; the same report [in French] is also housed in the Olgiati private archive, Social Service Library, Zurich. Both versions translated by Walter Reed.

9. Ibid.

10. Ruth Schütz Usrad, *Entrapped Adolescence* [in Hebrew: "Neurim be-malkodet"] (Tel Aviv: Miśrad ha-biṭaḥon, 1997), 54–56, passage translated by Brenda Weitzberg.

11. Ibid.

12. Edith Goldapper Rosenthal, private diary, 36–37, copy provided to the author by Edith Goldapper; an additional copy is archived at the United States Holocaust Memorial Museum (USHMM), Washington, DC. Passage translated by Walter Reed.

13. Ibid., 38–39.

14. Ibid.

15. Ibid.

16. Ibid.

17. Marrus and Paxton, *Vichy France and the Jews*, 228.

18. Ibid.

19. Ibid., 233–34.

20. Ibid., 257–58.

21. Donald A. Lowrie, memorandum from Geneva, Switzerland to Stacy Strong, general secretary, World's Committee of the YMCA, 10 August 1942, doc. 346, pp. 312–15, American Friends Service committee (AFSC) files, USHMM.

22. Ibid., 315.

23. Donald A. Lowrie, confidential report to Tracy Strong (General Secretary, World's Alliance YMCA, New York City), 22 August 1942, doc. 353, pp. 326–28, American Friends Service committee (AFSC) files, USHMM.

24. Secours Suisse, "Notiz betr. jüdische Kinder in Heimen des SRK, Kinderhilfe, im unbesetzten Frankreich" [Memorandum Regarding Jewish Children of the Secours Suisse in Unoccupied France] (based on oral report from Mme Dubois of 30 August 1942), 31 August 1942, unsigned staff report to Col. Remund of the Secours Suisse, Swiss Red Cross archives, copied by Dr. Theo Tschuy, Tschuy archive, AFZ, translated from German by Walter Reed.

25. Antonia Schmidlin, *Eine andere Schweiz: Helferinnen, Kriegskinder und humanitäre Politik (1933–1942)* (Zurich: Chronos Verlag, 1999), 275–77, translation by Walter Reed.

26. Marguérite Goldschmidt-Brodsky, handwritten copy of telegram to Max Gottschalk, 27 August 1942, Goldschmidt-Brodsky private archive.

27. Irène Frank, private diary, 83.

28. Ibid., 78.

29. Secours Suisse, "Memorandum regarding Jewish children of the Secours Suisse in unoccupied France," Tschuy archive, AFZ.

30. Ibid.

31. Esther Schärer, "Croix-Rouge suisse, secours aux enfants en France 1942–1945: sa formation, son activité, ses relations avec le gouvernement suisse, son rôle" (research paper, University of Geneva, Switzerland, October 1986), 88, archives of the International Committee of the Red Cross (ICRC), Geneva, Switzerland.

32. Rösli Näf, report, 15 September 1942, 5, copied by Dr. Theo Tschuy from Secours Suisse archives, Tschuy archive, AFZ.

33. Ibid., 6.

34. Goldapper Rosenthal, private diary, 39–40.

35. Rösli Näf, report, 15 September 1942, 6, Tschuy archive, AFZ.

36. Isi Bravermann Veleris, private files, documentation furnished to the author.

37. Rösli Näf, report, 6.

38. Ibid., 7.

39. Schütz Usrad, *Entrapped Adolescence*, 59.

40. Irène Frank, private diary, 93–94.

41. Goldapper Rosenthal, private diary, 41.

42. Mayor [unnamed] of Montégut-Plantaurel, signed declaration, 9 September 1942, departmental archive at Foix, France.

43. Serge Klarsfeld, *French Children of the Holocaust: A Memorial* (New York: New York Univ. Press, 1996), 8.

9. Hazardous Journeys across Well-Guarded Borders

1. Maurice Dubois, letter written in Toulouse to Marguérite Goldschmidt-Brodsky in Basel, 10 September 1942, Goldschmidt-Brodsky private archive.

2. Rösli Näf, report, in Richard Gilg, ed., "Le Secours Suisse aux Enfants dans le Sud de la France 1939 à 1947," 1990, Tschuy archive, AFZ.

3. Eleanor Dubois, "Memorandum Regarding Jewish Children of the Secours Suisse in Unoccupied France," 2, Dr. Theo Tschuy archive, Archiv für Zeitgeschichte (AFZ), Eidgenössische Technische Hochschule Zürich Zentrum, Zurich. Note: The reference to Donald A. Lowrie is somewhat in error: he was a representative of the YMCA, not chair of the American Unitarian Service Committee.

4. Antonia Schmidlin, *Eine andere Schweiz: Helferinnen, Kriegskinder und humanitäre Politik (1933–1942)* (Zurich: Chronos Verlag, 1999), 274–77.

5. Ibid.

6. Schmidlin, *Eine andere Schweiz*, 274–77.

7. Ibid., 227. Max Zürcher had been appointed by Col. Remund as "Délégué général" in May 1942 to supervise the Secours Suisse in Vichy France and to carry out relations with Vichy authorities.

8. Esther Schärer, "Croix-Rouge suisse, secours aux enfants en France 1942–1945: sa formation, son activité, ses relations avec le gouvernement suisse, son rôle" (research paper, University of Geneva, Switzerland, October 1986), 92, archives of the International Committee of the Red Cross (ICRC), Geneva, Switzerland.

9. Ruth Schütz Usrad, *Entrapped Adolescence* [in Hebrew: "Neurim be-malko-det"] (Tel Aviv: Miśrad ha-biṭaḥon, 1997), 61, passage translated by Brenda Weitzberg.

10. Ibid.

11. Rösli Näf, report, 15 September 1942, 7, Tschuy archive, AFZ.

12. Henri Chaim Storosum, letter to author, 10 September 2007.

13. P. Pucheu (Interior Ministry state secretary), memorandum to the regional prefects of the Unoccupied Zone, 2 January 1942, Ariège departmental archive at Foix, France, document no. SW 115, translated by Walter Reed.

14. File 5W120, departmental archives of Ariège at Foix, France.

15. Letter from the delegate (unnamed) of Mission de Restauration Paysanne in the Ariège department to the Ariège Prefect, 29 March 1943, Ariège Department archive, France.

16. Eugene Lyrer, statement to French policemen in Gendarmerie Nationale search report, 23 February 1943, Ariège Department archive in Foix.

17. Michael R. Marrus and Robert O. Paxton, *Vichy France and the Jews* (New York: Basic, 1981), 171.

18. Listed by Serge Klarsfeld, archives of Mémorial de la Shoah, Paris.

19. Arie (Leo) Grossmann, letter to the author, 24 December 2006.

20. Listed by Serge Klarsfeld, archives of Mémorial de la Shoah, Paris.

21. Edith Goldapper Rosenthal, private diary, 42, translation by Walter Reed.

22. Schütz Usrad, *Entrapped Adolescence*, 61.

23. Col. Hugo Remund, letter to E. de Haller (chief of the Swiss government overseeing aid societies), 21 November 1942, copied from Secours Suisse archives by Dr. Theo Tschuy, Tschuy archive, AFZ.

24. Jean-Jacques Pétris, *Le Maquis de Roquefixade*, 1999, http://www.histariege .com/le_maquis_de_roquefixade.htm.

25. Rösli Näf, "Die Schweizerische Kinderhilfe in Frankreich, 1939/40–1947," 48, Dok 4426, Swiss Red Cross archive, copied by Dr. Theo Tschuy, Tschuy archive, AFZ.

26. Marrus and Paxton, *Vichy France and the Jews*, 308–9.

27. Almuth Königshöfer, border police interrogation statement, 15 September 1942, Swiss archives at United States Holocaust Memorial Museum (USHMM), Washington, DC.

28. Dr. Ruth Fivaz-Silbermann, e-mail report to Dr. Theo Tschuy, 15 April 2003, provided to the author by Dr. Tschuy.

29. Lucien Wolfgang, autobiography statement, 1990s, Alex Frank archive, USHMM.

30. Irène Frank, private diary, 100.

31. Peter Salz, autobiography written in 1985, and Margot Kern, autobiography written in 1985, Alex Frank archive, USHMM; see also Ruth Fivaz-Silbermann, e-mail report to Dr. Theo Tschuy, 15 April 2003, Dr. Theo Tschuy archive, AFZ.

32. Various letters from Goldschmidt-Brodsky private archive.

33. Canton of Geneva, records furnished to Dr. Theo Tschuy by Ruth Fivaz-Silbermann, Tschuy archive, AFZ.

34. Hans Garfunkel, letter from Büren to Marguérite Goldschmidt-Brodsky in Basel, 28 January 1943, Goldschmidt-Brodsky private archive.

35. Näf, "Die Schweizerische Kinderhilfe in Frankreich," 48, Tschuy archive, AFZ.

36. Goldapper Rosenthal, private diary, 43.

37. Inge Schragenheim, autobiography written in the 1990s, Alex Frank archive, USHMM.

38. Information regarding Lewin-Schragenheim derives from: Leo Lewin, autobiography, 23 January 1993, Alex Frank archive, USHMM; and Ruth Fivaz-Silbermann, study of Canton of Geneva records, Tschuy archive, AFZ.

39. Inge (Schragenheim) Nowakowska, autobiography prepared for La Hille reunion, Kibbutz Lehavoth Habashan, Israel, May 1985, Tschuy archive, AFZ; also in Alex Frank archive, USHMM.

40. Ibid.

41. Canton of Geneva, records, Tschuy archive, AFZ.

42. Plt. Schaufelberger of the Schweizerisches Armeekommando, letter to Division de Police, Dept. de Justice et Police, 3 February 1943, Bern in Schweizerisches Bundesarchiv, Bestand E 4264 (-), USHMM.

43. Lixie Grabkowicz, autobiography, written in the 1990's, Alex Frank archive, USHMM.

44. Schütz Usrad, *Entrapped Adolescence*, 68.

45. Ibid.

46. Ibid., 69.

47. See Grabkowicz, autobiography; and Schütz Usrad, *Entrapped Adolescence*.

48. Irène Frank, private diary, 100–101.

49. Kurt Moser, private diary, entry on 30 December 1942.

50. Ibid.

51. Ibid.

52. Ibid.

53. Sebastian Steiger, *Die Kinder von Schloss La Hille* (Basel: Brunnen-Verlag, 1992), 252–54.

54. Schütz Usrad, *Entrapped Adolescence*, 62.

55. Inge Joseph Bleier and David E. Gumpert, *Inge, A Girl's Journey through Nazi Europe* (Grand Rapids, MI: William B. Eerdmans, 2004), 179–81.

56. Ibid.

57. Germaine Hommel, report to Marthe Terrier, 8 January 1943, Swiss Red Cross archives, Tschuy archive, AFZ.

58. Bleier and Gumpert, *Inge*, 187–90.

59. Germaine Hommel, report to Marthe Terrier, 8 January 1943, Tschuy archive, AFZ.

60. Bleier and Gumpert, *Inge*, 194–200.

61. Hommel, report to Marthe Terrier, Tschuy archive, AFZ.

62. Ibid.

63. Ibid.

64. Kurt Moser, private diary.

65. Listed by Serge Klarsfeld, archives of Memorial de la Shoah, Paris.

66. Schmidlin, *Eine andere Schweiz*, 402n89.

67. Bleier and Gumpert, *Inge*, 204–14.

68. Hommel, report to Marthe Terrier, Tschuy archive, AFZ.

69. Schmidlin, *Eine andere Schweiz*, 309.

70. Ibid., 309–11.

71. Ibid., 312.

72. Näf, "Die Schweizerische Kinderhilfe in Frankreich," 50, Tschuy archive, AFZ.

73. Schmidlin, *Eine andere Schweiz*, 312.

74. Ibid., 313.

75. Ibid., 314–15. All the children in question were already incarcerated in not very pleasant Swiss internment camps; fortunately, neither they nor the godparents ever learned of de Haller's proposal.

10. The Noose Tightens and More Try to Escape

1. Edith Goldapper Rosenthal, private diary, 44–45.

2. Antonia Schmidlin, *Eine andere Schweiz: Helferinnen, Kriegskinder und humanitäre Politik (1933–1942)* (Zurich: Chronos Verlag, 1999), 305 and 311.

3. Inge Berlin Vogelstein, e-mail message to author, 19 February 2006.

4. Alex Frank, interview by Marion Rager in Berlin, 23 March 1998, titled "Alltag und Widerstand im NS-Regime-Erinnerungen Berliner Antifaschisten," Alex Frank private archive, United States Holocaust Memorial Museum (USHMM), Washington, DC.

5. Ibid.

6. Inge Vogelstein, personal letter to the author, 27 February 2006.

7. Alex Frank, conversation with the author, 1998; Alex Frank, interview by Rager, 18, Alex Frank private archive, USHMM.

8. Inge Vogelstein, personal letter to author, 27 February 2006.

9. Alex Frank, interview by Rager, Alex Frank private archive, USHMM.

10. Margrit Tännler, "Rapport Januar bis Juni 1943, Colonie d'enfants du Château de La Hille, Montégut-Plantaurel (Ariège)," 2, Dr. Theo Tschuy archive, Archiv für Zeitgeschichte (AFZ), Eidgenössische Technische Hochschule Zürich Zentrum, Zurich, translated by Walter Reed.

11. Ibid.; see also "Procès verbal of the Gendarmerie Nationale, Pailhès," 23 February 1943, file no. SW119, Ariège departmental archives, Foix, France.

12. Serge Klarsfeld, *French Children of the Holocaust List*, 272, Memorial de la Shoah archives, Paris.

13. Tännler, "Report of January to June 1943," 2, Tschuy archive, AFZ.

14. Anne-Marie Im Hof-Piguet, *La filière en France occupée, 1942–1944* (Yverdon-les-Bains, Switzerland: Parcours-Éditions de la Thièle, 1985), 92.

15. Michael R. Marrus and Robert O. Paxton, *Vichy France and the Jews* (New York: Basic, 1981), 304.

16. Goldapper Rosenthal, private diary, 46.

17. Ibid., 47.

18. Ibid., 49.

19. Ibid., 47, 49.

20. Kurt Moser, private diary, entry on May 24, 1943.

21. Ibid.

22. Ibid.

23. Ibid., dates of late June–July 1943.

24. Fritz Wertheimer, handwritten letter, 15 November 1942, Wertheimer family private records, copy furnished to the author by Peter Wertheimer, his nephew.

25. "Bericht über die Kinderkolonie des Schweizer Roten Kreuzes in Montégut-Plantaurel" [Report about the Children's Colony of the Swiss Red Cross at Montégut-Plantaurel (Ariège)], n.d., CCXVIII-2, p. 6, Archives du Centre de Documentation Juive Contemporaine, Paris, translation by Walter Reed.

26. Ibid., 7.

27. Werner Epstein, "My Life from 1942–1985," handwritten autobiography, Alex Frank archive, USHMM.

28. Goldapper Rosenthal, private diary, 50.

29. Ibid.

30. Werner Epstein, letter to Edith Moser, Alex Frank archive, USHMM, translated from German by Walter Reed.

31. Epstein, "My Life from 1942–1985."

32. Marrus and Paxton, *Vichy France and the Jews*, 325–29.

33. Information from the arrest record of the Gendarmerie Nationale, 15 September 1943, departmental archive, Foix, France.

34. Goldapper Rosenthal, private diary, 52.

35. Ibid.

36. Im Hof-Piguet, *La filière en France occupée, 1942–1944*, 109–10.

37. Ibid., 110.

38. Ruth Schütz Usrad, *Entrapped Adolescence* [in Hebrew: "Neurim be-malkodet"] (Tel Aviv: Miśrad ha-biṭaḥon, 1997), 92–103, passage translated by Brenda Weitzberg.

39. Ibid., 102.

40. Ibid.

41. Betty Schütz Bloom, interview titled "Sisters in Distress," *Jewish Chronicle* (London), 14 February 1997, 32.

42. Schmidlin, *Eine andere Schweiz*, 317.

43. "Victoria Cordier" (obituary), *Horizons et débats*, no. 21 (July 2003).

44. Im Hof-Piguet, *La filière en France occupée, 1942–1944*, 111.

45. Ibid., 112–13.

46. Ibid., 113–14.

47. This was not the Saint-Cergues near Annemasse where Addi's sister and others had crossed.

48. Ibid., 115.

49. Inge Joseph Bleier and David E. Gumpert, *Inge: A Girl's Journey through Nazi Europe* (Grand Rapids, MI: William B. Eerdmans, 2004), 230–42.

50. Ibid., 246–48.

51. Im Hof-Piguet, *La filière en France occupée, 1942–1944*, 116–17.

52. Goldapper Rosenthal, private diary, 56–57.

53. Ibid., 58.

54. Ibid.

55. Edith Lefort (née Moser), "My Life," autobiography, Alex Frank private archive, USHMM.

56. Edith Moser, "Tagebuch von Edith Moser," personal diary, Alex Frank archive, USHMM.

57. Ibid.

58. Ibid., 17.

59. Ibid., 18.

60. Ibid., 19–28.

61. Ibid., 62–67.

62. Ibid., 68–69.

63. Ibid., 71–72.

64. Ibid., 73–77.

65. Ibid., 79–80.

66. Victoria Cordier, "Ce que je n'oublierai jamais . . ." [I shall never forget this . . .] (self-published, n.d.), 97–98, Tschuy archive, AFZ.

67. Ibid., 97–98.

68. Goldapper Rosenthal, private diary, 83.

69. Ibid., 85–87.

70. Stadtpolizei Zürich, Kopie für Ter. Kdo. 6, 15 December 1943, USHMM.

71. Goldapper Rosenthal, private diary, 88.

72. Stadtpolizei Zürich, Kopie für Ter. Kdo. 6, 15 December 1943, USHMM.

73. Ibid.

74. Goldapper Rosenthal, private diary, "volume 1," 89–94, and "volume 2," 1–8, translated by Walter Reed. Note: The diary is a single volume, but it is labeled internally "*Buch I*" and "*Buch II*" (volume 1 and volume 2). "Volume

1" is titled, "France-Switzerland—1943–44"; "Volume 2" is titled, "Fribourg, Switzerland—1944."

75. Tännler, "Report of January to June 1943," 3, Tschuy archive, AFZ.

76. Marrus and Paxton, *Vichy France and the Jews*, 335.

77. Gret Tobler, personal diary, Cummins family records, graciously furnished to the author by Gret's niece Ursula Cummins, with permission to publish, translated from German by Walter Reed.

78. The entire report of this escape derives from Gret Tobler, personal diary, translated from German by Walter Reed.

79. Mme Fivaz-Silbermann, notes, Archives d'État de Genève, R. 14.4.03, Tschuy archive, AFZ.

80. Im Hof-Piguet, *La filière en France occupée, 1942–1944*, 133–34.

81. Ibid., 134.

82. Cordier, "Ce que je n'oublierai jamais . . . ," 121, Tschuy archive, AFZ.

83. Im Hof-Piguet, *La filière en France occupée, 1942–1944*, 135–36.

84. Ibid.

85. Cordier, "Ce que je n'oublierai jamais . . . ," 121, Tschuy archive, AFZ.

86. Ibid.

87. Im Hof-Piguet, *La filière en France occupée, 1942–1944*, 137.

88. Ibid., 138–39.

89. Ibid., 139.

11. Hidden and Surviving in France until the End

1. Michael R. Marrus and Robert O. Paxton, *Vichy France and the Jews* (New York: Basic, 1981), 305–6.

2. Ruth Herz, autobiography, Alex Frank archive, United States Holocaust Memorial Museum (USHMM), Washington, DC.

3. Lixie Grabkowicz (Alix Kowler), autobiography prepared for La Hille reunion, Kibbutz Lehavoth Habashan, Israel, May 1985, Alix Kowler personal files.

4. Lixie (Alix) Grabkowicz, autobiography, Alex Frank archive, USHMM.

5. Frieda Steinberg Urman, letters to the author, 11 November 2000, 12 December 2001, and 20 May 2003; Frieda Steinberg, autobiography, Alex Frank archive, USHMM.

6. Extensive unpublished documentation regarding Peter Landesmann-Bouché, Bouché-Landesmann family private files, access generously provided to the author by grandson Damien Bouché-Landesmann.

7. Susan Zuccotti, *The Holocaust, the French, and the Jews* (New York: Basic, 1993), 274–76.

8. Henri Chaim Storosum, letters to the author, 14 November 2000, 11 February 2002, and 10 September 2007.

9. Anne-Marie Im Hof-Piguet, *La filière en France occupée*, 1942–1944 (Yverdon-les-Bains, Switzerland: Parcours-Éditions de la Thièle, 1985), 109.

10. Background and documents about Mme Authié's clandestine activities furnished to author by her daughter, Mme Lucette Franco; additional documents obtained from Foix, France departmental archives and Mr. Jean-Jacques Pétris.

11. Ilse Brünell autobiography, Alex Frank archive, USHMM.

12. Ruth Schütz Usrad, *Entrapped Adolescence* [in Hebrew: "Neurim be-malkodet"] (Tel Aviv: Miśrad ha-biṭaḥon, 1997), 88–89, passage translated by Brenda Weitzberg.

13. Ibid., 120.

14. Ibid., 132.

15. Ibid., 133–36.

16. Lilly Felddegen, letter to US State Department, 14 May 1941, Felddegen private archive, USHMM.

17. Jack Blatt, handwritten letter to Lilly Felddegen, 22 February 1941, Felddegen private archive, USHMM.

18. United States Committee for the Care of European Children, undated immigration list of 38 children, plus the Kantor siblings and Wolpert, Felddegen private archive, USHMM.

19. Various documents, Felddegen private archive, USHMM.

20. United States Committee for the Care of European Children, press release, n.d., marked "for release upon arrival of 'Serpa Pinto' Thursday, June 25 or Friday, June 26," archived at YIVO Institute for Jewish Research, New York.

21. Lilly Felddegen, letter to Renée deBecker, 23 April 1943, Felddegen private archive, USHMM.

22. Isidor Ganzman, letter to Belgian Rescue Committee, 13 January 1939, Felddegen private archive, USHMM.

23. Ibid.

24. H. K. Travers, Chief, Visa Division, Department of State, Washington, letter to "Mrs. Albert Felddegen" [Lilly Felddegen], 24 July 1942, Felddegen private archive, USHMM.

25. Lucien Lazare, *Rescue as Resistance: How Jewish Organizations Fought the Holocaust in France*, trans. Jeffrey M. Green (New York: Columbia Univ. Press, 1996), 198.

26. Delphine Deroo, *Les enfants de la Martellière* (Paris: Editions Grasset et Fasquelle, 1999), 145.

27. Ibid.

28. Cordula Kappner, *Von Burgpreppach über Auschwitz in das Konzentrationslager Sachsenhausen—der Weg des Kindes Gerhard Eckmann—Eine Spursuche* [From Burgpreppach via Auschwitz to the Concentration Camp Sachsenhausen—The Path of Young Gerhard Eckmann—Researching the Trail] (self-published).

29. Henri Brunel, response letter to questionnaire sent by Dr. Theo Tschuy, 10 July 2003, Dr. Theo Tschuy archive, Archiv für Zeitgeschichte (AFZ), Eidgenössische Technische Hochschule Zürich Zentrum, Zurich, Switzerland.

30. Pierre Tisseyre, conversation with the author, June 2007.

31. Frieda Rosenfeld Schaefer, letter to the author, 11 August 2008.

32. Cilly Stückler Ratzenberger, "Life History, 1942 till Now," 1985, Alex Frank private archive, USHMM.

33. Fanny Kuhlberg Rubin, autobiography, 1985, Alex Frank private archive, USHMM.

34. Frances Weinberg, conversation with the author, June 2007.

35. Guy Haas, e-mail to the author, 10 August 2003.

36. Ibid.

12. New Faces at La Hille

1. Edith Goldapper, letter to Marguérite Goldschmidt-Brodsky in Basel, 23 September 1943, Goldschmidt-Brodsky private archive.

2. Robert Weinberg, family history report, 9 July 2003, sent to Dr. Theo Tschuy, Dr. Theo Tschuy archive, Archiv für Zeitgeschichte (AFZ), Eidgenössische Technische Hochschule Zürich Zentrum, Zurich.

3. Ibid.

4. Ibid.; see also Sebastian Steiger, *Die Kinder von Schloss La Hille* (Basel: Brunnen Verlag, 1992), 307 et seq.

5. Robert Weinberg, family history report, 9 July 2003, sent to Dr. Theo Tschuy, Tschuy archive, AFZ.

6. Steiger, *Die Kinder von Schloss La Hille*, 313.

7. Brigade of Merens, Procès Verbal of the Weinberg children's interrogation by the Brigade of Merens, 13 November 1942, Foix departmental archives, Foix, France.

8. Connie Van Praag (originally Gonda Weinberg), letter to the author, 15 July 2001; other correspondence from Van Praag with the author.

9. Fernand Nohr, autobiography, 10 January 2000, Alex Frank personal archive, United States Holocaust Memorial Museum (USHMM), Washington, DC.

10. Ibid.

11. Ibid.

12. Richard Gilg, ed., "Le Secours Suisse au Sud de la France, 1939 à 1947," 1990, 101, Tschuy archive, AFZ.

13. Josette Mendes Zylberstein, letter to Theo Tschuy, 14 July 2003, Tschuy archive, AFZ.

14. Testimony of Josette Mendes Zylberstein with Rosa Moreau, June 2007, archive of Museum at Montégut-Plantaurel, France.

15. Testimony of Paulette Abramovicz Erpst with Rosa Moreau, May 2007, archive of Museum at Montégut-Plantaurel, France; Paulette Erpst, letter to the author, May 2000.

16. Information from contemporary group photo furnished by Rosa Marimon Moreau.

17. Isi Bravermann (Veleris), interview, transcribed by "Mme Persitz," 1 April 1994, DCL11–12, Centre de Documentation Juive Contemporaine, Paris.

18. Ibid.

19. Irène Kokotek Nathan, letter to the author, 20 July 2008; Guita Kokotek Vormes, e-mail message to the author, 12 November 2005.

20. Statement by Esther Hocherman/Edith Jankeliewicz, in Steiger Briefsammlung, 1985, Tschuy archive, AFZ.

21. Eva Fernanbuk/Chava Brafmann, autobiography, Tschuy archive, AFZ.

22. Statement by Esther Hocherman/Edith Jankeliewicz, in Steiger Briefsammlung, 1985, Tschuy archive, AFZ.

23. Jeanette Bettelheim, *Les Oranges de Don Quich* (Netanya, Israel: Société d'Editions Infos, 1993), 40–42.

24. Irène Kokotek Nathan, interview with the author, Vannes, France, summer 2007.

25. Irène Kokotek Nathan, letter to the author, 20 July 2008.

26. Peter Bergmann, autobiography, April 1985, Alex Frank archive, USHMM.

27. Rosa Marimon Moreau, letter to the author, 4 January 2001.

28. Conchita Palau Romeo, interview by Rosa Moreau, 1 August 2008, Menthon-le-Annecy, France; and Jaime Palau [son], interview by Rosa Moreau, 1 May 2008, Annecy, France, archive of Montégut-Plantaurel Museum.

29. Esther Schärer, "Croix-Rouge suisse, secours aux enfants en France 1942–1945: sa formation, son activité, ses relations avec le gouvernement suisse, son rôle" (research paper, University of Geneva, Switzerland, October 1986), 127, archives of the International Committee of the Red Cross (ICRC), Geneva, Switzerland.

13. Those Who Helped and Those Who Hindered

1. Alex Frank, letters to members of the Belgian Comité d'Assistance aux Enfants Juifs Réfugiés from Seyre, copies of these letters are housed at Felddegen private archive, United States Holocaust Memorial Museum (USHMM), Washington, DC, and in Goldschmidt-Brodsky private archive.

2. Secours Suisse, meeting minutes, 20 February 1941, 5, Felddegen archive, USHMM.

3. Rösli Näf, undated report (August 1941?), Dr. Theo Tschuy archive, Archiv für Zeitgeschichte (AFZ), Eidgenössische Technische Hochschule Zürich Zentrum, Zurich.

4. Académie de Toulouse in Foix, appointment letter to René Vigneau, 29 November 1941, Ariège departmental archive, France.

5. Olga Authié (cabinet secretary at the Ariège Préfecture), various refugee registration lists, Ariège Préfecture archives, Foix, France.

6. Relevant documents provided to the author by Olga Authié's daughter, Lucette Franco, at her home in Foix, France, 14 September 2005, and by Jean-Jacques Pétris.

7. Relevant documents copied by author from the Ariège departmental archives.

8. Fritz Wertheimer, letter to Karl Wertheimer in Colombia, South America, 15 November 1942, copy provided to author Walter Reed in e-mail dated 28 October 2009 by Fritz's nephew Peter Wertheimer.

9. Michael R. Marrus and Robert O. Paxton, *Vichy France and the Jews* (New York: Basic, 1981), 218–19.

10. Lotte Nussbaum, letter to Lilly Felddegen and Renée deBecker, 30 January 1941, Felddegen private archive, USHMM.

11. Ibid.

12. Antonia Schmidlin, *Eine andere Schweiz: Helferinnen, Kriegskinder und humanitäre Politik (1933–1942)* (Zurich: Chronos Verlag, 1999), 199 and 202.

13. Richard Gilg, letter to Dr. Theo Tschuy, 27 January 2003, Tschuy archive, AFZ.

14. Ibid.

15. Schmidlin, *Eine andere Schweiz*, 207–8.

16. Max O. Zürcher and R. Olgiati, "Report about the Events at La Hille and Elsewhere," Swiss Red Cross archives, Tschuy archive, AFZ.

17. Swiss Red Cross, minutes of Red Cross meeting, 26 January 1943, Archives of the Swiss Red Cross, Protokolle 1943, Band II, Tschuy archive, AFZ.

18. Ibid., 8.

19. Ibid., 10.

20. Ibid.

21. Walter Stucki, letter to Hugo Remund, January 13, 1943, 3, archives of the Swiss Red Cross, Tschuy archive, AFZ.

22. Ibid., 4.

23. Rösli Näf, review of events, part of staff members' recollections quoted in Richard Gilg, ed., "Le Secours Suisse aux Enfants dans le Sud de La France," 1990, 135, Tschuy archive, AFZ.

14. The Heroes of La Hille

1. Debórah Dwork, *Children with a Star: Jewish Youth in Nazi Europe* (New Haven, CT: Yale Univ. Press, 1991), 65.

2. Ibid.

3. Marguérite Goldschmidt-Brodsky, letters to US Consul Walter H. Sholes in Basel, Switzerland, 27 and 31 August 1942; US Consul Walter H. Sholes, reply letters, 17 and 20 October 1942, and 4 November 1942 (which contained a copy of a letter from US Ambassador S. Pinkney Tuck from Vichy France dated 27 October 1942), all related to possible rescue of the La Hille children, Goldschmidt-Brodsky personal archive.

4. Alexander Frank, handwritten letter to Lilly Felddegen in New York, 24 February 1941, Felddegen private archive, United States Holocaust Memorial Museum (USHMM), Washington, DC.

5. Meir Wagner, *The Righteous of Switzerland: Heroes of the Holocaust* (Hoboken, NJ: Ktav, 2001), 87.

6. Victoria Cordier, "Ce que je n'oublierai jamais . . ." [I shall never forget this . . .] (self-published, n.d.), Dr. Theo Tschuy archive, Archiv für Zeitgeschichte (AFZ), Eidgenössische Technische Hochschule Zürich Zentrum, Zurich.

7. Jean-Jacques Pétris, *Egon Berlin, L'enfant juif de Roquefixade* [Egon Berlin, the Jewish Youngster of Roquefixade] (privately published, Saint-Paul de Jarrat, 2001), 34.

8. Ibid., 35.

9. Ibid., 37–44.

10. Jean-Jacques Pétris, e-mail message to the author, 14 February 2003.

11. Alex Frank, letter to the author, 18 October 1997.

12. Joseph Dortort, e-mail message to author, 15 February 2007.

13. Lucien Wolfgang, autobiography, Alex Frank private archive, USHMM.

14. Edgar Chaim, autobiography from "Les Enfants de La Hille 1942–1985," compiled on the occasion of a survivor reunion in Israel in 1985, Tschuy archive, AFZ.

15. After the Liberation

1. From the author's personal observation as an American soldier in Europe at war's end.

2. Peter Salz, handwritten letter to Alex Frank, 16 July 1945, Alex Frank private archive, United States Holocaust Memorial Museum (USHMM), Washington, DC.

3. Werner Epstein, handwritten autobiography prepared for La Hille reunion, Kibbutz Lehavoth Habashan, Israel, May 1985, Dr. Theo Tschuy archive, Archiv für Zeitgeschichte (AFZ), Eidgenössische Technische Hochschule Zürich Zentrum, Zurich.

4. Friedl Steinberg Urman, letter to the author, 14 August 1999.

5. Friedl Steinberg Urman, letter to the author, 24 August 1999.

6. Ibid.

7. Lotte Nussbaum, handwritten letter from Zurich to Alex Frank, 24 February 1946, Alex Frank private archive.

8. Ibid.

9. Lotte Nussbaum, autobiography prepared for La Hille reunion, Kibbutz Lehavoth Habashan, Israel, May 1985, Tschuy archive, AFZ.

10. Else Rosenblatt, autobiography prepared for La Hille reunion, Kibbutz Lehavoth Habashan, Israel, May 1985, Tschuy archive, AFZ.

11. Fanny Kuhlberg Rubin, autobiography prepared for La Hille reunion, Kibbutz Lehavoth Habashan, Israel, May 1985, Tschuy archive, AFZ.

12. Edith Jankielewicz, autobiography prepared for La Hille reunion, Kibbutz Lehavoth Habashan, Israel, May 1985, Tschuy archive, AFZ.

13. Margot Kern, autobiography prepared for La Hille reunion, Kibbutz Lehavoth Habashan, Israel, May 1985, Tschuy archive, AFZ.

14. Peter Salz, autobiography prepared for La Hille reunion, Kibbutz Lehavoth Habashan, Israel, May 1985, Tschuy archive, AFZ.

15. Ruth Schütz Usrad, autobiography prepared for La Hille reunion, Kibbutz Lehavoth Habashan, Israel, May 1985, Tschuy archive, AFZ.

16. Betty Schütz Bloom, autobiography prepared for La Hille reunion, Kibbutz Lehavoth Habashan, Israel, May 1985, Tschuy archive, AFZ.

17. Cilly Stückler Ratzenberger, autobiography prepared for La Hille reunion, Kibbutz Lehavoth Habashan, Israel, May 1985, Tschuy archive, AFZ.

18. Jacques Roth, autobiography prepared for La Hille reunion, Kibbutz Lehavoth Habashan, Israel, May 1985, Tschuy archive, AFZ.

19. Inge Schragenheim Nowakowska, autobiography prepared for La Hille reunion, Kibbutz Lehavoth Habashan, Israel, May 1985, Tschuy archive, AFZ.

20. Ruth Herz Goldschmidt, autobiography prepared for La Hille reunion, Kibbutz Lehavoth Habashan, Israel, May 1985, Tschuy archive, AFZ.

21. Edith Goldapper Rosenthal, autobiography prepared for La Hille reunion, Kibbutz Lehavoth Habashan, Israel, May 1985, Tschuy archive, AFZ.

22. Hans Garfunkel, autobiography prepared for La Hille reunion, Kibbutz Lehavoth Habashan, Israel, May 1985, Tschuy archive, AFZ.

23. Leo Lewin, personal communication and visit with the author in February 2005. See also Vera Friedländer, *Die Kinder von La Hille: Flucht und Rettung vor der Deportation* (Berlin: Aufbau Taschenbuch Verlag, 2004), 302–3.

24. Hanni Schlimmer Schild, autobiography prepared for La Hille reunion, Kibbutz Lehavoth Habashan, Israel, May 1985, and updates provided in 2003, Tschuy archive, AFZ.

25. Herbert Kammer, conversations with the author; see also "Mother, Son, Hitler Refugees Reunited after Nine Years," *Milwaukee Sentinel*, 22 April 1948, n.p.

26. "Dr. Herbert Kammer to Retire," *The Fur Rancher* (Fall 1994), 4.

27. Alex Frank, "Report on the meeting at Montégut-Plantaurel and Seyre on June 1–4.93," Alex Frank private archive, USHMM.

28. Alfred Eschwege, excerpt from unpublished letter to the *Chicago Tribune*, 12 May 1999, Alfred Eschwege personal files.

29. Rivka Paz, letter to the author, 12 February 2001.

30. Ibid.

31. Lotte Nussbaum, autobiography, Tschuy archive, AFZ.

32. Joseph and Fred Findling, interview by Regina Illmann, September 2000, Toulouse, France, Alex Frank private archive, USHMM.

33. Hanni Schlimmer Schild autobiography, Alex Frank private archive, USHMM.

34. Henri Brunel, response to questionnaire from Dr. Theo Tschuy, 10 July 2003, Tschuy archive, AFZ.

35. Betty Schütz Bloom, autobiography prepared for La Hille reunion, Kibbutz Lehavoth Habashan, Israel, May 1985, Tschuy archive, AFZ.

Index

Goldschmidt-Brodsky, Marguérite, *53*; actions and heroism of, 222–23; Baroness Ferstel and, 17; CAEJR role of, 10; in Cahors, 48; on deportations, 112; Maurice Dubois's letters to, 118; escape attempts and, 127–28, 130; Felddegen's letters to, 71–72, 74–75; flight from Belgium (1940) and, 34–35; Alexandre Frank's letter to, 91, 101; fundraising by, 22; on funds entrusted to DeWaay, 45; funds for books from, 94; Edith Goldapper's escape and, 167–68; on internment camps in France, 36; Joint Distribution Committee of New York and, 54; letter from boys at Seyre colony, 48; letter of commendation for Gaspard DeWaay, 48; placement of children by, 27, 28; Secours Suisse and, 52–54, 55; in Switzerland, 55

Göring, Hermann, 6–7

Gottschalk, Max: actions and heroism of, 222, 223; CAEJR and, 9–10; deportations and, 112; emigration to United States and, 69, 75, 76; flight from Belgium and, 35; Alexandre Frank's letter to, 61

Grabkowicz, Lixie (Kowler): on Bertrand Elkan, 147; on emigration to Belgium, 17; escape attempt by, 131–34; on hiding in France, 178; letter to parents, 90; Ruth Schütz and, 184, 185

Grossmann, Leo, 122–23, 212

Grossmann, Willy, 48–49, 122–23, 212

Groupement de Travailleurs Étrangers (GTE), 120–22

group homes, in Belgium, 27–29

Grynszpan, Herschel, 6

GTE (Groupement de Travailleurs Étrangers), 120–22

guides. *See passeur* (illegal border guides)

Gumpert, David E., 18, 136

Haas, Guy (Günther), 65, 195–96

Hahn, Henriette, 30

Haller, Edouard de: Bern meeting of 1942, 119–20; on escape attempts, 157, 219; on roundups, 112; Strauss group escape attempt and, 142, 273n75

Hanukkah, 29

Hartmann, Walther Georg, 142, 219

Haskelevicz, Elias: on Château de La Hille work crew, 82; evacuation to France and, 36; photographs of, *28, 41, 96*; in Vichy France internment camps, 50–51

Haulot, Arthur, 42

Hebrew Immigrant Aid Society (HIAS), 101, 102, 191, 223

Heide-lez-Anvers (Antwerp), 23–24

Helft, Inge, *176*; death in Auschwitz, 242, 251; entry into Belgium by, 30; escape attempt by, 134, 136–40, 143

Herbst, Adolf, 30

heroes of the Children of La Hille, xi, xv, 221–33; Belgian rescuers as, 222–24; children and teenagers as, 228–33; French citizens as, 228; in French resistance, 229–30, *230*, 232; parents as, 221–22; service in Allied forces, 231–32; Swiss citizens as, 224–28

Walter W. Reed (originally Werner Rindsberg) grew up in Mainstockheim, a Bavarian village near Würzburg and experienced Nazi persecution of Jews, including his own arrest as a fourteen-year-old on Kristallnacht, November 9–10, 1938. In 1939 his parents sent him to Belgium and he was able to flee to Vichy France with nearly 100 child companions when Germany attacked Belgium in May 1940. After immigrating to New York in 1941 he served as an American soldier from 1943 to 1946, and as an interrogator of German prisoners in General Patton's Third Army after the liberation of Paris in 1944. A graduate of the University of Missouri School of Journalism, he pursued a forty-year career in public relations. Having reconnected with his La Hille companions in 1997, he became their voluntary convener/coordinator and organized several survivor reunions. His parents and two younger brothers were deported and murdered in Poland in 1942. Since 1998 he has been a frequent speaker about the Holocaust in the United States and in Europe.